Guide to America's Outdoors

Western Canada

Guide to America's Outdoors
Western Canada

By Bob Devine
Photography by Raymond Gehman

NATIONAL
GEOGRAPHIC
WASHINGTON, D.C.

Contents

Cover: Hiking Sentinel Pass above Minnestimma Lake, Banff National Park, Alberta
Page 1: Bull elk with antlers in velvet, Banff National Park, Alberta
Pages 2-3: Evening alpenglow at Lake Victoria, Yoho National Park, British Columbia
Opposite: Pisew Falls Provincial Park, Manitoba

Treading Lightly in the Wild

Spreading fleabane, Nairn Falls PP

NATIONAL GEOGRAPHIC GUIDE TO AMERICA'S OUTDOORS: WESTERN CANADA takes you to the pristine and most peaceful natural areas of a region famed for rugged coastlines, glistening ice fields, snowcapped peaks, churning rivers, and swaying grasslands. And, of course, such iconic wildlife as polar bears, caribou, and bison.

Visitors who care about this spectacular region know they must tread lightly on the land. Ecosystems can be damaged, even destroyed, by thoughtless misuse. Many have already suffered from the impact of tourism. The marks are clear: litter-strewn acres, polluted waters, trampled vegetation, and disturbed wildlife. You can do your part to preserve these places for yourself, your children, and all other nature travelers. Before embarking on a backcountry visit or a camping adventure, learn some basic conservation dos and don'ts. Leave No Trace, a national educational program, recommends the following:

Plan ahead and prepare for your trip. If you know what to expect in terms of climate, conditions, and hazards, you can pack for general needs, extreme weather, and emergencies. Do yourself and the land a favor by visiting if possible during off-peak months and limiting your group to no more than four to six people. To keep trash or litter to a minimum, repackage food into reusable containers or bags. And rather than using cairns, flags, or paint cues that mar the environment to mark your way, bring a map and compass.

Travel and camp on solid surfaces. In popular areas, stay within established trails and campsites. Be sure to choose the right path, whether you are hiking, biking, skiing, or riding. Travel single file in the middle of the trail, even when it's wet or muddy, to avoid trampling vegetation. If you explore off a trail in pristine, lightly traveled areas, have your group spread out to lessen impact. Good campsites are found, not made. Travel and camp on sand, gravel, or rock, or on dry grasses, pine needles, or snow. Remember to stay at least 200 feet from waterways. After you've broken camp, leave the site as you found it.

Pack out what you pack in—and that means *everything* except human waste, which should be deposited in a hole dug away from water, camp, or trail, then covered and concealed. When washing dishes, clothes, or yourself, use small amounts of biodegradable soap and scatter the water away from lakes and streams.

Be sure to leave all items—plants, rocks, artifacts—as you find them. Avoid potential disaster by neither introducing nor transporting non-native species. Also, don't build or carve out structures that will alter the environment. A don't-touch policy not only preserves resources for future generations; it also gives the next guy a crack at the discovery experience.

Keep fires to a minimum. It may be unthinkable to camp without a campfire, but depletion of firewood harms the backcountry. When you can, try a gas-fueled camp stove and a candle lantern. If you choose to build a fire, first consider regulations, weather, skill, and firewood availability. Where possible, employ existing fire rings; elsewhere, use fire pans or mound fires. Keep your fire small, use only sticks from the ground, burn the fire down to ash, and don't leave the site until it's cold.

Respect wildlife. Though they may appear tame, animals in the wild are just that. Watch wildlife from a distance (bring binoculars or a tele-photo lens for close-ups), but never approach, feed, or follow them. Feeding weakens an animal's ability to fend for itself in the wild. If you can't keep your pets under control, leave them at home.

Finally, be mindful of other visitors. Yield to fellow travelers on the trail, and keep voices and noise levels low so that all the sounds of nature can be heard.

With these points in mind, you have only to chart your course. Enjoy your explorations. Let natural places quiet your mind, refresh your spirit, and remain as you found them. Just remember, leave behind no trace. ■

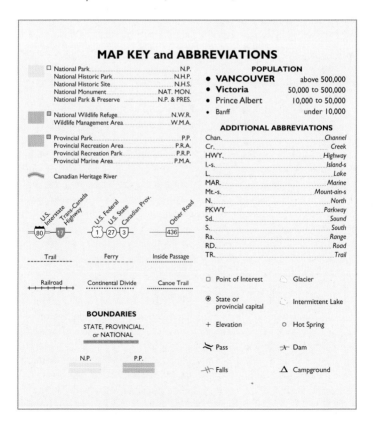

MAP KEY and ABBREVIATIONS

National Park..N.P.
National Historic Park...............................N.H.P.
National Historic Site................................N.H.S.
National Monument...............................NAT. MON.
National Park & Preserve ....................N.P. & PRES.

National Wildlife Refuge............................N.W.R.
Wildlife Management Area.........................W.M.A.

Provincial Park..P.P.
Provincial Recreation Area.........................P.R.A.
Provincial Recreation Park.........................P.R.P.
Provincial Marine Area..............................P.M.A.

Canadian Heritage River

U.S. Interstate   Trans-Canada Highway   U.S. Federal   U.S. State   Canadian Prov.   Other Road
80   17   1   27   3   436

Trail   Ferry   Inside Passage

Railroad   Continental Divide   Canoe Trail

BOUNDARIES

STATE, PROVINCIAL,
or NATIONAL

N.P.   P.P.

POPULATION

● **VANCOUVER**   above 500,000
● **Victoria**   50,000 to 500,000
● Prince Albert   10,000 to 50,000
● Banff   under 10,000

ADDITIONAL ABBREVIATIONS

Chan....................................Channel
Cr..Creek
HWY...................................Highway
I.-s.......................................Island-s
L...Lake
MAR....................................Marine
Mt.-s...................................Mount-ain-s
N..North
PKWY..................................Parkway
Sd.......................................Sound
S...South
Ra.......................................Range
RD.......................................Road
TR..Trail

☐ Point of Interest   Glacier

⊛ State or   Intermittent Lake
   provincial capital

+ Elevation   o Hot Spring

⤳ Pass   ⤙ Dam

⊬ Falls   △ Campground

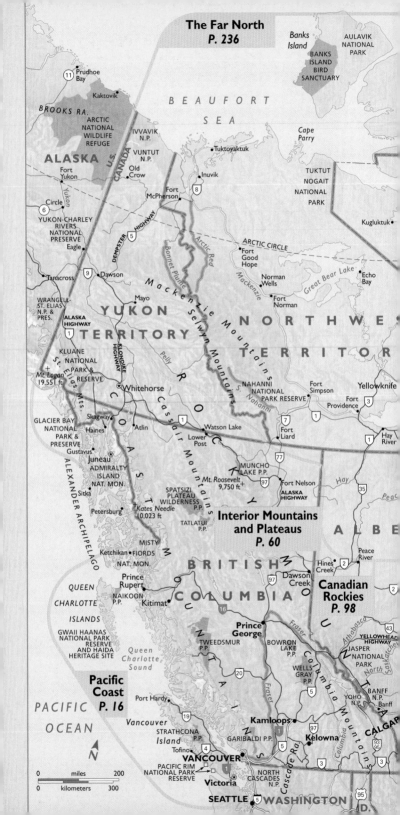

The Far North
P. 236

Banks Island

AULAVIK NATIONAL PARK

BANKS ISLAND BIRD SANCTUARY

BEAUFORT SEA

Cape Parry

TUKTUT NOGAIT NATIONAL PARK

11 Prudhoe Bay

Kaktovik

BROOKS RA.

ARCTIC NATIONAL WILDLIFE REFUGE

ALASKA

Fort Yukon

6 Circle

IVVAVIK N.P.

VUNTUT N.P.

Old Crow

Tuktoyaktuk

Inuvik

8

Fort McPherson

Kugluktuk

ARCTIC CIRCLE

Fort Good Hope

Norman Wells

Great Bear Lake

Echo Bay

YUKON-CHARLEY RIVERS NATIONAL PRESERVE

Eagle

Tanacross

9 Dawson

5 DEMPSTER HIGHWAY

Mayo

Bonnet Plume

Arctic Red

Mackenzie

Selwyn Mountains

Fort Norman

WRANGELL-ST. ELIAS N.P. & PRES.

YUKON

ALASKA HIGHWAY

1

TERRITORY

KLUANE NATIONAL PARK & RESERVE

Mt. Logan 19,551 ft

St. Elias Mts.

KLONDIKE HIGHWAY

Whitehorse

Pelly R.

Cassiar Mountains

NORTHWEST

TERRITOR

NAHANNI NATIONAL PARK RESERVE

Nahanni

Fort Simpson

Yellowknife

Fort Providence

3

1

COAST

Skagway

Haines

Atlin

1

Watson Lake

Lower Post

7

Fort Liard

1

Hay River

GLACIER BAY NATIONAL PARK & PRESERVE

Gustavus

Juneau

ADMIRALTY ISLAND NAT. MON.

77

MUNCHO LAKE P.P.

Mt. Roosevelt 9,750 ft

97

Fort Nelson

35

Hay

Peac

Sitka

ALEXANDER ARCHIPELAGO

Petersburg

SPATSIZI PLATEAU WILDERNESS P.P.

Kates Needle 10,023 ft

ALASKA HIGHWAY

Interior Mountains and Plateaus
P. 60

ALBE

TATLATUI P.P.

MISTY FIORDS NAT. MON.

Ketchikan

BRITISH

C

Peace River

2

QUEEN

Prince Rupert

NAIKOON P.P.

Kitimat

COLUMBIA

Hines Creek

CHARLOTTE

ISLANDS

GWAII HAANAS NATIONAL PARK RESERVE AND HAIDA HERITAGE SITE

97

Dawson Creek

2

Canadian Rockies
P. 98

TWEEDSMUIR P.P.

Prince George

BOWRON LAKE P.P.

YELLOWHEAD HIGHWAY

43

JASPER NATIONAL PARK

Queen Charlotte Sound

WELLS GRAY P.P.

Columbia Mountains

North Saskatche

Pacific Coast
P. 16

PACIFIC

OCEAN

Port Hardy

20

Fraser

5

BANFF N.P.

YOHO N.P.

Banff

Vancouver Island

19

STRATHCONA P.P.

Kamloops

97

Kelowna

CALGAR

Tofino

GARIBALDI P.P.

5

93 95

PACIFIC RIM NATIONAL PARK RESERVE

VANCOUVER

1

NORTH CASCADES N.P.

3

Cascade Ra.

Columbia R.

Victoria

95

SEATTLE

5

WASHINGTON

ID.

0 — miles — 200
0 — kilometers — 300

N

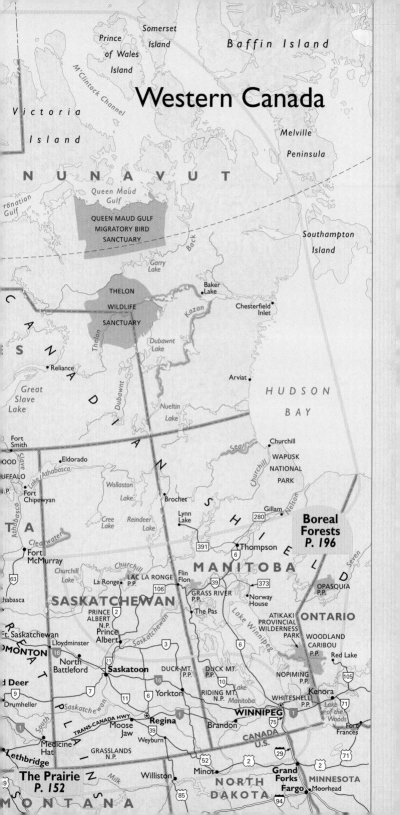

Western Canada

NUNAVUT

Baffin Island

Somerset Island

Prince of Wales Island

Victoria Island

M'Clintock Channel

Melville Peninsula

Coronation Gulf

Queen Maud Gulf

QUEEN MAUD GULF MIGRATORY BIRD SANCTUARY

Southampton Island

Garry Lake

Baker Lake

Chesterfield Inlet

THELON WILDLIFE SANCTUARY

Dubawnt Lake

Kazan

Back

Reliance

Arviat

HUDSON BAY

Great Slave Lake

Dubawnt

Nueltin Lake

Fort Smith

WOOD BUFFALO N.P.

Eldorado

Fort Chipewyan

Lake Athabasca

Slave

Wollaston Lake

Brochet

Churchill

Seal

WAPUSK NATIONAL PARK

Gillam

Nelson

280

Boreal Forests P. 196

Cree Lake

Reindeer Lake

Lynn Lake

391

Thompson

6

OPASQUIA P.P.

Seven

Athabasca

Clearwater

Fort McMurray

Churchill Lake

Churchill

LAC LA RONGE P.P.

La Ronge

Flin Flon

MANITOBA

63

SASKATCHEWAN

106

GRASS RIVER P.P.

39

373

Norway House

ONTARIO

C A N A D I A N   S H I E L D

PRINCE ALBERT N.P.

Saskatchewan

The Pas

ATIKAKI PROVINCIAL WILDERNESS PARK

WOODLAND CARIBOU P.P.

Red Lake

N. Saskatchewan

Prince Albert

2

3

Lake Winnipeg

6

NOPIMING P.P.

105

EDMONTON

Lloydminster

North Battleford

16

11

Saskatoon

DUCK MT. P.P.

DUCK MT. P.P.

10

RIDING MT. N.P.

Lake Manitoba

Kenora

Lake of the Woods

Red Deer

7

16

Yorkton

WHITESHELL P.P.

75

9

Drumheller

11

6

Saskatchewan

TRANS-CANADA HWY

Moose Jaw

Regina

1

Brandon

WINNIPEG

1

Fort Frances

A L B E R T A

Medicine Hat

South Saskatchewan

39

Weyburn

CANADA

52

U.S.

29

71

Lethbridge

GRASSLANDS N.P.

Milk

The Prairie P. 152

Williston

Minot

2

Grand Forks **Fargo**

94

2

MINNESOTA

Moorhead

9

85

NORTH DAKOTA

MONTANA

Sanctuary from Civilization

WE WERE HIKING THE EAST BANK of the Slims River in Kluane National Park and Reserve when a grizzly walked out from behind some trees 50 feet away. My companions and I had been on high alert, having just come across fresh bear tracks, but the nearness of the griz shot a jolt of adrenaline straight to my knees. We shouted, waved our arms, and held our packs above our heads to appear larger—a common method of discouraging bear attacks. It worked: After 15 seconds or so, the grizzly bolted into the trees.

Exhilarated and unnerved by the encounter, I began to wonder if we venture into the wild in search of such run-ins or in spite of them. A bit of both, I suppose. Most of us do not consciously seek out (nor obsess upon) danger as we explore the natural world, but all of us quest for the untamed—the realm our ancestors roamed for millions of years before the advent of industrial civilization.

We may be looking for scenic beauty, but we could find that in the countryside or a formal garden. We may be hiking or canoeing for exercise, but we could get that in a gym. We may be camping or backpacking to spend time with family or friends, but we could achieve the same goal in a city or at the beach. Something more profound—something less ex-

Amethyst Lake, backed by The Ramparts

plicable—must be pulling us toward places like the wildlands of Western Canada, where shopping malls, car horns, and factory exhaust can be left far behind for the sight of glacier-draped mountains, the call of loons, and the warm fragrance of sun-drenched wildflowers.

Granted, we set aside wilderness to protect our watersheds, to perpetuate the existence of native animal and plant species that have commercial value, to filter pollutants from our air and water, and to conserve biological diversity and the crucial genetic resources it encompasses. These are the practical reasons for saving the wild.

But we also preserve wilderness because wild places resonate in our souls. Though most of us now live in thoroughly domesticated settings, spending great chunks of time in office and factory (or in the virtual reality of television and computer), we remain flesh-and-blood creatures whose species evolved in intimate contact with the natural world.

That's why we belong in the valleys, prairie grasslands, coastal rain forests, rolling aspen parklands, arid badlands, and other varied habitats of Western Canada. When we hike along a Kluane park river valley greened by trees and grassy meadows and populated by moose and eagles—and by at least one curious grizzly bear—we are not visiting an exotic foreign land. We're going home.

Bob Devine

Discovering Western Canada

WESTERN CANADA IS A STELLAR DESTINATION for nature lovers. Like the Amazon, the outback, and Siberia, it holds vast expanses of sparsely populated and little developed lands and waters. Even lightly settled Montana is 66 times more densely populated than the Northwest Territories, where 42,000 people occupy 452,000 square miles. If you want to get away from it all, the wilds of Western Canada are a great place to start.

This book defines Western Canada as everything from the western shore of Hudson Bay to Alaska and the Pacific Ocean, including islands off the British Columbia coast. Western Canada also runs south to the tip of Vancouver Island and the Strait of Juan de Fuca, and as far north as Aulavik National Park above the Arctic Circle. In geopolitical terms, the region comprises the Yukon Territory, British Columbia, the Northwest Territories, Alberta, Saskatchewan, Manitoba, and the western reaches of Nunavut, Canada's newest province.

If you don't own an ice ax and can't tell the tracks of a grizzly from those of a black bear, you may be wondering if Western Canada is too wild and woolly for you. It's not: Anyone of average fitness can enjoy the majority of sites profiled in these pages. Many destinations bracket the rigor spectrum, from viewing displays in a visitor center to mountaineering on isolated glaciers. A few sites offer untouched wilderness; accessible mainly by raft, canoe, or bush plane, they are best visited by organized tour. Happily, many outfitters and wilderness lodges stand ready to guide travelers to a safe, pleasurable exploration of these isolated areas.

Not surprisingly for its size—nearly twice that of India—Western Canada encompasses an extraordinary diversity of landscapes. Each chapter in this book covers a distinct biogeographic region. Because these are broadly defined, each division contains nearly infinite local variations. For example, the prairie—often thought of as monotonous—is far from uniform: Grasslands can be shortgrass, mixed-grass, or tallgrass. In some places they give way to desert, and even to sparsely vegetated dune fields. In other places the dry prairie is pocked by verdant oases in the form of rivers, lakes, and creeks. Parts of the prairie sport mountains and high plateaus—forested islands brimming with wildlife.

The Pacific Coast, the subject of Chapter 1, is a small but rich area that runs from the Washington State border in the south to the Alaska Panhandle in the north and from the Queen Charlotte Islands in the west to the Coast Mountains in the east. The mountainous terrain—many peaks exceed 10,000 feet—creates dramatic altitude changes and rain shadows, which in turn foster habitats ranging from old-growth temperate rain forest to sunny islands and alpine tundra.

The Interior Mountains and Plateaus (Chapter 2) occupy the midsection of British Columbia. Here mountains, lakes, and elevated rolling hills are wedged between the Coast Mountains and the Rockies; they run the length of British Columbia and just slightly into the Yukon.

Hiking Great Glacier Trail below Mount Sir Donald, Glacier National Park

The Canadian Rockies (Chapter 3) straddle the border between British Columbia and Alberta in the south, then angle across northeast B.C. This region of supreme montane scenery harbors some celebrated natural treasures, among them Banff, Jasper, and Yoho National Parks.

The Prairie (Chapter 4), described above, runs from the Rockies east across southern Alberta, southern Saskatchewan, and southwest Manitoba.

The Boreal Forest (Chapter 5) arcs from extreme southeast Manitoba northwest across central and northern Manitoba and Saskatchewan. This is a land where dense conifer forests and a bounty of lakes blanket the almost incomprehensibly ancient bedrock of the Canadian Shield.

The Far North (Chapter 6), basically everything north of the first five regions, encompasses more than half of Western Canada. A broad band of taiga—stunted conifers mixed with bogs, lakes, and wetlands—makes up the southern portion. North of that, beyond the limits of tree growth, is tundra; this harsh but exhilarating realm of ground-hugging plants extends to the Arctic Ocean and out onto its islands. The far north is nearly roadless and little developed, but those who find a way there discover off-world scenery and a surprising variety of wildlife.

I could rhapsodize about Western Canada's caribou herds, tide pools, 300-foot cedars, flower-filled subalpine meadows, and mournful wolf

Great blue heron on Wickaninnish Beach, Pacific Rim National Park

howls, but I'd rather use the remaining space to warn you about the area's potential discomforts and dangers. Many visitors worry about the weather, but most of the region (except its high latitudes and altitudes) enjoys warm, sometimes hot summers with plenty of sunshine. Naturally, local variations, off-season travel, and the ever present threat of the unexpected dictate that you come prepared for foul weather.

Boaters take note: Most Western Canadian waters are bone-chillingly cold. Capsizing in the middle of a large lake means hypothermia and death within minutes, so stay close to shore. Bugs abound in spring and summer, their marshaling points (any body of water) duplicating those of outdoors enthusiasts. Arm yourself with insect repellent, a head net, and bug jacket as needed. Black bears and grizzlies are present by the tens of thousands. Along the coastal edges of the far north lives the most fearsome of them all: the polar bear.

Finally, if you plan to drive the area's remote roads, many of them gravel, pack the usual emergency gear plus an extra spare tire, a tow rope, and extra windshield-washing supplies. Protect your headlights with a mesh or plastic cover, slow down when passing on gravel roads, and fill up with gas whenever you can; as I may have mentioned, civilization is a long way off. ■

Pacific Coast

Sunset over Wickaninnish Bay, Vancouver Island

WESTERN CANADA'S PACIFIC COAST is synonymous with wildness and the great outdoors. Instead of thronged beaches, you can expect to find unpopulated shores. Rather than tidy little towns, you'll encounter dense, disheveled forests. And in place of the beach bunnies and broad-shouldered hunks who constitute the coastal wildlife much farther south, you'll see bald eagles and bears.

Canada's wild western coast lies entirely within the province of British Columbia. The shore stretches 790 miles (1,270 km) south to north, from the southern end of Vancouver Island, just across the Strait of Juan de Fuca from Washington State, to the Alaska Panhandle.

Taking the Pacific Coast's east-west measure, of course, is more problematic. Just what constitutes the "coast"? Anything below high-tide mark? Any site that borders salt water, even if it lies at the end of an ocean inlet 50 miles (80 km) from the sea? Any area within a 10-mile (16 km) radius of a souvenir shop selling driftwood carved in the shape of dolphins?

A typical dictionary definition—"the edge or margin of the land next to the sea"—provides little precision. But don't fault the lexicographers. The truth is, no precise definition exists.

For the most part, you'll know the coast when you see it. You'll know you're there when you witness breakers 20 feet high hurling themselves against the rocks in Pacific Rim National Park Reserve; when you spot killer whales breaching in Johnstone Strait; and when you gaze up at that quintessential coastal rain forest tree, a 200-foot-tall Sitka spruce, while you're sea kayaking through Gwaii Haanas National Park Reserve.

A sea kayak is just one of the many vehicles that visitors use to explore Canada's Pacific Coast. By shanks' mare you can stroll barefoot on the beach, hike shoreside trails, or explore tide pools. By car you can motor along scenic roads skirting the Pacific. And by boat your options are virtually limitless, allowing you to take whale-watching trips; to sail on

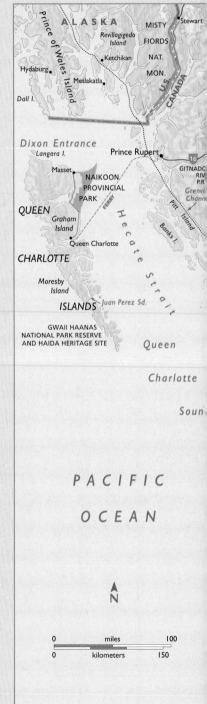

Algae-covered rocks, Moresby Island, Gwaii Haanas

Black-tailed deer and mortuary poles, Anthony Island

an old packet freighter through the islands of Pacific Rim National Park Reserve; to soak in a hot spring perched at the ocean's edge; and to scuba dive in clear waters teeming with aquatic life.

The western slopes of the Coast Mountains belong to the coast. The southwest corner of Garibaldi Provincial Park, an undisputed mountain redoubt, lies within half a dozen miles of salt water, yet the park's high country includes 8,000-foot (2,440 m) peaks towering above alpine meadows more typical of Rocky Mountain landscapes hundreds of miles inland. Perhaps the broadest possible definition of the Canadian Pacific coast is therefore the best one: The region includes everything from isolated islands to rugged cliffs, cascading waterfalls, racing rapids, thick forests of pine, and snowcapped peaks.

Diversity does not guarantee docility, however. For that reason, visitors will benefit from bearing a few natural hazards in mind. Much of this region can be classified as rain forest; this means that steady drizzle, sudden downpours, and rainstorms are the order of the day (in three seasons, at least; summers tend to be fairly dry). Littered with islands and deeply incised with bays, sounds, inlets, and straits, the ragged coastline also creates extreme tides and strong currents—be alert and informed if you plan to explore via small boat, canoe, or kayak.

These tides can endanger people on land as well; beach hikers have been known to find themselves cut off fore and aft by an incoming tide. Beware of sneaker waves, too; though rare, these unpredictable large waves can take beachcombers or children by surprise. A final hazard is rain forest trees washed into the sea, where they roll about in the surf, posing significant peril to waders or swimmers—the latter restricted to those few souls brave or foolhardy enough to venture into this icy water. ■

Pacific Rim National Park Reserve

■ 149,000 acres ■ Southwest coast of Vancouver Island, 65 miles (105 km) west of Port Alberni ■ Best months June-Aug. ■ Camping, hiking, boat tours, kayaking, wildlife viewing, tide-pooling, hot springs ■ Adm. fee ■ Reservations required to hike West Coast Trail ■ Contact the park, Box 280, 2185 Ocean Terrace Road, Ucluelet, BC V0R 3A0; phone 250-726-7721. http://parkscan .harbour.com/pacrim

ONLY ONE PAVED ROAD, Hwy. 4, accesses the wild, virtually undeveloped west coast of Vancouver Island. The Pacific Rim Hwy. leads to the popular Long Beach Unit of Pacific Rim National Park Reserve. Neither of the reserve's other two units—the rugged West Coast Trail and the Broken Group Islands—is easily accessible, but all offer enough sites and activities to capture the beauty and diversity of the island's untamed coast.

You can explore Pacific Rim by car, foot, floatplane, tour boat, or kayak. Some hikes trace sandy beaches. Others wind along rocky shores where waves explode against barnacled rocks and bright sea stars steal through quiet tide pools. If you venture out in a boat or kayak, you'll

Sunrise through conifers and fog, Pacific Rim National Park Reserve

cruise through a maze of small islands dotted with conifers and occupied by seals and sea lions. Just behind the beaches sprawls the temperate rain forest, where trails thread moss-festooned cedars and hemlocks.

It's just a five-hour drive from the Long Beach Unit to high tea at the Empress Hotel in Victoria, but as you wander Vancouver Island's wild west you'll feel 1,000 miles—and 1,000 years—removed from civilization.

What to See and Do

Arriving at the Park

In **Port Alberni,** at the head of Alberni Inlet about 115 miles (118 km) northwest of Victoria, decide whether to reach Pacific Rim by land or water. Hwy. 4 curves 65 (105 km) miles to the park through forested mountains and along Sproat Lake and Kennedy Lake. Or you can board one of two packet freighters (*Lady Rose*

Marine Services 250-723-8313 or 800-663-7192) for a half-day voyage that is even more scenic than the land route. The ships don't carry cars, so someone in your party will have to drive to Ucluelet—or you can make do without your own vehicle (limited shuttle-van service available in park).

The coastal freighters—the 105-foot, 100-passenger M.V.

Lady Rose and the 128-foot, 200-passenger M.V. *Frances Barkley*—depart from the Port Alberni docks. In the first two hours, as you pass through the long, narrow inlet, you'll likely see cormorants, Canada geese, and deer; with luck you'll spot black bears and trumpeter swans. The freighter stops at the occasional settlement or logging camp to unload supplies.

Upon entering **Barkley Sound,**

Bald eagle in western hemlock, Pacific Rim

the ship heads south to Bamfield or northwest to Ucluelet, depending on the itinerary you've chosen. Either way, for the next few hours you'll cruise amid the Broken Group Islands that dot the sound —some barely big enough to host a harbor seal, others blanketed with cedar, hemlock, and spruce. Watch for bald eagles, common loons, and Steller sea lions. You may even see a porpoise or gray whale.

West Coast Trail

The fishing village of **Bamfield** is the northern gateway to the West Coast Trail, southernmost of the park's three units. This storied coastal route curves 47 miles (76 km) south to Port Renfrew. The trail passes through total wilderness, so experienced hikers able to walk long distances through rough terrain with a heavy pack will enjoy ample wildlife, deserted beaches, and unspoiled rain forest. Do not attempt the West Coast Trail unless you are a fit, well-equipped veteran with a park permit.

The rugged trail leads past cliffs, waterfalls, caves, sea arches, sea stacks, and beaches. Crossing ravines requires climbing down (and up!) a total of 25 ladders of 100 feet each. Be prepared for uneven ground, slippery conditions on muddy trails, and steep slopes. You'll have to wade rivers and creeks, be prepared to meet black bears and cougars, and be able to pull yourself hand over hand via cable car across two ravines.

The rains are heavy, averaging 120 inches per year, with frequent morning fog. Summer's average high temperature is 57°F.

Parks Canada admits only 8,000 hikers per year. It's best to apply in advance for a permit. Hikers who simply show up unannounced could face waits of one to three days during peak periods.

Hikers can pick up the trail's northern end at **Pachena Bay** (3.1 miles/5 km south of Bamfield) or its southern end at the **Gordon River Trailhead** (3.1 miles north of Port Renfrew). As well as these two points, hikers may exit at **Nitinat Lake.** Transportation to the West Coast Trail is subject to change, so call for updated schedules.

Broken Group Islands

On the freighter to Ucluelet, the ship slaloms through the Broken

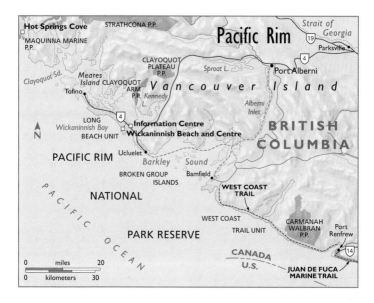

Group Islands—approximately 100 islands sprinkled across Barkley Sound. If this whets your appetite, return aboard a tour boat from Ucluelet or Bamfield for a closer look. The inner islands offer protection from the force of the Pacific, but the outermost islands are fully exposed.

For the most intimate contact with these islands, paddle among them in a sea kayak (novice paddlers should go with a guided tour). A number of outfitters sponsor kayak trips into the Broken Group; ask the park for contact information.

Long Beach Unit

If you arrive by freighter from Port Alberni, you'll disembark in **Ucluelet,** a fishing village at the mouth of Barkley Sound on the Pacific. At the dock, catch the Long Beach Link Shuttle van *(250-726-7790)* for the 5-mile (8 km) ride to the Long Beach Unit

or the 26-mile (42 km) ride to the town of Tofino. Van service is limited, so many visitors drive instead. It takes about 90 minutes to drive the 70 miles (113 km) from Port Alberni on Hwy. 4—a paved road through a mountain pass. When you come to a T-intersection, turn left and go 5 miles (8 km) to Ucluelet.

A right turn on Hwy. 4 at the T-intersection takes you into the park's Long Beach Unit. An information center *(250-726-4212. mid-June–mid-Sept.)* sits just inside the park. The highway proceeds 15 miles (24 km) into the park, threading the forest and skirting the seashore. Other than one campground and some park facilities, the landscape remains deliciously undeveloped.

To reach the unit's eponymous beach, continue on Hwy. 4 to the first available side road branching to the coast. This 2-mile (3.2 km) spur leads to **Wickaninnish**

Beach and Wickaninnish Centre (*mid-March–mid-Oct.*). Looking northwest from the center, you can scan the 6.4-mile (10 km) sweep of **Long Beach** (Wickaninnish Beach is its southernmost portion). Creeks carve the sand en route to the Pacific, driftwood logs jut from the beach like breaching whales, and the barks of sea lions drift in from offshore rocks. Two spur roads farther along the highway provide access to other parts of Long Beach. Of the nine short walking trails here, two—the **Half Moon Bay Trail** and the **Florencia Trail**—lead hikers to the beaches of Florencia Bay.

If you can tear yourself away from Long Beach, check out the rocky headlands that start just south of Wickaninnish Centre. You can reach them by taking the half-mile **South Beach Trail.** At several points you can walk down to pools and channels rich with

anemones, gooseneck barnacles, and sunflower stars—the largest and fastest starfish in North America. Don't overlook the broad, shallow channels where camouflaged flounders ripple over the sandy bottom and Dungeness crabs come to molt.

South Beach waits at trail's end. It's cozy, hemmed in by massive rocks, including a double arch. The beach consists of smooth pebbles that ring like chimes as waves jostle them together. At the northwest end of South Beach, the surf rampages through surge channels—narrow, rock-walled cuts in the bedrock—shaking the earth and shooting spray 50 feet (15 m) high.

Forest and Bog

Inland attractions of the Long Beach Unit include the **Rain Forest Trail**—two half-mile loops that start at the same trailhead. In

Hot Springs Cove

To luxuriate in seaside hot springs, take an excursion from Tofino to Hot Springs Cove, 25 miles (40 km) north of town in Maquinna Provincial Park (*250-391-2300*). The hot springs are minutes away by floatplane, but take a tour boat if you have the time.

The half-day exploration of Vancouver Island's west coast on the way to and from Maquinna is memorable. You weave among islands bristling with cedars and spruce, glimpsing bald eagles or perhaps even a fledgling. Grab a ringside seat for the spring migration of 20,000 gray whales, a show that peaks from mid-March to mid-April as the 45-foot leviathans hug the fertile coastal waters en route to summer feeding areas up north.

Once you disembark at the Maquinna Provincial Park dock, take the easy, 1-mile boardwalk trail that leads through the forest to the hot springs. The toasty water—80°F to 120°F (27°C to 49°C)—runs down a gentle hillside, forming pools where rocks slow its passage. The lowest pools lie near sea level and are sometimes invaded (and cooled) by a high-tide surge of ocean water.

On the lookout for gray whales in Clayoquot Sound

common with most of the park's trails, this one is primarily boardwalk and steep wooden stairs, with only a few small sections of dirt and gravel. The trail loops amid old-growth western redcedar, Sitka spruce, and western hemlock. Invigorated by some 120 inches of rain a year, lush vegetation sprouts from decaying logs, cracks in the rocks, lightning-singed tree trunks, and the branches of standing trees—as well as from the ground.

Another half-mile interpretive loop is the **Bog Trail,** a wheelchair-accessible path that winds along boardwalks through a downright soggy area. Here the heavy rains have produced a radically different natural community. The high water table and acidic conditions make life hard or impossible for most plants, but sphagnum moss thrives under such conditions, blanketing the bog's surface.

Park officials ask visitors not to stray off the boardwalk; like most of Pacific Rim's delicate ecosystem, the sphagnum-covered ground (it quivers like Jell-O) is extremely fragile. ∎

Gray whale fluke

Juan de Fuca Marine Trail

■ 29 miles (47 km) long ■ Southwest British Columbia, 35 miles (56 km) northwest of Victoria ■ Best season summer ■ Hiking, backpacking, tide-pooling, wildlife viewing ■ Contact BC Parks, 2930 Trans-Canada Hwy., Victoria, BC V9B 6H6; phone 250-391-2300. http://wlapwww.gov.bc.ca/bcparks

THE JUAN DE FUCA MARINE TRAIL takes hikers along a narrow strip of coastal wilderness parallel to Hwy. 14. Starting at China Beach, the marine trail runs some 29 miles northwest along the shore of the Strait of Juan de Fuca to Botanical Beach, just south of Port Renfrew. Blessed with sandy beaches, rocky bluffs, ample wildlife, and some outstanding tide pools, the shoreline is largely wild. The forest behind the shore features some old-growth and some older second-growth. The road and evidence of recent logging in spots are the only notable signs of civilization.

Experienced and fit backpackers with plenty of time can hike the entire trail, but they must deal with bears, tides, unpredictable weather, and sometimes tricky creek crossings. For an abbreviated challenge, try a long day hike over a section of the main trail; one popular stretch (12 moderately hard miles/19 km, one way) lies between **Sombrio Beach** and Botanical Beach. You can arrange a van shuttle back to your car.

Travelers with less time or experience can partake by stopping at any of four access points along Hwy. 14. One of the more appealing is **China Beach,** located near the southern end of the marine trail. A 15-minute stroll from the parking lot leads you down a trail of gravel and stairs through a mossy Sitka spruce forest full of 8-foot-diameter trees to the beach. Once there, you can walk northwest a few hundred yards to a waterfall at one end of the beach or troop far along the soft sands to the southeast.

The highlights of the marine trail, Botanical Beach and Botany Bay, lie near its northern end. Drive several miles south of Port Renfrew on a gravel road to the trailheads. For a fine loop, take the trail down to Botany Bay, turn southeast along the shore to Botanical Beach, then go back to the parking lot on the **Botanical Beach Trail.** You could complete this easy loop in an hour, but allot some extra time for lingering.

You'll want to linger at **Botany Bay,** where the deep, dark forest hovers over the beach. Huge slabs of furrowed stone angle from the sand and the nearshore waters. If the tide allows and you step carefully on the slippery rocks, you can walk out along these natural stone ramps to observe the intertidal life and snarling surf. Just offshore, sea stacks topped with trees guard the mouth of the bay.

The scenery at **Botanical Beach** equals and perhaps surpasses that of Botany Bay. When you emerge from the forest, stop and survey the burly bluffs, the massive and elaborate rock formations, and the sight of the Olympic Peninsula's snowy mountains visible across the mouth of the Strait of Juan de Fuca. You'll probably spend most of your time looking down—the tide pools are fantastic. (Try to arrive during low tide.)

These tide pools are no mere holes in the rocks; they are smoothly shaped wild aquariums that appear to have been formed by the hands of a giant potter. Some are oval; others are nearly perfect circles. They range in size from goldfish bowls to deep pools more than 20 feet across. The denizens of that limpid water include orange sea stars, shore crabs, gooseneck barnacles, and vast, spiny blooms of purple sea urchins. You may spy black bears, river otters, and raccoons foraging in the pools. ■

Gulf Islands & San Juan Islands

■ Southwest British Columbia, northwest Washington State, in straits between Vancouver Island and mainland Washington ■ Best months May-Sept. ■ Camping, hiking, boating, kayaking, tide-pooling, fishing, biking, whale-watching, wildlife viewing, fishing, wildflower viewing, boat tours ■ Contact Saltspring Island Visitor Information Centre, phone 866-216-2936, www.saltspringtoday.com; or San Juan Islands Visitor Information Service, P.O. Box 65, Lopez Island, WA 98261, phone 888-468-3701 or 360-468-3663, www.guidetosanjuans.com

ACCESSIBLE ONLY BY BOAT OR SMALL PLANE, the southern Gulf Islands and San Juan Islands are places apart. Though ferries make the main islands easy to visit—they've even been developed, in a semiwild sort of way— these ships bypass the vast majority of islands, which remain largely or entirely unpopulated. Even Saltspring Island—the most populous Gulf Island of all—scatters a scant 10,000 residents across 44,800 acres.

Plugged into the ferry system or not, settled or unpeopled, all the larger islands offer an enticing brew of forest, mountain, and coast. This archipelago of hundreds of islands straddles the border between Canada and the United States. The southern Gulf Islands have been approved as

White picket fence around officers' quarters, San Juan Island National Historic Park

Canada's next national park; the San Juan Islands lie in U.S. waters. The islands range in size from rocks that rise above the water only at low tide to 17-mile-long (27 km) landmasses crowned by 2,000-foot mountains.

The islands are bounded by the British Columbia mainland to the east, the Washington mainland to the south, and Vancouver Island to the west. The southern Gulf Islands cluster off the southeastern tip of Vancouver Island, adjacent to the San Juans. Protected from ocean storms by Vancouver Island and the Olympic Mountains, the Gulf and San Juan Islands boast some of the region's driest and sunniest weather (18 to 30 inches/46 to 76 cm of rain a year, almost all of it in winter).

You'll find most of the archipelago's roads and tourist facilities on those islands that are serviced by ferries. If you have a hankering to explore some of the other islands, you can hire a water taxi, charter a boat, or view them in passing while on a ferry or a whale-watching cruise.

What to See and Do

Saltspring Island
You can see a fair bit of the archipelago from the mountaintops of Saltspring Island, at 69 square miles the largest of the Gulf Islands. The most accessible summit, which you can ascend in your car, is 1,980-foot (600 m) **Baynes Peak,** located in **Mount Maxwell Provincial Park** *(250-391-2300).*

Return to sea level for the island's best hiking, found amid the second-growth forest and along a striking stretch of shore in **Ruckle Provincial Park** *(250-391-2300)* in southeast Saltspring. Walk the coastal trail, which hugs spectacularly sculpted bedrock right at the water's edge. If you scramble about in the intertidal area, you'll come across narrow channels and tide pools packed with anemones, mussels, and other marine life.

Classic tide-pooling is a terrestrial affair. It involves standing on intertidal rocks exposed by low tide and gazing into pools of water filled with life. However, several Saltspring outfitters offer an unorthodox option: tide-pooling from a kayak, with or without a guide.

In a kayak you can skim over the clear, shallow water close to shore and glimpse the lives of the intertidal and subtidal communities. You'll likely see a 2-foot-diameter sunflower star crawling about in search of prey, huge purple sea urchins, a rock sea cucumber, or a long-legged kelp crab using its claws to bring food to its mouth. These kayak excursions are hardly confined to this unusual method of tide-pooling. As you paddle along the coast, dipping in and out of little coves, you'll often

spy bigger game, too, such as bald eagles and harbor seals. For sure you'll see cobble beaches, rock cliffs, and conifer forests sprinkled with arbutus trees (called Pacific madrones by Americans).

North Pender and South Pender

Just east of Saltspring lie North Pender and South Pender Islands, separate but very close and connected by a short wooden bridge. Seven parks and more than 20 beach access points make for plenty of outdoor recreation. South Pender is the wilder of the two islands, with only a few hundred people living there—not that North Pender's population of 2,573 makes it Tokyo. To get your bearings (and some grand views) on South Pender, take one of two steep, 45-minute trails to the 800-foot (244 m) summit of **Mount Norman,** located in **Mount Norman Regional Park** *(250-478-3344).* One trail-

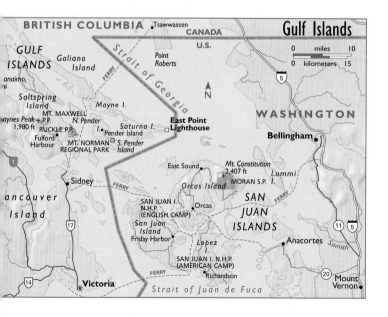

head is about a quarter mile south of the bridge from North Pender, on Ainslie Point Rd. The other lies off Canal Rd. about 1.5 miles (2.4 km) from the bridge. On the way to the summit you'll pass through woodlands of maple, fir, and cedar sprinkled with wildflowers. A platform at the summit leans over the cliff and serves up expansive vistas of the islands and beyond.

Saturna Island

East of the Pender Islands is Saturna Island, perhaps the most scenic of the major southern Gulf Islands, due largely to its low population: 326 people at last count. Motor along **East Point Road** on the north shore, enjoying the ocean views, accessible beaches, and relative lack of houses. Watch the water for orcas (killer whales), seals, and bald eagles.

For better chances of spotting orcas, go to the **East Point Lighthouse,** where pods often appear from May to November. On the northwest end of the island a 1-mile trail loops through the woods and marshes of **Winter Cove Provincial Marine Park,** whence fine views open of the Strait of Georgia.

Whale-watching

For a 90 percent chance of seeing orcas, between mid-May and mid-July take one of the whale-watching trips that ply the southern Gulf and San Juan Islands. Boats provide a better opportunity than land-based whale-watching because they can head for places where whales have been spotted and stay with a pod for an hour or two. You'll get a close look at these beautiful animals, with their smooth, gleaming skin and those intricate black-and-white markings. They typically engage in a variety of behaviors: jumping out of the water and reentering with a cannonball splash, spy-hopping (rising vertically from the water as much as 6 feet/1.8 m), slapping the water with their long pectoral fins, and hammering the surface with their flukes (tails).

These boat tours focus on orcas, but you'll see other wildlife and skirt many small isles thronging the archipelago. You may also spot pilot whales, harbor porpoises, minke whales, and Dall's porpoises (often mistaken for baby orcas because of their black-and-white markings). Some trips out of Friday Harbor, the main town on San Juan Island, take in the islands and reefs of **San Juan Islands National Wildlife Refuge** *(360-457-8451)*. Scan the Pacific madrones and Douglas-firs for bald eagle nests. Seabirds, including auklets, cormorants, and crowd-pleasing puffins, also nest in the refuge. Harbor seals often haul out on the rocks to bask in the sun.

San Juan Island

If you're ready to land on the American side of the archipelago, start with 55-square-mile San Juan Island, which anchors the San Juans. You can hike along untouched coastline or through pretty woods at **American Camp,** a unit of **San Juan Island National Historic Park** *(350-378-2240)*. Look for deer, fox, bald eagles, and listen for the resonant hammering of the pileated woodpecker. A few minutes' drive east from American Camp takes you to **Cattle Point,** land's end for southern San Juan

Lime Kiln Lighthouse, Lime Kiln Point State Park, San Juan Island

Island. Walk to the top of the nearby knob to see the San Juans, the
Olympic Mountains, and even distant Mounts Baker and Rainier.

Orcas Island

Of the three other San Juan Islands
served by the ferry—Orcas, Lopez,
and Shaw—rugged **Orcas Island**
offers the most outdoor attractions.
Its literal high point is **Mount
Constitution,** which crowns
5,176-acre **Moran State Park**

(360-376-2326). Energetic hikers
can huff and puff their way to the
2,407-foot summit, but most visitors drive. Climb the old stone
lookout tower at the top for a 360-
degree view of the Canadian Coast
Mountains, Vancouver Island, the
Gulf Islands, and Mount Rainier.

Orcas Island also harbors many
pockets of wild forest and coastline awaiting discovery by those
who drive or cycle its back roads.
A stellar example lies a few hun-

Pod people: Watching orcas swim past Lime Kiln Point State Park

dred yards from the village of **Eastsound.** Travel south on Prune Alley along the eastern shore of **East Sound** to the end of the road. Continue along the shore on foot and in a few minutes you'll enter **Madrona Point,** a hideaway named for the groves of Pacific madrones (aka arbutus trees). You can identify these handsome trees by their bright yellow-orange-brown trunks and branches and their ever peeling bark. A network of informal trails crisscrosses the point. Walk down to a few of the secluded coves on the sound. Some of the little plots of sandy beach are so packed with clams that nearly every one of your steps will stimulate buried clams to spout, sometimes as high as eye level. The rocky beaches shelter an abundance of tide-pool life, including sea urchins, barnacles, sea stars, and, in places, an exceptional diversity and number of crabs. ■

George C. Reifel Migratory Bird Sanctuary

■ 850 acres ■ Southwest British Columbia, 22 miles south of Vancouver ■ Best months Oct.-March ■ Hiking, bird-watching ■ Adm. fee ■ Contact the sanctuary, British Columbia Waterfowl Society, 5191 Robertson Rd., Delta, BC V4K 3N2; phone 604-946-6980. www.pyr.ec.gc.ca/wildlife/habitat/mbs-george_e.htm

Sandhill crane

IF THE SIGHTS AND SOUNDS of thousands of snow geese lifting into a cold winter sky set your pulse racing, head for the George C. Reifel Migratory Bird Sanctuary, part of the Alaksen National Wildlife Area at the mouth of the Fraser River.

The snow geese may be the most renowned birds at the sanctuary, but they are hardly alone out there. This patchwork of mudflats, fresh water, brackish and salt marshes, and upland fields attracts the largest wintering population of waterfowl in Canada; 37 species of ducks, geese, and swans have been sighted in the George Reifel sanctuary.

Nor are waterfowl the only beneficiaries of this prized delta habitat. More than 268 bird species have shown up, and many are either residents or regular visitors.

A network of dikes allows you to hike in the sanctuary. Several lookout points and an observation tower enhance your viewing opportunities. And what opportunities they are. Trumpeter swans sail atop the open water, blowing their resonating bugles. Long-billed dowitchers, their straight bills rhythmically jabbing down and up like sewing machine needles, probe the mudflats for juicy marine worms. Peregrine falcons hit the afterburners and rocket at speeds greater than 100 miles per hour (161 kmph) in pursuit of a duck dinner. For bird-watchers, the biggest problem seems to be aching arms—a symptom of holding up their binoculars so long.

The traditional human travel month of July is the quietest time to visit the sanctuary, because there's relatively little avian activity. The migrants start arriving in the late summer and fall and peak in early November, depending on that year's weather. Many of these migrants winter at Reifel, typically remaining until late March. ■

Rafting on Green Lake

Garibaldi Provincial Park

■ 466,229 acres ■ Southwest British Columbia, 40 miles (64 km) north of Vancouver ■ Best months July-Sept., Jan.-March ■ Camping, hiking, backpacking, mountain climbing, skiing, wildlife viewing ■ Camping fee ■ Contact BC Parks, phone 604-898-3678. wlapwww.gov.bc.ca/bcparks

THIS IS THE COAST? Instead of Pacific breakers, you'll see waves of 8,000-foot peaks, glaciers clinging to their flanks…high valleys in which the green of alpine meadows mixes with the blue-green of glacial lakes…low valleys bristling with thick forests of Douglas-fir, western redcedar, and western hemlock. How can Garibaldi Provincial Park, this protected mountain refuge, be considered part of the British Columbia coast?

Well, the park's southwest corner comes within 5.6 miles of salt water, and the nearby Pacific determines the park's climate, flora, and fauna.

The park was connected to the coast early on. In 1860, a naval captain surveying Howe Sound in the Strait of Georgia dubbed one of the area's tallest peaks, 8,786-foot-high Mount Garibaldi, after the famous Italian patriot. The name stuck—and was recycled 67 years later, when the views from the summit spurred the creation of Garibaldi Provincial Park.

Visitors lacking advanced outdoor skills should approach Garibaldi from the west; trackless wilderness lies to the east. Starting in Vancouver, drive about 40 miles north on Hwy. 99 and you'll arrive at the southwest corner of the park. From there the highway continues along Garibaldi's western border. In five places spur roads thrust east into the park, each leading to one of the five developed areas within Garibaldi. However, in this case "developed" doesn't mean snack bars and interpretive centers—merely established trails and the occasional campground.

Peak ritual: Adding to the cairn at the summit of Whistler Mountain

What to See and Do

The park's two tallest peaks—9,485-foot Wedge Mountain, reached via its own trailhead just north of Whistler, and 8,786-foot Mount Garibaldi, reached via the Diamond Head trail—lure many climbers to take in the vistas from above. Other visitors access the trails via five spur roads.

The northernmost spur road leaves Hwy. 99 about 8 miles (13 km) north of Whistler, leads a few miles into the park, and ends at a trailhead. From there a 4-mile (6.5 km) trail ascends to the **Wedgemount Lake area.** This demanding trail gains about 4,000 vertical feet and, near the end, traverses a treacherous, rock-strewn slope. The payoff: a 1,000-foot waterfall, a chance to see mountain goats, and superb high-country views.

The next spur road to the south starts in the ski resort of **Whistler Village** and once led to the trailhead for the **Singing Pass area.** Part of the road is unstable, however, so it has been closed to vehicles. The hike to this celebrated alpine haven now includes several miles of the old road, making it a tough, 15-mile (round-trip) trek.

A couple of miles south of Whistler, the third spur threads east 5 miles from Hwy. 99, dead-ending at a parking lot whence you can walk into the **Cheakamus Lake area.** A pleasingly flat trail follows the **Cheakamus River** beneath a high canopy of old-growth western redcedar, Douglas-fir, and western hemlock. In that deep shade, skunk cabbage, ferns, kelly green moss, and devil's club higher than your head prosper. The milky green glacial river flows in contrast to the clear creeks feeding it, their crystalline waters soon lost in the opaque flow. About 2 miles along is a campground at the west end of the 4-mile-long lake, hemmed in by 2,000-foot (610 m) mountains. The trail continues along the lakeshore for another 2 miles, then ends at a second campground.

Black Tusk/Garibaldi Lake Area

Seven miles (11km) south of the Cheakamus turnoff, you'll arrive at the fourth of the spur roads into Garibaldi. This 1.5-mile drive takes you to the trail that penetrates the heart of the park: the Black Tusk/Garibaldi Lake area.

The trail to Garibaldi Lake, about 6 miles with an elevation gain of 2,500 feet, climbs relentlessly for the first 4 miles. The grade is humane, though; it won't

Grizzly Bear Range

Garibaldi Provincial Park lies near the southern boundary of grizzly bear country. A few of these awesome carnivores inhabit the northern sections of Washington, Idaho, and Montana, and some live in isolated pockets farther south, notably in Yellowstone National Park. But almost the entire North American population of *Ursus arctos* resides in western Canada and Alaska.

It wasn't always so. Grizzlies once ranged as far east as Manitoba and western Iowa—and as far south as Mexico.

leave your legs shaking. Plus the scenery—a forest of monumental old-growth western redcedar and Douglas-fir—rewards the effort. At the end of this push, you pass the **Barrier,** a wall of volcanic rock, and the trail levels out as it leads from Barrier Lake to Lesser Garibaldi Lake to the most storied place in the park: Garibaldi Lake.

On the lake's west bank is a ranger station and a big (for the backcountry) campsite. A smaller camping area lies about a mile away, at Taylor Meadows. Glaciers and knife-point peaks encircle the 1,000-foot-deep, miles-long lake.

When you tire of soaking up the scenery from the Garibaldi Lake Campground (which may take a week), walk a mile northwest to **Taylor Meadows.** The meadows are a painter's palette of colors, including the drooping magenta blooms of Lewis's monkey flower; the dainty pink petals of mountain heather; the purple-blue of arctic lupine; and the incandescent yellow of glacier lilies, pushing up through the snow in a rush

Singing Pass and Overlord Mountain (and its glacier) from atop Whistler Mountain

to reproduce during the short high-country summer. The flowers here peak in mid-July and August.

Another fine hike—though a much harder one—takes you 3 miles (4.8 km) north from Garibaldi Lake to the base of the **Black Tusk,** a dramatically isolated volcanic tower that you can climb if you're so inclined—and suitably equipped. Thirty minutes after leaving the lake, the trail enters subalpine meadows ablaze with wildflowers and dotted with small, blue-black alpine lakes and ponds.

At times the path climbs up through steeply angled mountain-side flower gardens that make you feel as if you're ascending a waterfall of blossoms.

You don't have to climb the Black Tusk to get fabulous views. About halfway up the Black Tusk trail, branch off to the east and proceed about 1.5 miles (2.4 km) to the crest of **Panorama Ridge.** As wizened conifers give way to tree line, the trail winds through ground-hugging alpine plants; it then curves past **Mimulus, Black**

Windsurfing competition in Squamish River Estuary, Howe Sound

Tusk, and **Helm Lakes,** the views improving with every step. As you approach the **Helm Glacier,** the trail turns south and starts climbing Panorama Ridge.

The final half mile gets very steep and involves scrambling over loose rocks and sometimes slogging through snow, even in summer. Once you've reached the summit—a fairly flat knob about the size of a badminton court—you'll be able to see for dozens of miles in all directions. Directly below the ridge to the south sprawls Garibaldi Lake, its light blue-green glacial water the color of a tropical sea (though a good deal colder, to be sure).

The Black Tusk juts skyward not far from your 7,000-foot (213 m) perch, its elevation not much higher than yours. Also near eye level are the snowy tops of **Gentian Peak, Helm Peak, Mount Price,** and a skyline of other peaks, many draped with aqua-flecked glaciers. As you eat your lunch here, you can drink in the scenery.

Diamond Head Area

Mamquam Rd., southernmost of the five spur roads into Garibaldi, cuts off Hwy. 99 about 2 miles north of the town of Squamish. It meanders east 10 miles (16 km) to the Diamond Head area. From Hwy. 99 the road follows the Mamquam River and Ring Creek before crossing into the park and rising into the high country. The views en route are arresting, especially as you near the end-of-the-road parking lot, above 3,000 feet.

To truly see the Diamond Head area, hike northeast 3 miles to **Red Heather Meadows,** an expanse of summer wildflowers and, as promised, red heather. Four miles farther up Paul Ridge the trail hits **Elfin Lakes.** Here you can shed your pack and laze by the small, icy lakes, eyeing Columnar Peak, Mamquam Icefield, Opal Cone, and the Gargoyles (rock formations carved into weird shapes by erosion). Many people camp near Elfin Lakes and follow trails deeper into the park. ■

Brandywine Creek, Brandywine Falls Provincial Park

Skookumchuck Narrows

■ 304 acres ■ Southwest British Columbia on Sunshine Coast, 50 miles (80 km) northwest of Vancouver ■ Year-round ■ Hiking, tidal rapids ■ Contact BC Parks, Box 220, Brackendale, BC V0N 1H0; phone 604-898-3678. http://wlapwww.gov.bc.ca/bcparks/explore/parkpgs/skook.htm

A BOTTLENECK IN SECHELT INLET, **Skookumchuck Narrows** gets its name from the Chinook word for "rapid torrent" or "strong water." Shookum-chuck Narrows Provincial Park lies on the inland side of the Sechelt Peninsula, near Egmont. A 2.5-mile/4 km (one-way) forest trail climbs to viewpoints above the narrows.

Try to visit the narrows just before the tide shifts from outgoing to incoming or vice versa (consult a tide table). Scan the tide table for a significant change—from, say, a low tide of 4 feet to a high tide of 12 (1.2 m to 3.7 m). If the tide is going out, head for **North Point** (the first lookout you reach) to view the action; if it's coming in, the best vantage point is at **Roland Point,** another ten minutes down the trail.

When the tide shifts, 200 billion gallons of water are forced through a shallow channel just 200 yards (183 m) wide, turning the placid inlet into a raging river: The water swirls and churns through at 15 to 20 mph (24 to 32 kmph). Even in places where there are no rocks, white-water rapids appear. Huge eddies send water surging back against the flow. Whirlpools carve spinning holes, some 50 feet (15 m) across and 6 feet (1.8 m) deep. Logs sucked into the maelstrom of the narrows at the changing of the tide—when the water level on one side can be 6 feet higher than on the other—may twist and spin for an hour without making any progress.

Skookumchuck Narrows in full flow spurs humans to full folly. Kay-akers "play" in the waves, and according to one story some off-duty Coast Guardsmen once piloted a rescue boat into the narrows during a big tidal change. The boat flipped, and the red-faced rescuers had to be rescued. ■

Jervis & Princess Louisa Inlets

■ Southwest British Columbia, 50 miles ((80 km) northwest of Vancouver ■ Best months June–mid-Sept. ■ Wildlife viewing, boat cruises, waterfalls ■ Contact BC Parks, Box 220, Brackendale, BC V0N 1H0; phone 604-898-3678. http://wlapwww.gov.bc.ca/bcparks/explore/parkpgs/princesl.htm

THE MAGICAL MARINE JOURNEY through Jervis Inlet and its tributary, Princess Louisa Inlet, begins on the coast of the Strait of Georgia and ends deep in the Pacific Ranges of the Coast Mountains. Several touring companies based around the Sechelt Peninsula run excursion boats that make this all-day, roughly 100-mile (161 km) round-trip voyage through British Columbia's fjord country.

Some trips leave from **Pender Harbor,** a bay strewn with islands and coves on the western coast of the peninsula. Half an hour after leaving Pender you enter Jervis Inlet, which zigzags 35 miles (56 km) northeast through the coastal range. This marine trail is lined by 5,000-foot (1,525 m) mountains, which seem to lean over the water. About 10 miles (16 km) up Jervis you'll pass **Mount Churchill,** a 6,502-foot (1,980 m) Matterhorn-shaped peak that is the highest on the inlet.

Near sea level you'll see heavily forested mountains, the dark green brightened by the yellow-orange flashes of Pacific madrones; deer grazing in meadows or swimming across the inlet; shoreline rocks festooned with sea stars, barnacles, and oysters; and bald eagles trolling for fish. Above all, you'll see waterfalls—dozens of them if it has rained recently or if the snow is melting in the high country. Wispy white stripes that stand out brilliantly against the dark rock faces, many of these cascades snake hundreds of feet down the slopes.

About three hours into the trip you'll pass through Malibu Rapids and enter Princess Louisa Inlet, a slender, 5-mile-long (8 km) fjord that cuts through massive mountains (some higher than 7,000 feet/2,134 m). "Perhaps an atheist could view it and remain an atheist," wrote Erle Stanley Gardner of the site, "but I doubt it."

At the end of the inlet, **Chatterbox Falls** descends nearly a mile before diving 120 feet (37 m) into the inlet. Most trips stop at **Princess Louisa Marine Provincial Park** for passengers to explore the old-growth forest or stand near the bottom of the falls and get drenched. ■

Beach camping at Chatterbox Falls, Princess Louisa Marine Provincial Park

Strathcona Provincial Park

■ 618,600 acres ■ Southwest British Columbia, central Vancouver Island, 25 miles (40 km) west of Courtenay ■ Best months May-Sept. ■ Hiking, camping, climbing, boating, kayaking, canoeing, fishing, wildlife viewing, wildflower viewing ■ Contact BC Parks, Box 1479, Parksville, BC V9P 2H4; phone 250-954-4600. http://wlapwww.gov.bc.ca/bcparks/explore/parkpgs/strathco.htm

UNLIKE MANY PLACES BILLED AS THE "Canadian Alps," Strathcona Provincial Park comes by the comparison honestly. Six of Vancouver Island's seven highest peaks—including the 7,201-foot-tall Golden Hinde—rise from the park, while Canada's highest cascade, 1,443-foot Della Falls, dives off a cliff here. Strathcona has alpine tundra, alpine lakes, and an ice field. The park's dense conifer forests, its flowered subalpine meadows, and its horned peaks crowned with snow all project the gestalt of the Swiss Alps.

The vast majority of the park is wilderness. If you enjoy route-finding with a 60-pound (27 kg) pack, you'll love all this backcountry. You can even learn this skill on site by signing up for a program at Strathcona Park Lodge *(250-286-3122)*, an outdoor education and adventure-vacation center on Upper Campbell Lake, just outside the park.

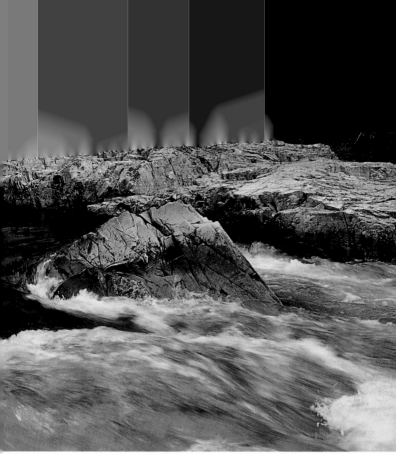

Lower Myra Falls, south end of Buttle Lake, Strathcona Provincial Park

What to See and Do

For car-camping and superb day hikes, Strathcona offers the Forbidden Plateau and the Buttle Lake area, both on the park's east side.

Paradise Meadows is the main gateway to the **Forbidden Plateau** —actually a gentle land known for its wildflower displays. The easy, 1.4-mile **Paradise Meadows Loop** provides a lovely introduction to the meadows: It circles through a summer riot of pink heather, lupines, violets, and monkey flowers. Equally easy but longer is the **Lake Helen McKenzie Loop,** a jaunt of three or four hours: It splits from the Paradise Meadows loop a few hundred yards from its start and curves south through meadows and forests to reach the lake.

Drive 30 miles (48 km) west from Campbell River on Hwy. 28 to reach the spur road skirting Buttle Lake's east bank. Along the lake's 15-mile (24 km) length are campgrounds, boat launches, picnic areas, and a number of good day hikes. A couple of miles south of Hwy. 28, savor the cool mist of **Lupin Falls.** Easy trails of half an hour include the **Auger Point Trail,** which explores woods recovering from a 1984 fire, and the **Wild Ginger** and **Shepherd Creek** loops, which slip through the forest along the Ralph River. ∎

Lenses peeled for orcas, Johnstone Strait

Johnstone Strait

■ Southwest British Columbia, northeast shore of Vancouver Island, 20 miles (32 km) east of Port McNeill ■ Best months June-Sept. ■ Boating, kayaking, whale-watching, wildlife viewing ■ Contact Tourism Vancouver Island, 335 Wesley St., Ste. 303, Nanaimo, BC V9R 2T5; phone 250-754-3500. www.islands.bc.ca

SEEING ORCAS (KILLER WHALES) in the wild is an unforgettable experience. First you spot the blows, or steamy exhalations, of orcas surfacing in the distance. As they near your boat or vice versa, their sleek, gleaming dorsal fins can be seen jutting from the water like black sails. As the whales get closer, you can make out their black-and-white markings and hear the creatures spout. They may slap the water with their tails, spy-hop (rise vertically several feet out of the water), or breach (leap clear out of the water and come back down with an impressive splash).

Johnstone Strait and vicinity is one of the best places in the world to view orcas. Tucked into the lee of Vancouver Island, this narrow channel lies in the protected waters of the Inside Passage, making for comfortable orca-watching. Because migrating salmon funnel through the strait from June to September, many of the killer whales drawn to British Columbia waters gather here to feed on the fish. Others descend upon the locale to scratch an itch—literally. Nearby Robson Bight Ecological Reserve is a sheltered bay (off-limits to visitors) whose seafloor is covered with gravel, pebbles, and barnacle-encrusted rocks; apparently the orcas take a singular delight in rubbing themselves upon these each summer.

Local observers have cataloged the animals according to their whereabouts and behavior (see sidebar opposite). A number of operators offer boat trips into Johnstone Strait, usually with naturalist guides aboard. Some vessels are fitted with hydrophones; these let passengers listen to the whales' complex vocalizations as they echolocate and communicate with one another. You may also spot Steller sea lions, humpback whales, harlequin ducks (look for their court-jester markings), harbor seals, pods of up to 100 dolphins, and bald eagles. ■

Orchestrating Orcas

The orcas that cruise British Columbia waters belong to three groups that seldom if ever mix: residents, transients, and offshores. Untrained observers won't see any difference among these populations, but whale researchers can discern slight distinctions, such as the shape of the dorsal fins, that indicate genetic dissimilarities.

More significant, the populations have different territories, behaviors, vocalizations, and diets. Offshores, for example, stay in the open ocean, where they travel in large groups of 25 or more. The 400 or so transients include 200 that stick closer to shore and another 200 that roam the coast in pods of two to four. The more social residents number 300; they hug the coast but remain in much smaller territories than the transients. Each resident pod consists of a mother and all of her offspring. While orca-watching in Johnstone Strait, the Gulf Islands, or the Queen Charlottes, you will sight residents almost exclusively.

Residents favor a diet of fish, mostly salmon. Though less is known about offshores, they too subsist mainly on fish. Transients, on the other hand, are wolves of the sea that merit the orca's other name—killer whale: Hunting in packs of four or five, they crave warm-blooded prey. Transients eat sea lions, dolphins, harbor seals, and the calves of large whales. There have been no confirmed attacks on humans by any orca.

Transients are crafty hunters, as evidenced by their cautious method of killing sea lions, a prey that can brandish wicked teeth and weigh more than half a ton. Members of the transient pack take turns hammering the sea lion with their powerful tails or leaping into the air and landing on the victim with their 10- to 11-ton bodies. Only after the sea lion has been stunned and rendered helpless do the transients risk moving in for the kill.

Orca pod, Johnstone Strait

British Columbia Inside Passage

■ 315 miles (507 km) long ■ Western British Columbia, between Port Hardy, on northern end of Vancouver Island, and Prince Rupert, on mainland central coast ■ Best months mid-May–late Sept. ■ Kayaking, wildlife viewing, ferry cruise ■ Contact BC Ferries, 1112 Fort St., Victoria, BC V8V 4V2; phone 250-386-3431 or 888-223-3779 (in B.C.). www.bcferries.com

THE INSIDE PASSAGE IS A WATER ROUTE that runs along the Pacific coast from Washington to Alaska. "Inside" because for the most part the passage threads the many coastal islands and is thus protected from the rough seas that sometimes afflict coastal waters exposed to open ocean.

Thousands of watercraft—from kayaks to cruise ships—travel the Inside Passage every year. Cruise passengers who partake exclusively of the blandishments aboard miss out on the sublime scenery outside: a realm of misty forests, snow-topped mountains, and restless seas inhabited by eagles, grizzly bears, salmon, humpback whales, and orcas.

To cruise a prime stretch of the Inside Passage aboard a comfortable but not opulent vessel, take BC Ferries' *Queen of the North.* This 410-foot (125 m) ship transports up to 110 vehicles *(reservations required)* and 650 passengers through the Inside Passage between Port Hardy, on the northern tip of Vancouver Island, and Prince Rupert, a mainland port just

Sunset view of Coast Mountains

south of Alaska. The ferry plies this route year-round, but the summer schedule caters to those who want to soak in the scenery of the Inside Passage. From mid-May to late September, the *Queen of the North* cruises only by daylight—a commodity in ample supply in the northern summer. The vessel leaves one port at 7:30 a.m. and arrives in the other at 10:30 p.m., then begins the 15-hour return trip the next morning.

Passengers have a number of options as they head out of Port Hardy. Some focus entirely on the Inside Passage, going up on the *Queen of the North* one day and coming back the next. These folks can get an overnight cabin aboard the ferry or reserve lodging in Prince Rupert. Other passengers extend their exploration by taking a ferry west from Prince Rupert to the Queen Charlotte Islands or driving east on Hwy. 16 into the British Columbia interior. One-way passengers can reserve a day cabin, but they certainly don't need one. You can find good seats inside and outside from which to enjoy the sights; outside provides the best views, but bring warm, waterproof clothing and look for seats out of the wind.

The northbound journey begins as the *Queen of the North* pulls out of the terminal at Bear Cove, across Hardy Bay from downtown Port Hardy. An hour out you'll see the flash of the lighthouse on **Pine Island,** which marks the entrance to the Inside Passage. This islet is one of only a few known nesting sites in the region of the rhinoceros auklet, a pigeon-size seabird. In breeding season, the male birds grow a pale yellow horn at the

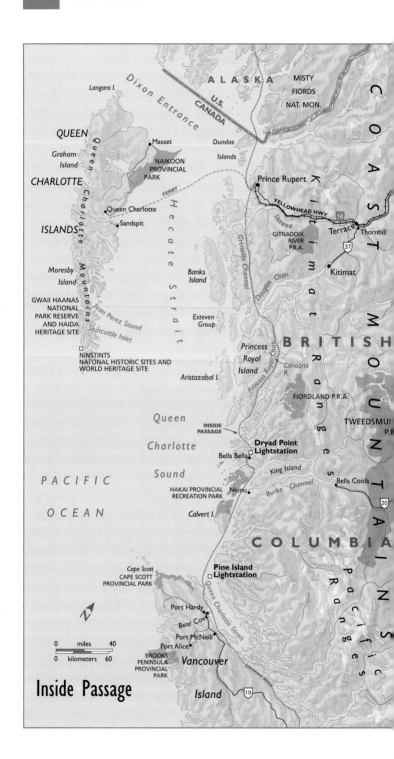

ALASKA

MISTY
FIORDS
NAT. MON.

U.S.
CANADA

Langara I.

Dixon Entrance

QUEEN

Graham
Island

CHARLOTTE

Masset

NAIKOON
PROVINCIAL
PARK

Dundas

Islands

Prince Rupert

Kitimat

YELLOWHEAD HWY

FERRY

Skeena

ISLANDS

Queen Charlotte

Sandspit

GITNADOIX
RIVER
P.R.A.

Terrace

Thornhill

16

COAST

37

Moresby
Island

Hecate Strait

Banks
Island

Kitimat

Queen Charlotte Mountains

Juan Perez Sound

Kuncuttle Inlet

Esteven
Group

Grenville Channel

Douglas Chan.

MOUNTAIN

GWAII HAANAS
NATIONAL
PARK RESERVE
AND HAIDA
HERITAGE SITE

NINSTINTS
NATONAL HISTORIC SITES AND
WORLD HERITAGE SITE

Aristazabal I.

Princess
Royal
Island

Canoona R.

BRITISH

Princess Royal Chan.

FIORDLAND P.R.A.

Queen

INSIDE
PASSAGE

Charlotte

Dryad Point
Lightstation

Bella Bella

King Island

TWEEDSMUI
P.

Sound

PACIFIC

HAKAI PROVINCIAL
RECREATION PARK

Namu

Burke Channel

Bella Coola

20

OCEAN

Calvert I.

COLUMBIA

Cape Scott
CAPE SCOTT
PROVINCIAL PARK

Pine Island
Lightstation

Pacific

Port Hardy

Bear Cove

Queen Charlotte Strait

Port McNeill

Port Alice

BROOKS
PENINSULA
PROVINCIAL
PARK

Vancouver

Ranges

0   miles   40
0   kilometers   60

Island

19

Inside Passage

base of their orange bills—hence "rhinoceros." Not far past Pine Island the ship crosses **Queen Charlotte Sound,** one of two stretches where the B.C. portion of the Inside Passage ventures "outside," exposed to the open ocean. Glance at the bow waves every now and then to see if a playful dolphin or porpoise is surfing them.

After about an hour and a half of open water the ship tucks in behind **Calvert Island** and starts up **Fitz Hugh Sound.** Now you're in classic Inside Passage territory, cruising up a channel flanked closely by land on both sides, the Coast Mountains looming to the east and the densely forested islands pressing in from the west. This is the temperate rain forest, one of the most biologically productive ecosystems on the planet. You'll see western redcedars, Douglas-firs, Sitka spruce, and other tree species 5 or 6 feet (1.5 or 1.8 m) in diameter and more than 200 feet (61 m) tall.

Near the end of the 40-mile-long (65 km) sound you'll pass **Namu** on the mainland, formerly a cannery site and now a resort and fishing lodge. The first orca taken from the wild for exhibition was caught near here, and thus got its now famous name, "Namu." Between 1965 and 1978 some 60 orcas in B.C. and Washington waters were captured to display in aquariums and zoos, but public outrage put an end to the practice in this region. You stand a fair chance of seeing a pod of these sleek cetaceans as they patrol parts of the Inside Passage. Sometimes they will play with a ship, rocketing back and forth beneath it at the speed of a dolphin—which is not surprising if you know that orcas to the dolphin family and technically are not whales.

About an hour past Namu, you begin slaloming past thickets of small islands. Just south of **Dryad Point** the ship squeezes through the narrowest channel of the trip, a mere 800 feet (244 m) wide. As you continue amid the islands keep an eye out for sea lion colonies, which are common on the rocky shores. You may hear their boisterous barking long before you see them. Bounty hunters used to shoot sea lions in order to protect salmon fisheries, but research showed that sea lions took less than 3 percent of the annual commercial catch (the misguided practice was discontinued in 1964). Watch for bald eagles, too; they typically space their nests about 3 miles (4.8 km) apart, leaving each family ample territory.

Midway along the eastern shore of **Princess Royal Island** you'll pass the **Canoona River.** As with most rivers that feed into the Inside Passage, salmon throng the mouth of the Canoona during the spawning season, in late summer. Among the black bears that come for the easy fish dinners you may spot a white bear. Often mistaken for albinos, these are a rare subspecies known as Kermode bears.

Nearing the end of the cruise, the ship runs up 45-mile-long (72 km) **Grenville Channel,** an unusually beautiful stretch of the Inside Passage. The channel narrows to 1,400 feet wide, with steep mountains hovering 3,500 feet above you. The mountains thrust so suddenly from the water that the ship can travel close to them with no risk of running aground; you may feel as if you're hiking through the lush forest sliding past the railing. From Grenville Channel it's a short haul into Prince Rupert. ▪

Gwaii Haanas National Park Reserve & Haida Heritage Site

■ 364,500 acres (islands) 1,300 square miles (ocean) ■ Western British Columbia, southern tip of Queen Charlotte Islands/Haida Gwaii, about 100 miles (161 km) offshore ■ Best months May–Sept. ■ Camping, boating, kayaking, tide-pooling, fishing, wildlife viewing, boat tour, ecotours ■ Adm. fee. ■ Visitor quotas, so reserve in advance; also reserve in advance for guided tours and space on ferry ■ Access to Gwaii Haanas by boat or plane only ■ Contact the park, P.O. Box 37, Queen Charlotte City, BC V0T 1S0; phone 250-559-8818. http://parkscan .harbour.com/gwaii

ONCE KNOWN TO THE OUTSIDE WORLD as the Queen Charlotte Islands, **Haida Gwaii**—the "islands of the people"—make up a misty, rugged, densely forested island archipelago rising out of the Pacific 100 miles off central British Columbia. They have also been dubbed the "Canadian Galápagos" for their large number of endemic species, or species that exist nowhere else. Wildlife aplenty, both endemic and not, still inhabits the lands but especially the waters of Haida Gwaii, where visitors may see orcas, spawning salmon, Steller sea lions, humpback whales, dolphins, basking sharks, harbor seals, gray whales, and other seafaring creatures.

The Charlottes began to take shape about 120 million years ago, when the offshore Pacific plate began subducting, or sliding, beneath the continental North American plate, pushing up the edge of North America in a number of high points connected to the mainland by tundra. Then, about 10,000 years ago, the ice sheets melted, water flooded the tundra (turning it into today's Hecate Strait), and the high points became isolated islands.

What to See and Do

Haida Gwaii is the realm in which the Haida, a First Nations people, have lived for 10,000 years. These days they live north of Gwaii Haanas, but evidence of their past and ongoing presence is everywhere in Gwaii Haanas National Park Reserve and Haida Heritage Site. One of the most obvious signs is their famous heraldic poles (not "totem" poles). In five village sites you'll meet Watchmen—Haida who live at important village sites from May to September to safe-guard their cultural and physical heritage. As they keep watch, they often share Haida culture and history with travelers.

Gwaii Haanas National Park Reserve and Haida Heritage Site protects the southern 15 percent of the Charlottes' landmass, which comprises hundreds of islands that stretch over some 55 miles. "Protects" is the key word. A local, national, and international effort to shield this fabled place from clear-cutting, which has devastated the

Low-tide treasures at Burnaby Island: Sea stars, bat stars, and blood stars

Crepuscular sky and water at Rose Harbor, Kunghit Island

northern Charlottes, led to the park's establishment in 1988. Since then it has been essentially left undeveloped. You won't find visitor centers (except at the Sandspit Airport and in Queen Charlotte City), roads, or hiking trails, except in a private inholding at Rose Harbour, where visitors can rent a guesthouse and kayaks, buy meals, and sign up for boat tours. There is a Parks Canada warden station at **Huxley Island,** north of Burnaby

Island in Juan Perez Sound, and another at **Ellen Island** in Rose Harbour. The only way into Gwaii Haanas is by water or air.

Do the Charlottes sound remote? You'd better believe it. Venture heedlessly into this wilderness and you may never come out. Big tidal fluxes, strong currents, mercurial weather, bears, and the low probability of rescue make Gwaii Haanas a challenge. Fortunately, the Archipelago Management

Board—jointly run by the Canadian government and the Council of the Haida Nation—has licensed some two dozen companies to operate tours through the protected area, encouraging non-adventurers to visit. You can fly over the islands in a floatplane and perhaps land for a glimpse at ground level, but it's much better to take a kayak, sailboat, or powerboat trip. Not only are these organized trips safe, but you stand to learn a good deal about the islands from your captain/guide.

Whether you go with an operator or not, pad your schedule—and stay flexible. In summer, rain, fog, and wind can cause delays of hours or even days. Even on the drier, eastern side of the archipelago, it rains more days than it doesn't. And the west coast is the wettest place in Canada, receiving as much as 157 inches a year. That (and its steep cliffs, big waves, and brutal winds) may explain why few people venture there.

Why go to the trouble of reaching this remote spot? To answer that question, take a look around. You're standing on the deck of a 70-foot ketch, sailing close to the jigsaw-puzzle shoreline of **Skincuttle Inlet,** gazing at forest ferns and preposterously large trees, some of them 10 feet in diameter. From a hemlock, a bald eagle stares down at you with appraising eyes. With 1.5 million seabirds nesting in the Charlottes (about half of them in Gwaii Haanas), you spot all sorts of birds as you pass a rocky islet: common murres, pelagic cormorants, rhinoceros and Cassin's auklets, and perhaps a puffin. This area is home to 80 percent of Canada's tufted puffins and 100 percent of its horned puffins. You can recognize the crowd-pleasing bird by its massive, yellow-orange, crab-pincer bill.

Or perhaps you're on a kayak tour when you spy a steamy geyser blow from the surface of **Juan Perez Sound.** It's a 35-foot minke whale, preparing for another feeding dive. The orcas that cruise Gwaii Haanas occasionally attack minke whales. Humpback whales, dolphins, porpoises, and harbor seals round out the list of commonly seen marine mammals.

A different cohort of marine life awaits when you steer your kayak down **Burnaby Narrows—** a shallow, half-mile-long, 150-foot-wide channel connecting Skincuttle Inlet and Juan Perez Sound. Burnaby Narrows reputedly con-

Island Invaders

You're kayaking the eastern shore of the Queen Charlotte Islands, down south in Gwaii Haanas National Park Reserve and Haida Heritage Site, when you pause to admire a Sitka black-tailed deer. The animal is lovely and graceful. It's also destroying the park.

On the Charlottes, Sitka black-tailed deer are an invasive alien species: They are not native to this place, and they are causing it harm. People brought them to the islands in the 19th century; the deer then spread to every forested island in the archipelago. They have reduced the abundance of trees, shrubs, ferns, and herbs. In some places, they have eaten devil's club and skunk cabbage almost out of existence, altering the ecosystem.

Remote islands are especially vulnerable to invasion because their plants and animals have evolved in isolation and therefore often lack defenses against non-native species. In Hawaii, for example, where no native plant has thorns, the native flora is being devastated by non-native grazing animals introduced by humans.

Similarly, certain age-old behaviors can make animals vulnerable to invasives. This became evident in the Charlottes in the mid-1990s, when non-native rats invaded Langara Island and began preying on ground-nesting murrelets. As the seabird population plunged, so did Langara's famed population of peregrine falcons; the rats had been poaching a dietary mainstay of the raptors.

Bald eagle on Moresby Island, Gwaii Haanas park

tains more animal life per square inch than any other marine site in the world. As you glide over the clear water you'll see moon snails, rockfish, sea cucumbers, red crabs, softball-size sea urchins, and a riot of sea stars in a rainbow of colors and a spectrum of sizes.

You may even see a furry, four-legged visitor; black bears often forage in the intertidal areas of Gwaii Haanas. If you know black bears, you'll notice that this one is different. If you don't know black bears well, your naturalist-guide may point out that the bears on the Charlottes are larger than black bears elsewhere in North America, and that they have larger teeth and unusually long snouts. Scientists think these island bears evolved such features to capture intertidal prey, especially crabs.

Other endemic species that have flourished in the isolation of the Charlottes include unique flowering plants, a subspecies of dusky shrew, a subspecies of the short-tailed weasel, and a sub-species of an extinct caribou. On the flip side, animals that live in similar mainland habitats, such as grizzlies and elk, are not native to Haida Gwaii. Unfortunately, a number of these non-natives— raccoons, squirrels, Sitka deer, and three species of rat—have invaded the islands since the late 1800s. They got here with human help, both deliberate and accidental, and they are now causing serious harm to the environment (see sidebar, opposite).

Where to go from Burnaby Narrows? What place to explore the next day, and the next? Hard to say; with so many operators offering so many itineraries, the possi-bilities are nearly limitless. Maybe you'll go ashore on **Moresby Is-land** and hike up a peak in the San Christoval Mountains; options include 3,700-foot Mount Moresby and 3,684-foot Mont de la Touche. Perhaps you'll laze in the warm pools on **Hotspring Island,** resting from a long day's paddling. Or you may simply stop at some islet yet to be named, sit back, and watch sunset redden the water. ■

Interior Mountains
and Plateaus

Mountains, water, and sky, Muncho Lake Provincial Park

ANY AREA THAT'S MORE THAN 1,000 miles by 300 miles
is bound to have variety. Whether it's boreal forest,
prairie, or Arctic tundra, a chunk of land this size will
contain many different animals, plants, and habitats.
But even for a region so vast, the interior mountains
and plateaus of western Canada encompass extraordinary
diversity. Travelers encounter skyscraping mountains
and broad, flat valleys; temperate rain forests and sandy
deserts; cold alpine tundra and hot, dry grasslands;

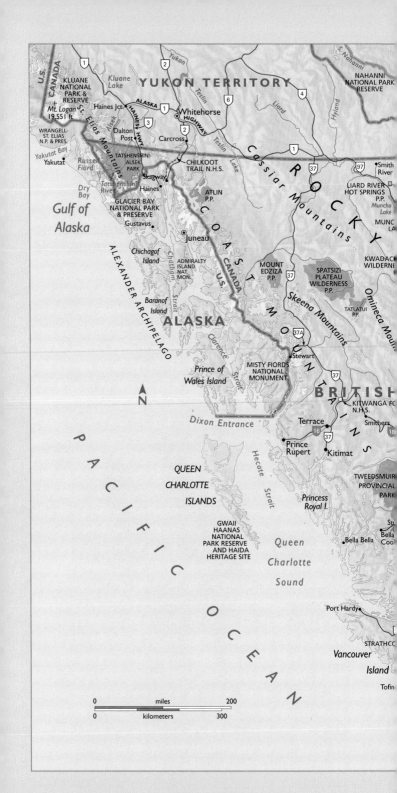

cathedral forests canopied by towering western redcedar; and boggy boreal forests of scraggly, 15-foot (4.6 m) black spruce.

This interior plateau spans central British Columbia from the Coast Mountains in the west to the Rocky Mountains in the east. South to north it stretches from the U.S. border, the Okanogan Valley, and the Frazer River up through British Columbia to the southwest corner of the Yukon, the ice fields of the St. Elias Mountains, and the Tatshenshini River.

The climate is almost as varied as the topography, but there are some broad patterns. The tall, wide Coast Mountains cast a sizable rain shadow, which is responsible for fairly dry weather for some distance to the east. The Rockies also cast what could be called a cold shadow to the west: They interfere with the flow of cold, continental Arctic air masses.

Annual rainfall ranges widely, from scores of inches on the western slopes of some of the mountains to just 10 inches (25.4 cm) —the average precipitation level of a desert—in the Thompson River Valley. (This dry, cool area produces some of Canada's leading wines.)

Many of the areas in this region are remote and hard to get to, but they are hardly off limits. The province of British Columbia has established (and actively protects) more than 625 parks and ecological reserves, providing some services and penetration to these wilderness areas.

Travelers can start in the far south with two British Columbia provincial parks—E. C. Manning

Rapids of the Ashnola River, Cathedral Provincial Park

and Cathedral. Snuggled up against the U.S. boundary, these gems represent the last gasp of the Cascade Range, which extends a mountainous arm from Washington up into Canada.

A couple of hundred miles north, visitors will encounter the Columbia Mountains and the Frazer Plateau. This area is anchored by Tweedsmuir Provincial Park to the west and Wells Gray Provincial Park to the east. Both are big parks with vast expanses of trackless wilderness, but each offers front-country areas for less ambitious visitors.

The northern half of British Columbia is almost devoid of roads, except for the thoroughfares that serve logging, mining, and oil and gas development. The one road whose entire length is paved is the Alaska Hwy., which winds across the northeast corner of the province. Along this road you can visit two provincial parks, Muncho Lake and Liard

River Hot Springs. The former is large and scenic; the latter is petite but exquisite and filled with delightful hot springs.

The region's final geographic jump veers westward to Tatshenshini-Alsek Park, nestled in far northwest British Columbia, then hurdles the provincial boundary to adjacent Kluane National Park and Reserve in the extreme southwest corner of the Yukon Territory. The Tat-Alsek, as the park is known, is a totally wild land—one that is typically reached by floating the namesake rivers. Kluane has a facade of front-country amenities, but the lion's share of the park is utterly remote backcountry. Combined, Tat-Alsek, Kluane, and their neighbors across the Alaska border—Glacier Bay National Park and Wrangell-St. Elias National Park and Reserve—are thought to constitute the largest protected wilderness area in the world. ■

E.C. Manning Provincial Park

■ 176,000 acres ■ Southwest British Columbia, 100 miles (160 km) east of Vancouver ■ Best months mid-May–mid-Oct. ■ Camping, hiking, boating, canoeing, mountain biking, horseback riding, cross-country skiing, wildlife viewing, wildflower viewing ■ Contact the park, Box 3, Manning Park, BC V0X 1R0; phone 250-840-8836. wlapwww.gov.bc.ca/bcparks/explore/parkpgs/manning.htm

JUST NORTH OF E. C. MANNING PROVINCIAL PARK the Cascade mountains begin drooping into the flatlands of the Kamloops Plateau. Even within the park boundaries the change can be seen. In the heart of Manning grow Engelmann spruce, lodgepole pine, and Douglas-fir—typical Cascades species. But toward the northeast boundary of the park, black cottonwood appears along the waterways and ponderosa pine occupies the slopes—trees that prefer drier climates and lower elevations. Tellingly, it is in Manning that the Pacific Crest Trail ends its 2,650-mile (4,265 km) run from the U.S.-Mexico border, here presumably because the crests are beginning to dwindle.

Manning offers numerous amenities, but the park has more than enough wild to go around: 7,000-foot (2,134 m) peaks, fish-filled rivers, forested glacial valleys, and prolific wildlife. There's a great diversity of animals and plants because, west to east, the park spans an ecological divide, creating a spectrum of flora and fauna that ranges from coastal species to sagebrush-country species. Manning's wildflower displays are among the finest in British Columbia.

What to See and Do

The visitor center and nearby Manning Park Resort, off Hwy. 3 between Hope and Princeton, serve as the staging area for many park activities. From here the bulk of the park sprawls south and west toward North Cascades National Park in Washington.

Delve into this area by heading west on Gibson Pass Road. After about a mile (1.6 km) you'll come to the start of the 1.2-mile (1.9 km) **Canyon Nature Trail,** a loop that follows the west bank of the Similkameen River and comes back down the east bank, with 17 marked stations keyed to an interpretive booklet.

Across the road is the horse corral, which offers guided rides *(fee)* along the park's equestrian trails. Another interpretive loop, the 0.3-mile (0.5 km) **Rein Orchid Trail,** starts a quarter mile farther down the road. Boardwalks circle through a bog, where beavers labor at dawn and dusk and the orchids bloom white in early summer.

Lightning Lake

About a mile farther down the road lies **Lightning Lake,** a hot spot of outdoor recreation. You can rent canoes at the resort *(250-840-8822)* and paddle this 1.5-mile-long (2.4 km) lake or stroll

Hiking the Heather Trail, E. C. Manning Provincial Park

around it on the 5.6-mile (9 km) **Lightning Lake Loop.** At the far end of the lake you can hitch up with the **Lightning Lake Chain Trail** and continue southwest several miles to Flash, Strike, and Thunder Lakes. Whether canoeing or hiking, watch for ducks and loons. Around Rainbow Bridge at dusk you may glimpse beavers

sculling across the water. Black bears sometimes use this trail, too, so stay alert and adhere to bear safety procedures (see pp. 84-85).

One of the most popular hikes available here grinds up to the summit of **Frosty Mountain;** at 7,900 feet (2,408 m) it's the highest point in the park. Two routes leaving from the Lightning Lake day-

Kayaking on Lightning Lake, E. C. Manning Provincial Park

use area reach the top: one a 14-mile (22.5 km) route that simply goes up and back, the other a somewhat longer loop (17 miles/27.3 km). In either case, your legs and lungs will have to endure an elevation gain of nearly 4,000 feet (1,219 m), but the views and flower-packed meadows will amply reward your effort.

Skyline I Trail

The Skyline I Trail also originates at Lightning Lake. This moderately difficult hike leads through deep forest and along a high ridgeline that yields knockout views. The loop is 13 miles (21 km) long and gains 2,500 vertical feet (762 m).

Park at Spruce Bay, near the campground, and go south on Lightning Lake Chain Trail to the start of the Skyline I Trail. Take it northwest up the heavily forested slope. Within a couple of miles the grade steepens. Hairy woodpeckers hammer away at the dead standing

trees from a 1994 fire, and mule deer often graze on the tender new grass below.

Just above the burn, the skyline ridge begins. The gently rolling ridge serves up a diet of grand views and beaming wildflowers. Except for a few misshapen whitebark pines, the trees are left behind. Here, look out over the glaciers, avalanche chutes, lakes, cirques, rivers, and hundreds of miles of the North Cascades wilderness. In the hotter, drier areas look for the red of Indian paintbrush and the yellow of stonecrop. Occasionally a small patch of tiger lilies will appear, their showy, speckled orange flowers waving atop 3-foot (0.9 m) stems. Look for a northern gos-hawk to glide past at eye level.

As the trail starts a gradual descent, it passes through sprawling meadows. Wetter and better protected from the elements than their counterparts above, these meadows produce more robust plants, such as the waist-high hellebore—a poisonous plant easily identified by its large, deeply grooved, spiraling leaves—and the head-high cow parsnip. Black bears crave the cow parsnip found here, so keep an eye out and make noise so you don't surprise some bruin.

After about 6.5 miles (10.5 km), you'll intersect the Skyline II Trail. Stick with Skyline I, which makes a turn to the north. Now the trail descends several miles through forest to the **South Gibson Trail** and **Strawberry Flats.**

Located at the confluence of alpine, interior, and coastal plant zones, the flats contain more than 150 species of plants, about a quarter of all the floral species present in the park. Among the botanical highlights are bluebells, skyrockets, mountain forget-me-nots, tiger lilies, and, of course, strawberries. From Strawberry Flats continue about 2 miles (3.2 km) east on the South Gibson Trail back to Spruce Bay.

Blackwell Peak

To the north of the visitor center lies what is perhaps the park's most renowned feature—the subalpine wildflower meadows of the Blackwell Peak area. Across the highway from the resort, a paved road snakes 6 miles (10 km) up a steep grade to **Cascade Lookout.** As you stand there admiring the vistas, Cascade golden-mantled ground squirrels and yellow-pine chipmunks will skitter around your feet in search of crumbs and handouts. Enjoy their antics, but please don't feed them.

Another hustler might swoop down on you from the sky. This gray-bodied, black-winged member of the jay clan is the Clark's nutcracker. During the short pine nut season, Clark's nutcrackers

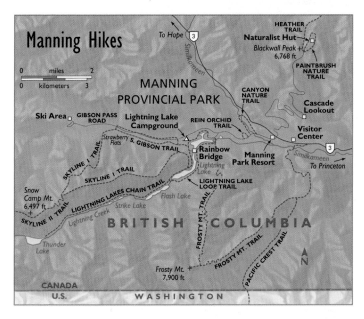

gather and bury thousands of seeds in different places. Come winter, they follow their mental maps and successfully return to about 90 percent of their caches.

From Cascade Lookout a gravel road leads 4.5 miles (7 km) up to Blackwell Peak, where wildflower havens extend north for about 15 miles (24 km). The first wave of blossoms hits as the last snow melts. Yellow avalanche lilies, white spring beauties, and creamy western anemones rush into the sunlight. The second and bigger blossoming occurs in midsummer. Indian paintbrush, lupine, yellow arnica, and many other species hurry to reproduce before the snow returns.

To learn more about the lives of the beautiful flowers, take one of the many interpretive walks that naturalists lead in the park *(check the boards for announcements).* One of their favorite routes follows the 1-mile (1.6 km) loop of the **Paintbrush Nature Trail.** Naturalists talk about the ubiquitous "moptops," which are the fluffy seedheads that remain after the large white blossoms drop from western anemones. Guides point out white Indian paintbrush, an uncommon relative of the prolific red paintbrush. They explain how stonecrop survives on the hot, rocky slopes.

Feel the lance-shaped leaves of the stonecrop; they're leathery and succulent, designed to retain moisture. The leaves around the base of lupines are curved up to catch water, and woolly pussytoes bristle with fuzz that diffuses UV rays. Such adaptations are common in the windswept, nearly treeless environment on the ridgetops, where plants have to make the most of what little water comes their way. To see more wildflowers, hike a few miles north on the moderately difficult **Heather Trail,** which wanders for 13 miles (21 km) amid tens of thousands of acres of hillside.

Though they get most of the attention, wildflowers aren't the

Rowboats for rent, Manning Provincial Park

View from Manning's Cascade Lookout

only forms of life that inhabit Blackwall Peak. Hoary marmots (aka whistle pigs) and pikas scurry among the rocks, squabbling over territory and gathering edible plants from the meadows. And you can't help noticing the work of the pocket gopher. The long rows of turned-over soil that stripe the meadows result from the gopher's digging. This plowing is essential to the well-being of all the wildflowers.

Not all the Clark's nutcrackers hang out at Cascade Lookout. They're up here, too, thanks to the abundance of whitebark pines, whose seeds constitute most of the nutcracker's diet. These hardy pines survive in harsh, high-elevation terrain because they're adapted to withstand brutal cold and wind. Still, the pines wouldn't make it without Clark's nutcrackers to spread their seeds.

Western Manning

Before you leave the park, stop in the westernmost part of Manning.

It consists of a long, narrow corridor along the **Sumallo** and **Skagit Rivers.** Near the rivers's confluence is **Sumallo Grove,** where visitors can take a half-mile (0.8 km) interpretive loop through a stand of gigantic western redcedar and Douglas-fir. Western redcedar are characteristic of cool, moist climates, so their presence in this portion of the park indicates that this river valley is an oasis of coastal habitat.

Coastal flora also prevails in neighboring **Rhododendron Flats.** You can immerse yourself in the beauty and fragrance of the blooming red rhododendrons if you walk the half-mile (0.8 km) loop through the flats in early to mid-June, when the flowers are at their peak. Several long trails leave from this area, including the 8-mile (12.9 km) **Skagit River Trail.** It starts in Sumallo Grove, crosses into adjacent **Skagit Valley Provincial Park** (604-924-2200), and continues down the lush valley of the Skagit. ■

Salmon Runs

ROMANCE, INTRIGUE, BATTLE, life
and death, a cast numbering a million
—a major salmon run would make a
great Hollywood spectacle. And you
don't even have to buy a ticket.

British Columbia features some of
the finest salmon runs in the world,
and the Fraser River system boasts
some of the finest salmon runs in
British Columbia. Emptying into the
Strait of Georgia, the Fraser extends
its veins as far north as the city of
Prince George, British Columbia.
Every year sockeye, pink, chinook,
coho, and chum salmon return to
the Fraser-Thompson network to
spawn. Some struggle upstream as
far as 850 miles (1,368 km).

The stars of the Fraser runs are
the sockeye. (The name apparently
derives from *sukkai,* the First Nations
word for this species.) Sockeye salmon
spawn in huge numbers and in several
places where visitors can watch them,
notably the Adams and Horsefly
Rivers. Both sites offer informational
signs, interpreters, and festivals to cel-
ebrate the return of the salmon *(for
information on the Adams, call 250-851-
3014; for the Horsefly, call 250-620-
3307).*

You won't see much unless you visit
during the height of a run. Peak times
can vary a bit from year to year, but
generally the Horsefly run goes full
bore in mid-September and the
Adams run in the second and third
weeks in October. The size of these
runs fluctuates dramatically from year
to year. The Adams and Horsefly
sockeye numbers follow a predictable
four-year cycle, featuring a huge, or
"dominant," run every fourth year. A
dominant run is expected in 2006.

These spawning spectacles are both
the culmination and the beginning of
one of nature's most renowned cycles.
The salmon fry emerge from their
gravel birthplaces and spend a year living in freshwater rivers and lakes before making the perilous journey to
the ocean; they transform into saltwater fish along the way. The mature
salmon spend two years at sea, then
make their way upriver to their birthplaces to spawn and die, setting the
stage for the next generation.

On average, for every 2,000 eggs
produced, only five will live to maturi-
ty—and only one adult salmon will
return to spawn. Nevertheless, dominant runs on the Adams number
about a million sockeye; the fish population is even higher on the Horsefly.

When visitors first set eyes on
a stretch of river or lake thronged
with spawning sockeye, most of them
tend simply to gape, overwhelmed
by the sheer numbers. Swimming
about in the clear, shallow water, the
salmon blur into a whole, like pixels
on a computer screen combining
into a single image. Once you've ab-
sorbed the big picture, however,
you can get down to the business
of salmon-watching.

Begin by focusing on a single fish.
Immediately you'll notice that the
sockeye's two-foot-long, six-pound
body is a brilliant scarlet, all except
for its pale green head (sockeye slowly
turn from silver to red as they swim
upriver). If the fish has a swollen belly,
it's a female; if it has a humped back,
a hooked mouth, and fang-like teeth,
it's a male.

The salmon will be engaged in different stages of spawning. That female

Sockeye salmon

fanning the gravel bottom with her tail is stirring up silt so the current will carry it away; if the silt isn't removed, it can fill the spaces among the bits of gravel and smother her eggs. Once she has her site prepared, she and a male will pair up and fan the clean gravel together until they have excavated a hole several inches deep.

In due time the female begins shuddering as if being electrocuted, until she squeezes out some orange eggs over the hole. Simultaneously, the male releases his milt over the eggs in order to fertilize them. Male and female repeat this process in other sites nearby until the female exhausts her supply of eggs. She then stands her ground and fiercely guards the nests for the rest of her life—a period of just two or three days. The male may join her or, if strong enough, pair up with other females before he dies.

As the spawning period nears its end, dead and dying sockeye float in the water like listless ghosts. Some will be eaten by bears, bald eagles, river otters, or other animals. Some decompose, nourishing the plankton that in turn will feed the newborn sockeye fry the next spring. Even in death, life is sustained.

Since the mid-1990s, the late-run sockeye have been returning earlier than normal. As many as 90 percent of the returning fish have been dying before spawning. Teams of Canadian and American scientists have launched a range of research programs to find the causes of this disturbing trend. *(For updates on the runs, contact Fisheries and Oceans Canada 604-666-0384. www.pac .dfo-mpo.gc.ca; or Adams River Salmon Society 250-955-0924. www. salmon society.com.)* ■

Cathedral Provincial Park

■ 82,667 acres ■ South-central British Columbia, on Washington State border
■ Park transportation available mid-May–mid-Oct. ■ Camping, hiking, wildlife
viewing, wildflower viewing ■ No private vehicles; no bicycles; no pets
permitted ■ Contact BC Parks, Box 399, Summerland, BC V0H 1Z0; phone
250-494-6500. wlapwww.gov.bc.ca/bcparks/explore/parkpgs/cathedra.htm; or
the Cathedral Lakes Lodge, phone 888-255-4453. www.cathedral-lakes-lodge
.com (park transportation and reservations)

CATHEDRAL PROVINCIAL PARK MAY MARK the northern end of the Cascade
Range, but as might be expected, these grand mountains go out with a
bang, not a whimper. In places you'll encounter flora, fauna, and terrain
typical of the drier transition landforms that lie between the Washington
Cascades and the interior plateaus of British Columbia. But the bulk of
the park features forests, stony pinnacles, meadows, lakes, and plenty
of wildlife.

The park is mostly wilderness; development is limited to a core area
consisting of a privately owned lodge, a park cabin, a bone-jarring dirt
road that labors up to the area, three campgrounds, and several delightful
trails. Be aware that you can't drive into the park on your own. Vehicles
must be left in the secure parking lot at the base camp, from which you
can hike into the park or pay to get a ride. It's a hard, all-day hike—some
10 miles (16 km), with a 4,200-foot (1,280 m) elevation gain—so most
people opt for the lodge's shuttle service *($55-$75 Can.)*. Reservations for
transportation should be made well in advance, and for the popular lodge
even further in advance.

What to See and Do

You can grasp the essence of
Cathedral Provincial Park by
exploring the **Cathedral lakes
area,** which is made up of six
different lakes in the center of the
park: Quiniscoe, Ladyslipper,
Scout, Pyramid, Glacier, and Lake
of the Woods.

Quiniscoe Lake anchors the
core area. Cupped by looming
mountains, the lake sits in a bowl
at about 6,800 feet (2,073 m). You
can savor views of the peaks as you
stroll along the easy 1-mile (1.6
km) trail that circles Quiniscoe.
Along the way look for bog

orchids and marsh marigolds in
the wetlands that edge the lake.

Several trails fan out from
Quiniscoe Lake. A relatively flat,
1-mile (1.6 km) path goes to **Lake
of the Woods,** and an equally easy
2-mile/3.2-km (one way) trail
leads through the forest to **Glacier
Lake.** Hikers looking to get their
blood pumping a little bit more
should try the moderately up-
and-down **Diamond Trail;** the
3-mile/5-km (one way) route
rings **Scout Mountain** and takes
hikers through some lovely
subalpine meadows.

Bighorn sheep, Cathedral Provincial Park

However, to take your exploration to a higher level, figuratively as well as literally, hike up into the alpine terrain—the tundra zone above timberline. And the best way to do this is to take the **Rim Trail.** This is the park's showcase route, running along the edge of the wall of mountains that enfolds Cathedral lakes. Three trails switchback up to the Rim Trail, making it possible to create a variety of loops, including a grand—daylong—tour of the entire rim.

For the latter, head out on the Diamond Trail and turn north toward Red Mountain. You'll wind your way through fields purpled by a sea of lupine blooms and flecked with the reds, yellows, whites, and blues of other wildflower species. Make sure to scan the sloping rock piles for pikas. You'll probably also see hoary marmots on those rocky slopes, as well as deer and moose on the grassy areas.

The trail crests on **Red Mountain,** where it levels out and then proceeds south on a broad ridge above Quiniscoe Lake. You're in the alpine region now, where brutal winters force plants to hug the ground for dear life. The low-growing vegetation offers visitors one welcome advantage; nothing gets in the way of the vistas.

At times during the next couple of miles glance to the west and see as far as Mount Baker, 100 miles (160 km) away in Washington. At other times the view extends far to the east, with Quiniscoe Lake in the foreground and in the background a vast expanse of mountain and forest.

Lowering your gaze you may find yourself staring into the eyes of a mountain goat. This creature will be easy to recognize: It'll be the only white, long-haired, black-horned, shaggy, goateed, 150-pound (68 kg) mammal around. During the summer males usually go their solitary way and females and their kids gather in groups of about ten. Watch mountain goats and witness their legendary strength and agility as they climb steep, stony cliffs that would give experienced rock climbers pause. In mid-to-late August also look for bighorn sheep up here in the high country.

Close to the southern end of the Rim Trail loop you pass the **Devil's Woodpile.** This formation of columnar-jointed basalt inspired the authors of the park's brochure to poetic flights of fancy uncharacteristic of most government publications; they describe the formation as "a tangled heap of rocks that might serve as the ingredients for Satan's blast furnace."

Not much farther down the path stands **Stone City,** which consists of monumental boulders of quartz monzonite over 200 million years old eroded by the wind into bizarre shapes. Name your own formations or see if you can find the Giant Hamburger or Smokey the Bear. Gaze south and deep into the Cascades; from here the Washington State border lies less than 5 miles (8 km) away. At Stone City the loop turns east on the **Ladyslipper Trail** and descends to Ladyslipper Lake. **Giant Cleft,** a deep fissure in the granite face of a mountain, lies about a mile to the south. ■

Caribou Meadows from Green Mountain Viewing Tower

Wells Gray Provincial Park

▪ 1.3 million acres ▪ East-central British Columbia, 100 miles (160 km) north of Kamloops ▪ Best months June-Sept. ▪ Camping, hiking, boating, white-water rafting, kayaking, canoeing, fishing, horseback riding, wildlife viewing, wildflower viewing ▪ High-clearance vehicles recommended for road to Trophy Meadows ▪ Contact BC Parks, Thompson River District, 1210 McGill Rd., Kamloops, BC V2C 6N6; phone 250-851-3000. wlapwww.gov.bc.ca/bcparks/explore/parkpgs/wells.htm

SOME PEOPLE REFER TO WELLS GRAY as the "waterfall park." But singling out this one—admittedly spectacular—aspect of this vast, multifaceted park does not do it justice. The park's 2,000 square miles encompass the Clearwater River drainage in the Cariboo Mountains, part of the Columbia Mountains system. Wells Gray is a rugged park, a place shaped by rivers, glaciers, and volcanic activity. The varied terrain supports an equally varied mix of wildlife, including wolves, moose, grizzly bears, lynx, mountain goats, and the last remaining intact herd of woodland caribou in British Columbia. At lower elevations you'll find cathedral old-growth forests of western redcedar, Douglas-fir, and hemlock, while in the alpine terrace visitors find hanging valleys and cirques.

Some 85 percent of this wilderness park is utterly undeveloped, accessible only to experienced backcountry travelers. The southern portion, though largely wild, has several access roads and a number of developed trails, campgrounds, and boat launches.

What to See and Do

The most popular area is known as the **Wells Gray Corridor.** Start at the visitor center (250-674-2646) in Clearwater, a town about 20 miles (32 km) south of the park.

Drive north up paved Clearwater Valley Road, which turns to gravel shortly after entering the park. At kilometer marker 37.7, turn south on Green Mountain Road, a steep

and narrow track that leads a couple of miles to the **Green Mountain Viewing Tower,** which provides a grand overview of the Battle, Flight, and 52 Ridge mountain ranges. Back on the main road, proceed to kilometer 42.2, the parking lot for the **Helmcken Falls Rim Trail.** This strenuous 6.2-mile (10 km) round-trip hike follows the **Murtle River** west to the point at which the river takes a 466-foot (142 m) dive, creating **Helmcken Falls,** the most storied of the waterfalls. If you'd like an effortless way to see the falls, drive across the Murtle River to kilometer 47.3 and turn west on the access road to the **Helmcken Falls viewing platform.**

Just past the viewing platform turnoff, the main road encounters the **Clearwater River** and goes north along the east bank of this beautiful waterway. For easy access to the river, try the very short **Bailey's Chute Trail loop** *(marker 59.3).* Here the chute forms a natural impasse to the spawning salmon.

At kilometer 67.9, just a couple of miles from the end of the road,

Sunset at Helmcken Falls, Wells Gray Provincial Park

you hit **Clearwater Lake.** This area brims with attractions, including two campgrounds, a boat launch onto the lake, the nice and easy **Lakeshore Trail,** and the harder but rewarding, 10.5-mile (17 km) **Chain Meadows Trail,** which leads to the Dragon's Tongue lava beds, Sticta Falls, and those fine meadows.

To see what many consider the best wildflower meadows in the Cariboo Mountains, head for **Trophy Mountain,** just northeast of the town of Clearwater. Branch off the Clearwater Valley Road and follow signs for 7 miles (11.3 km) to the parking lot. Though Trophy Mountain is one of the park's backcountry areas, some of its most appealing places are easily reached by day hikers. A half-mile (0.8 km) hike takes you to fields abounding with glacier lilies in June and later awash with arnica, daisy, lupine, and monkey flower blossoms. It's grizzly habitat, though, so behave accordingly. If you're up for a vigorous, 7.4-mile (12 km) round-trip trek, labor up to **Skyline Ridge** for views as fine as the name suggests. ■

Bowron Lake Provincial Park

■ 368,541 acres ■ East-central British Columbia, 70 miles (115 km) east of Quesnel ■ Best months mid-May–Sept. ■ Camping, kayaking, canoeing, fishing, wildlife viewing ■ Daily quotas for canoe departures; reserve well ahead ■ Contact BC Parks, Cariboo District, 281 1st Ave. N., Williams Lake, BC V2G 1Y7; phone 250-398-4414; 800-435-5622 for reservations. wlapwww.gov.bc.ca/bcparks/explore/parkpgs/bowron.htm

IF YOU DIDN'T KNOW BETTER, you could be forgiven for thinking that the arrangement of the lakes in Bowron Lake Provincial Park had been made just for canoeing and kayaking. The park's 11 lakes are laid out end to end in an almost perfect rectangle, so you paddle right back to where you started. Rivers and creeks provide much of what little connection is needed between lakes; the whole 72-mile (116 km) route requires just 7 miles (11.25 km) of portaging.

These waterways pass through eye-catching wilderness—and only one short stretch on the **Cariboo River** where you're going against the current. You paddle in the shadows of the 8,000-foot-high (2,438 m), glacier-streaked Cariboo Mountains. In the wetter valleys in the south and east, you'll canoe along banks overhung by big western redcedar and western hemlock. Some of the forested slopes are striped with avalanche chutes where frequent waves of snow have prevented the establishment of big trees, keeping the chutes clear for a garden of Indian paintbrush, buttercup, columbine, and other wildflowers. You can even hike the trail from **Unna Lake** to get a glimpse of the 80-foot (24 m) **Cariboo River Falls.**

Gliding through the sedge marshes, you'll stir up squadrons of dragonflies and damselflies and scolding blackbirds. A common sight, especially in the morning, are moose high-stepping through the shallow water as they feed on tasty sedges or willows. Beavers are everywhere, as are beaver dams, which you have to crawl over in a few places. In the spring be on the lookout for grizzly bears digging out roots and bulbs; in early fall they gather at the Bowron River to feast on the spawning sockeye salmon.

Start at the visitor center at Bowron Lake, where everyone traveling the circuit must register. Those without canoe or kayak can contract an outfitter or rent equipment and buy supplies from a couple of resorts or the store near the park entrance.

Your voyage will take six to ten days, depending on the weather—and how much, how hard, and how skillfully you paddle. You should have some canoeing and wilderness skills, but the circuit is moderately easy and you needn't be an expert. Plenty of established campsites, excellent portage trails, and metal containers to store food so bears can't get it, all make the trip easier. The park staff can't do anything about the weather or the bugs, however, so come prepared for both. ■

Lake and boreal forest, Bowron Lake Provincial Park

Tweedsmuir Provincial Park

■ 2.4 million acres ■ West-central British Columbia, 226 miles (365 km) west of Williams Lake ■ Best months mid-July–mid-Sept. ■ Camping, hiking, canoeing, fishing, horseback riding, skiing, wildlife viewing ■ Backcountry fee ■ Tweedsmuir North access by boat only ■ Contact Tweedsmuir South, Cariboo District, 281 1st Ave. N., Williams Lake, BC V2G 1Y7, phone 250-398-4414. wlapwww.gov.bc.ca/bcparks/explore/parkpgs/tweedsmu.htm; or Tweedsmuir North, Skeena District, 3790 Alfred Ave., Bag 5000, Smithers, BC V0J 2N0, phone 250-847-7320. wlapwww.gov.bc.ca/bcparks/explore/parkpgs/tweed.htm

ONE OF THE LARGEST OF British Columbia's several hundred parks, Tweedsmuir Provincial Park is so big that it is divided into south and north sections of roughly equal size. This division makes sense because access to the two sections is separated by 600 miles (966 km) of driving.

Tweedsmuir North

Though Tweedsmuir North is a scenic and unspoiled wildland, only about 250 boats per season visit. The main access route involves boating across a couple of lakes known for their strong winds and submerged trees—bathymetric maps are needed. Once in Tweedsmuir North, conditions don't get any easier: According to park literature, "Those not prepared to be completely self-sufficient or who do not wish to employ a professional guide should not contemplate a visit."

Tweedsmuir South

Most of Tweedsmuir South is as untouched as its northern counterpart—56,000 visitors annually—but you can drive there and it does have a few visitor facilities. If you enter on Hwy. 20 from the east, you'll have just climbed into the rounded Rainbow Range. From a trailhead at Heckman Pass you can choose among several trails that lead back into the range; the 10-mile (16 km) round-trip **Rainbow Trail** makes a suitable day hike.

To the west the highway plunges into the Atnarko River Valley, the bare slopes of the Rainbow Range giving way to Douglas-fir and aspen forests spiced with meadows. In the valley you'll find one of the park's two roadside campgrounds, a picnic area, some hiking—and bears. From August through October, when the salmon are running, grizzlies gather along the Atnarko River, so exercise caution. Black bears can be seen spring through fall.

The settlement of Stuie, where there's a lodge and other visitor facilities, makes a nice base for exploring the west side of the park. Among the day hikes in the area is the **Burnt Bridge Trail,** a loop that you can do in an hour and a half. Along the way there's a viewpoint overlooking the lush Bella Coola Valley. This trail follows part of the 215-mile (350 km) **Alexander Mackenzie Trail** from the Blackwater River to the spot where the intrepid Scottish-born explorer—in search of the Northwest Passage to the Pacific Ocean—was finally forced to turn his canoe around. ■

Mirror image of Muncho Lake

Muncho Lake Provincial Park

- 218,397 acres ■ North-central British Columbia, kilometer 681 of Alaska Hwy. ■ Best months June-Sept. ■ Camping, hiking, boating, canoeing, fishing, wildlife viewing, scenic drive, boat tour ■ Contact BC Parks, Peace-Liard District, Bag 1000, 4604 Sunset Dr., Fort Nelson, BC V0C 1R0; phone 250-774-7190. wlapwww.gov.bc.ca/bcparks/explore/parkpgs/muncho.htm

MUNCHO LAKE PROVINCIAL PARK serves up a visual feast. For more than 55 miles (88 km) the Alaska Hwy. curves through the park, treating motorists to one of the most beautiful stretches of that long road north.

The park's rumpled mountains—the northern tip of the Rockies—rise 8,000 feet, their wrinkled look the result of tectonic deformations that have folded the limestone. In the southern part of the park along the highway, you'll see a fine example in the aptly named Folded Mountain.

Clothed mostly in pine and spruce, the slopes sliding by your car window sport patches of moss campion, lousewort, wintergreen, asters, and lupine. Around the lake, where creeks enter and bogs are created, look for lady's slipper, wild rose, and bog orchids.

Muncho Lake is the park's scenic centerpiece: 7 miles (11.3 km) long, tinted green-blue by suspended minerals, framed by husky mountains, its cold water teeming with lake trout, arctic grayling, bulltrout, and whitefish. The lake is a great place to camp, hike, picnic, and fish. During the travel season a local operator runs boat tours of the lake *(for recommendations call Tourism Northern Rockies 250-774-2541).*

Wildlife seems to like the park as much as tourists do. Moose commonly are sighted in the marshy parts of the park. Bears ramble all over. Mountain caribou and Stone's sheep—a gray-to-almost-black version of the more familiar white Dall's sheep—often come down to the road to lick the salt left from winter road maintenance. ■

Grizzly mother and nine-month-old cub

Bear Necessities

WESTERN CANADA ENJOYS healthy populations of black, grizzly (brown), and polar bears. Most people agree that having these "charismatic megavertebrates" around is a good thing. Yet they are also predators capable of adding you to the food chain. Experts disagree how best to protect yourself from a bear attack, but this much is certain: Protecting yourself protects the bears as well, and the only way to guarantee safety from a bear is not to encounter one.

Before heading out, check with officials in the area for bear alerts and information on bear activity.

Camping

When camping, store food (day and night) in your vehicle or in the bear-proof containers provided by some parks. If neither is available, hang your food from trees. Don't cook, eat, or store food near your tent. This means all food or food products—even that

piece of gum in your shirt pocket. Don't sleep in the clothes you cooked in. Shun perfumes, skin lotions, soaps, or anything else that exudes a strong fragrance. In short, be careful to the point of paranoia about odors.

Choose your campsite with bears in mind: Look around for scat, tracks, or claw marks on trees. Don't camp on a game trail, in the middle of a patch of huckleberries, or next to a river choked with spawning salmon. Sleep in a tent; bears often check out people slumbering outdoors in sleeping bags, but rarely will they enter a tent (unless it contains food). Groups should arrange their tents in a line, not a circle; the latter can make a bear feel trapped. Leave your dogs at home; they antagonize bears (and are prohibited by most parks anyway).

Hiking

When hiking, observe the same kinds of precautions about smells that apply to camping. Traveling in a group is a good idea (bears very rarely charge groups of six or more). Making noise while walking also helps, so you don't surprise a bear. Carry your bear repellent spray and know how to use it; it does no good in your pack.

When bears hear humans approach, they almost always move away. (This is less the case with polar bears.) Specialists debate the effectiveness of bear bells and whistles, but they universally encourage the use of the human voice: shouting, yodeling, whatever. Near rushing water, pump up the volume to make yourself heard.

Let's be honest: Many of you are not going to walk through the woods shouting every minute; it just seems too weird. At the very least, though, take care to make noise under high-risk conditions. If the trail winds through dense shrubs known to be grizzly habitat, for example, or if you've come across fresh bear scat, let loose a hearty whoop now and then.

Encounters

What to do in the event of a bear encounter? The consensus breaks down a bit here, but most experts agree on a few basics. If you see a bear in the distance along your route, wait for it to move off, detour at least several hundred yards around it, or retreat and hike somewhere else.

If you blunder onto a bear up close, do not run. Your flight may label you as prey, and the bear can easily outrun you. Don't make eye contact, either; the bear may view it as a threat.

Beyond avoiding those two mistakes, things get complicated. You'll need to choose between two competing methods—and, to maximize response time, settle on one or the other before your hike.

Method one: Speak in a normal voice to identify yourselves as human, slowly backing away until the danger passes.

Method two: Intimidate the bear. Shout, hold your arms over your head to appear larger, wave—anything to appear dangerous. You can start with method one and switch to method two if the bear moves toward you.

Finally, what if the bear attacks? Use pepper spray if you've got it. Except in the case of polar bears, nearly all charges are bluffs, intended primarily to scare you off. Should the attack happen, though, you need to know whether you're facing a black bear or a grizzly. If it's a black bear, fight back: They're smaller and less ferocious fighters—and more likely than a grizzly to kill and eat you if you don't resist. If it's a grizzly, play dead: Curl up on the ground with your hands clasped over the back of your neck. Usually a grizzly will just leave, maybe after a few nuzzles. But (needless to say) wait until it's gone before moving.

Polar bears are another matter. Experts consider them by far the most dangerous of the three species, and far more likely than grizzlies and black bears to hunt meat. An encounter with a polar bear must therefore be avoided at all costs. (For a bit of safety advice, see the Churchill entry, on pages 242-48.)

To find out more about all three bear species, talk to park staffers, read handouts on bear safety, or consult the classic *Bear Attacks: Their Causes and Avoidance* (Herrero, 1985).

Keep in mind that the odds of being attacked by a bear are infinitesimally small—especially if you take precautions. Once you're aware of the dangers, you won't let an unreasonable fear of bears scare you away from the great outdoors of Western Canada. ■

Liard River Hot Springs Provincial Park

■ 2,673 acres ■ North-central British Columbia ■ Best months June-Sept.; campsite available May-Oct. ■ Bird-watching, wildlife viewing, hot springs ■ Contact BC Parks, Peace-Liard District, Bag 1000, 4604 Sunset Dr., Fort Nelson, BC V0C 1R0; phone 250-774-7190. wlapwww.gov.bc.ca/bcparks/explore/parkpgs/liard.htm

HOT SPRINGS ARE ONE OF NATURE'S sweetest luxuries. Can't you just feel that heat swaddling your tired body after a long day on the Alaska Hwy.? But lolling in the 108- to 126-degree (42º-52º C)water is not the best part of Liard River Hot Springs Provincial Park. It's the surrounding natural community that steals the show.

Stroll the boardwalks and see familiar boreal plants, such as the gigantic cow parsnip, that grow exuberantly due to the thermal influence. You can also see plants that look tropical and out of place in this cold, northern land, like ostrich fern. Aquatic plants include sundews, bladderworts, and butterwort, all carnivorous species. From the boardwalk between the bathing pools you can look out on the **Hanging Gardens,** a luxuriant cascade of wildflowers and exotic greenery growing on terraces of tufa (calcium deposits precipitating from hot springs water).

The warm swamps that are created by the thermal springs harbor animals, too. Beneath the boardwalk to Alpha Pool swim small lake chub endemic to the park. On a larger scale, moose are frequently seen as they graze in the swamps. Above the pools fly kingfishers, gulls, nighthawks, bohemian waxwings, and many other birds. ■

Stone Mountain Provincial Park

When you reach kilometer marker 595 on the Alaska Hwy., you'll be in Stone Mountain Provincial Park (250-774-7190). But sometimes there's another way to tell you've entered this 63,000-acre wilderness park—the roadside traffic jams of motorists watching Stone's sheep. A large population of these sheep (relatives of the bighorn) inhabits the park, and occasionally they display their climbing prowess on steep slopes visible from the highway.

To fully appreciate the park, get out of your vehicle; this is one of the north's easily accessible parks. Camp at Summit Lake, a deep blue beauty that lies along the Alaska Hwy. From the campground, day hikes lead to flower-fringed subalpine lakes and through grassy tundra, where you may see hoary marmots and golden eagles.

West of Summit Pass, at the Rocky Crest picnic area, the short **Erosion Pillars Trail** provides views of the eroded rock pillars known as hoodoos.

Rafting a river in British Columbia

Tatshenshini-Alsek Park

■ 2.3 million acres ■ Northwest British Columbia, 70 miles (113 km) south of Haines Junction, Yukon ■ Best months July-Aug. ■ Camping, white-water rafting and kayaking, wildlife viewing ■ Contact BC Parks, Skeena District, 3790 Alfred Ave., Bag 5000, Smithers, BC V0J 2N0, phone 250-847-7320. wlapwww.gov.bc.ca/bcparks/explore/parkpgs/tatshen.htm; or Glacier Bay National Park, Box 140, Gustavus, AK 99826, phone 907-697-2230. www.nps.gov/glba (additional rafting information)

THIS PARK GETS ITS NAME from the two major rivers that run through it: the **Tatshenshini** and the **Alsek.** Because most of the park's western side consists mainly of mountains, glaciers, and ice fields, almost everyone sees the park by water.

Visitors generally start on the Tatshenshini—the "Tat"—at Dalton Post, in Yukon Territory, about 50 miles (80 km) south of Haines Junction. From there it's 140 river miles (225 km) to Dry Bay on the Pacific Coast. After about 100 miles (160 km) the Tat joins the lower stretch of the Alsek.

The Tat-Alsek run involves a few Class III and sometimes Class IV rapids, as well as extremely remote wilderness travel. Don't attempt it on your own unless you've got high-level skills. It is suggested that you use an outfitter on this trip.

And what a trip it is: floating along beneath the broad shoulders of the St. Elias Mountains; passing the toes of enormous glaciers; delighting at merganser mothers pulling trains of fuzzy little ducklings; discovering grizzly tracks in the wet sand on the shore; watching bald eagles watch you; rafting among car-size icebergs on the lower Alsek; hiking along game trails amid a purple-pink forest of head-high fireweed. This park is a scenic slice of the region as it looked 5,000 years ago. ■

Following pages: Alpine wildflowers along Taku River, British Columbia

Kluane National Park and Reserve

■ 5.4 million acres ■ Southwest Yukon Territory, 100 miles (160 km) west of Whitehorse ■ Best months mid-June–mid-Sept. and Feb.-March ■ Camping, hiking, mountain climbing, boating, white-water rafting and kayaking, canoeing, ice fishing, horseback riding, cross-country skiing, snowshoeing, dogsledding, flight-seeing, wildlife viewing ■ Adm. fee ■ Contact the park, Box 5495, Haines Junction, YT Y0B 1L0; phone 867-634-7250. parkscan.harbour.com/kluane

ICE FIELDS AND LOFTY MOUNTAINS make up 75 percent of Kluane National Park and Reserve, part of which is in the Mount Logan ecoregion. The summits of the Icefield Ranges run around 15,000 feet (4,575 m), while Mount Logan, Canada's tallest and North America's second tallest mountain, tops out at 19,551 feet (5,959 m).

Kluane's other 25 percent, forming the eastern edges of the park, belongs in the St. Elias ecoregion. This is the area that the vast majority of visitors come to see—a realm of forested valleys, alpine meadows, mountain slopes tangled with alder and willow, swift rivers, and rocky peaks. Those rocky peaks average about 7,000 feet (2,134 m) and hide the Icefield Ranges from view.

Arms of Kaskawulsh Glacier, Kluane National Park and Reserve

Though this 25 percent isn't as inaccessible as the ice fields, it's hardly a city park. Only a handful of trails and a few dirt roads penetrate this million acres of front-country—an area larger than Yosemite National Park. Backcountry and front-country, ice fields and forests, Kluane is a vast wilderness. It combines with Wrangell-St. Elias and Glacier Bay National Parks in Alaska and Tatshenshini-Alsek Park in British Columbia to form the largest World Heritage site.

The western boundary of Kluane comes within 20 miles (32 km) of the Pacific. Moist ocean air drops up to 60 feet of snow annually on the ice fields, which in turn feed the glaciers that radiate from the ice fields like the spokes of a wheel. These enormous glaciers, some dozens of miles long with toes 100 yards high, grind down into the valleys.

Somewhere over Kluane that moist Pacific air meets dry Arctic air, producing a variety of climatic conditions. These conditions make Kluane perhaps the most biologically diverse area in northern Canada: It is home to more than 200 species of plants. But of greater interest to most visitors are the many high-profile animals that live there. Some 4,000 Dall's sheep inhabit the front-country slopes. The park also boasts a high concentration of grizzly bears, so behave accordingly (see pp. 84-85). Wolves, lynx, mountain bluebirds, moose, caribou, golden eagles, beavers, snowshoe hare, mountain goats, and an ark full of other species roam Kluane, too.

Mountain goat

What to See and Do

Haines Junction is Kluane's hub. The Alaska Hwy. comes into this little town from the east and leaves town heading north along the northeast boundary of the park. The Haines Road starts in town and runs south along the southeast boundary of the park.

Stop at the **visitor center** in Haines Junction for information, natural and cultural history displays, and the latest scoop regarding weather, trails closed due to bear activity, availability of trips on the Alsek, and so forth. Sometimes you'll even see a sign warning about bears in the vicinity of the visitor center itself.

With that in mind, your best bet might be to check at the visitor center for one of the excellent interpretive hikes; it's always safer to hike in a group, and you'll learn a lot more if you venture out with one of the park naturalists. Park staff also can provide literature about the many private operators who conduct a wide variety of trips into the park.

Heading south from Haines Junction on Haines Road, you may want to stop at the bridge over the Dezadeash River before you even get out of town. There begins the **Dezadeash River Trail,** an easy 3-mile (4.8 km) round-trip that runs along the swift-flowing river and through its wooded and marshy riparian zone. This is an interpretive trail with informative signs and observation platforms. The marshlands are home to moose, beavers, and muskrat. Many species of birds favor the trees where the wetlands meet the woods; cheer for the olive-sided flycatchers as they snag some of the mosquitoes that are trying to feast on you.

The Dezadeash River also serves as the departure point for one of Kluane's greatest adventures, one that you can enjoy even if you're not the sort of person who owns your own kayak: a raft trip down the **Alsek River** (see p. 87).

Go down the Dezadeash to where it joins with the Kaskawulsh River to create the Alsek and then head south on this big, braided river into the wild heart of Kluane. You'll see some imposing peaks, sand dunes, and likely some grizzlies, or at least their enormous paw prints in the wet sand; this is some of the finest grizzly habitat in Canada. Along the way hike up **Goatherd Mountain** to see mountain goats and most of the 40-mile (64 km) length of the Lowell Glacier.

Kathleen Lake

Back on Haines Road at the Dezadeash bridge, continue on this scenic drive south for about 16 miles (25 km) and take the short spur road down to Kathleen Lake. Located by this pretty lake are a vehicle-accessible campground (no hookups or running water), a picnic area, and the starting points of trails that range from the **Kokanee Trail,** a 0.3-mile (0.5 km) boardwalk along the lakeshore, to the **Cottonwood Trail,** a 53-mile (85 km) loop that takes 4 to 6 days to complete.

The 3-mile-long (4.8 km) **King's Throne Trail** makes a nice compromise, assuming you stop at the bottom of the cirque for which the trail is named; experienced hikers can go on to the top of King's Throne, but there's no established trail and the climb is a real kneebuster. Even the official version of the hike is strenuous—1,600 feet (488 m) elevation gain—and involves some mild route-finding during the final push up the rock-strewn slope to the cirque. Park interpreters regularly lead hikes up to King's Throne.

The King's Throne Trail starts out on the Cottonwood Trail, passing through a forest of white spruce, balsam poplar, and aspen. At ground level you'll see wildflowers, such as larkspur and monkshood, and bushes, such as soapberry. Another sight might well be bear tracks, either grizzly or black. The chances are especially high if the soapberries are ripe; bears crave these red berries and an adult can devour as many as 200,000 a day. Look closely at some of the tree trunks for a "bear tree," which are identified by the claw marks and by the hairs left behind when bears rub their backs on the bark.

After a mile or so the King's Throne Trail branches off from the Cottonwood Trail; don't miss the sign or you could go another 50 miles (80 km). The trail climbs moderately for a mile, then breaks out of the forest onto a steep, rocky slope dotted with stunted trees and clumps of wildflowers.

Stay on the switchbacks up toward the cirque, and along the

White-tailed ptarmigan

way you'll occasionally encounter a little sheltered garden of forget-me-nots, dwarf fireweed, lupine, and other flowers. Views improve from good to great as you ascend to the bottom of King's Throne, and another hour or two of labor to the top of King's Throne will be rewarded by fantastic vistas. By the way, almost since you left the forest you've been hiking up a rock glacier.

Unless hiking King's Throne with a park interpreter, the easiest way to learn about rock glaciers is to go back to the Haines Road and head south about 11 miles (18 km) to the **Rock Glacier Trail.** A thirty-minute stroll through the forest and a marsh will put you on the snout of a rock glacier.

As you walk a few hundred yards up through the jumble of gray, tan, and red rocks, interpretive signs explain the nature of this landform, which is fairly common in Kluane but uncommon generally. Over the last 8,000 years constant freezing and thawing have shattered the brittle bedrock from the steep peaks above into fragments. Lubricated by meltwater and riding a core of glacial ice, this growing mass of rock slowly flowed down the mountain, though recent warming has stabilized it. From the end of the trail you can look down on sprawling Dezadeash Lake and far to the east.

This stretch south of Haines Junction also serves as a popular winter sports area, especially in February and March, when there's enough daylight and the snow is still plentiful. You can try snowshoeing, dogsledding, ice fishing, and snow camping, as well as more

typical pursuits, such as cross-country skiing. If you're not wise in the ways of wilderness in winter, this might not be for you.

Sheep Mountain

To see a different side of Kluane, drive 43 miles (70 km) north from Haines Junction on the Alaska Hwy. to Sheep Mountain, where a small visitor center serves as a staging area for exploring this end of the park. This is a relatively dry region of Kluane in which the south-facing slopes often sport sage, winter fat, and other arid-land species. Dall's sheep thrive on this forage in the winter; Sheep Mountain supports an exceptionally high density of 18 sheep per square mile.

Whether you can see sheep from the deck of the visitor center depends on what time of year you're looking. The sheep use the southeast slopes of the mountain as winter range, in part because strong winds keep the plants fairly clear of snow. As the weather warms and the snow melts, the sheep move up the mountain, following the line of greening plants.

Eventually, in early or mid-June, the sheep move over the top and out of sight and usually don't return until late August. In May and early June you'll see a lot of lambs on the southeast slopes; not only is there good food but the slopes are steep and therefore the lambs are safer from predators. Look through the spotting scopes on the deck and you can watch these fluffy white bundles of energy frolicking.

A handful of trails and vaguely defined routes lead along the

Peaks of St. Elias Mountains, Kluane National Park and Reserve

Dall's sheep on alpine slope covered with summer grasses

Slims River, just south of Sheep Mountain, or up into the high country behind Sheep Mountain. One of the most appealing, a long day hike, is the 7.5-mile/ 12-km (one way), moderately difficult **Bullion Plateau Trail.** This path ascends to the lavishly vegetated subalpine and alpine Sheep-Bullion Plateau.

It is recommended that you hike this trail in groups of no less than four. Don't attempt the trail without first getting the latest information on bear activity from park staff.

If you see grizzlies on the plateau, they'll most likely be females with cubs—all the more fascinating and all the more dangerous. You don't want to get near a mama grizzly and her young, which she will protect ferociously. Though the valley bottoms offer even better habitat, female grizzlies are thought to bring their cubs up to the plateau to avoid male grizzlies, which sometimes kill cubs that they encounter.

The Ice Fields

If you find that you just can't leave Kluane without having at least glimpsed its hidden 75 percent—the great ice fields and sky-piercing peaks—consider a flight-seeing tour. Local operators fly both planes and helicopters over Kluane's frozen heartland. If you'd like to stay for a while, one tour company offers overnight trips (they recommend three nights) that include lodging on the ice in heated structures that are a cross between a tent and a quonset hut. During the day you can hang out or explore.

Mountaineering provides the ultimate ice field experience. Climbers come here from around the world, most intending to scale Mount Logan. Easier said than

The Urge to Surge

Forget their ponderous reputation: Research has revealed that glaciers don't always move at the speed of creeping ice. The Lowell Glacier, for example, has surged forth many times. Its most recent sortie occurred between 1725 and 1850, when the 40-mile-long (64 km) mass of ice rumbled down from its mountain home and across the Alsek River, blocking the river's flow. The water backed up more than 45 miles (72 km), drowning the area where Haines Junction sits today.

In 1850, the ice dam burst. Glaciologists speculate that the pent-up water poured out in just two days, creating a temporary freshet equal to that of today's Amazon River. Contemporary hikers on the Alsek Trail, just north of Haines Junction, can see enormous gravel ripples and wave-cut lake benches made by this and earlier great floods.

Kluane in particular boasts quite a number of surging glaciers. In 1966, in the northern part of the park, the Steele Glacier rambled 5 miles (8 km) in a couple of weeks. Other ice sheets in the park have advanced several miles in the course of a year—a pace fast enough that visitors could actually see and hear the ice moving.

According to the authors of a geology text entitled *The Earth's Dynamic Systems,* "glacial surges apparently result from sudden slippages along the bases of glaciers, caused by the buildup of extreme stress upstream. Stagnant or slow-moving ice near the terminus can act as a dam for the faster-moving ice upstream. If this happens, stress builds up behind the slow-moving ice, and a surge occurs when a critical point is reached."

In Kluane, the Donjek Glacier has surged twice in the last few years; it now infringes on the Donjek River. Another surge could clog the river completely and—shades of the Alsek—begin the formation of another time-bomb lake.

done. Not only is Mount Logan a lofty 19,551 feet, it's a whopping 12 miles (19 km) wide and some 18 miles (29 km) long, making it arguably the most massive mountain in the world.

Ascending this behemoth doesn't require spidering up a sheer rock cliff but it's one long, hard slog. A clue as to the arduous nature of the venture lies in the recommendation that climbers carry three weeks worth of provisions. One route up Mount Logan can be managed by novice climbers led by guides—but those novices had better be fit and prepared for hardship.

Telemark and heli-skiing are other activities undertaken here by growing numbers of enthusiasts. Imagine spending a week in an environment with no plants or animals. In parts of Kluane—on some of the peaks or on the Bagley Icefield—the average monthly temperatures are below freezing. The Bagley Icefield itself dates back before the last ice age. Who knows? You might even find a prehistoric mosquito frozen at your feet. ■

Canadian Rockies

Evening alpenglow on Continental Divide, Yoho National Park

THE SHINING MOUNTAINS—that's what some First Nations peoples once called the Canadian Rockies. (Canadians refer to their portion of the Rocky Mountains as "the Canadian Rockies," whereas Americans call their portion simply "the Rockies.") Canada's share of the range averages about 100 miles (160 km) across and runs from Waterton Lakes National Park on the Alberta-Montana border northeast toward the Yukon Territory. The beautiful and accessible parks for which the Canadian Rockies

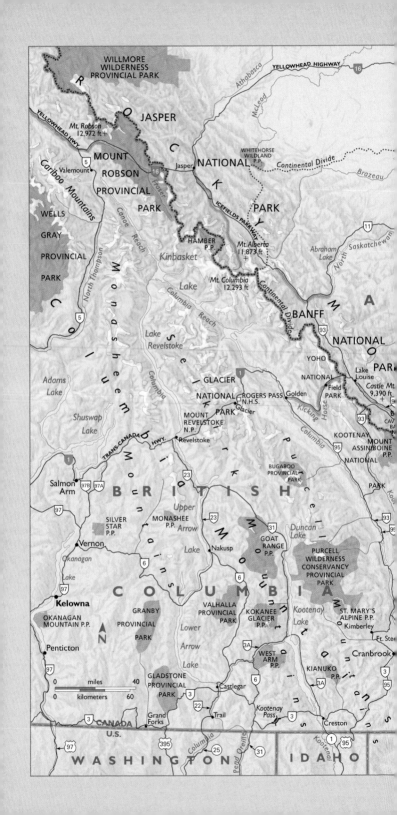

are famous are located primarily along the Alberta–British Columbia border in the range's southern half.

Shining Mountains remains an apt moniker. Those 10,000-, 11,000-, and 12,000-foot snow-and-ice-capped stones still jut proudly into the sky, as they have since the region's main mountain-building period between 140 million and 45 million years ago. During that time, the action of tectonic plates pushed what had been the Pacific Ocean's continental shelf inland. Over the ages, the layers of former seafloor broke apart and piled up into the towering range of sedimentary rock that constitutes today's Canadian Rockies. That's why the Burgess Shale—now 10,000 feet (3,050 m) above sea level—contains fossils of ancient corals, jellyfish, and other marine organisms from the Cambrian period.

But the ruggedly handsome sawtooth peaks that draw visitors to the Canadian Rockies were still a work in progress 45 million years ago. Only during the last two million years did the massive glaciers of the ice age refine the landscape, sharpening a peak here and carving a valley there. Even today, hundreds of glaciers continue to grind away the high country of the Canadian Rockies.

Sometimes visitors seem transfixed by the charisma—the sheer enormity and breathtaking beauty—of these ice-frosted mountains. Studies reveal that a large majority of visitors hardly explore the wilds at all, instead settling for a faraway look at the mountains from one of the tourist towns or from a car. As enjoyable as these views are, if that's the extent of your visit, you'll miss experiencing all the interesting

things that have been happening in the Canadian Rockies since the ice age ended some 10,000 years ago.

Once the climate had warmed and the glaciers had retreated to higher elevations, the ecological communities whose descendants we see today began to form. If you go camping or take some day hikes, you'll encounter a delicious diversity of life: subalpine meadows swimming with wildflowers; goshawks and woodpeckers gliding through the canopy of the lodgepole pine forest while wolves, elk, and black bears forage below; icy lakes greened by glacial silt, fringed by alder and willows, and patrolled by ospreys, bald eagles, and kingfishers; deep, narrow gorges that provide the clammy habitat favored by ferns and feather mosses; and, up above tree line, alpine meadows blanketed by ground-hugging plants such as

Pyramid Mountain and Patricia Lake, Jasper National Park

forget-me-not and moss campion, and roamed by a wide assortment
of animals including marmots, bighorn sheep, caribou, grizzlies, and
golden eagles.

As the presence of so much wildlife suggests, the Canadian Rockies
still harbor vast unspoiled tracts, despite the fact that logging, mining,
dams, and oil and gas development have scarred the areas beyond the
park boundaries.

Visitors with the determination and the knowledge to venture into
the backcountry will find utterly uncivilized places, some just 10 miles
(16 km) from the shops of Banff or Jasper. So instead of limiting yourself
to that grand view from the car or the restaurant window, let your feet
follow your eyes into the mountains for a closer look. ■

Waterton Lakes National Park

■ 129,300 acres ■ Southwest Alberta, 130 miles (209 km) south of Calgary
■ Best months June-Oct. ■ Camping, hiking, boating, kayaking, canoeing, fishing,
biking, cross-country skiing, wildlife viewing, boat tours, scenic drives ■ Adm.
fee ■ Contact the park, Waterton Park, AB T0K 2M0; phone 403-859-5133.
www.parkscanada.gc.ca/waterton

PEOPLE REFER TO WATERTON LAKES NATIONAL PARK as the place "where the
mountains meet the prairie." This phrase is true as far as it goes, but it
only hints at the tremendous biological and geographical diversity
packed into this relatively small national park. Ecosystems of the north,
south, east, and west converge here, at the Rocky Mountains' narrowest
point. The park harbors wet old-growth forest reminiscent of the Pacific
Northwest, the glaciated peaks and alpine meadows that characterize the
Rockies, and prairie grasslands like those that sweep the Great Plains.

Prince of Wales Hotel and Upper Waterton Lake

Such diverse—and healthy—habitat naturally shelters a variety of animals and plants. Grizzlies, bald eagles, lynx, bison, wolves, golden eagles, elk, bighorn sheep, and mountain goats are among the critters that call Waterton home. The assorted plants—nearly a thousand different species, a remarkable number—include lichen-cloaked Douglas-fir in the dense forest, alpine forget-me-not and sky pilot above tree line, and oat grass and fescue in the prairie.

Waterton features another sort of geographical diversity as well. When you pick up one of the park's map/brochures, you'll notice that it doesn't say "Waterton Lakes National Park" but "Waterton/Glacier International Peace Park." Acknowledging the close relationship between Canada and the United States—and that between Waterton Lakes National Park and its U.S. neighbor, Glacier National Park—the U.S. Congress and the Canadian Parliament created the international peace park in 1932. Originally a symbolic designation, today the two parks cooperate closely in managing a splendid ecosystem that bridges both countries.

What to See and Do

From the official entrance to the park, at the junction of Hwys. 5 and 6, a 5-mile (8 km) stretch of road runs south to the townsite, taking you from prairie to mountains in one short journey. Just inside the park entrance you'll skirt Lower Waterton Lake, the first and smallest of the chain of three lakes that gives the park its name; they get bigger and prettier as you head toward town.

A couple of miles before you reach the townsite, however, explore those rolling prairie hills by turning onto the **Red Rock Parkway.** For 9 miles (14.5 km) this narrow road slips along the north bank of Blakiston Creek until it ends at Red Rock Canyon. Pause at some of the pullouts. If it's late spring or summer, you'll be surrounded by fantastic wildflower displays as well as by prairie grasses dancing in the breeze. At any time of the year, you can gaze down on the wetlands and streamside forest of the creek or up to the edge of the Rockies, arching above the road like a tidal wave. Mount Blakiston, the park's highest peak at 9,527 feet, towers less than 3 miles (4.8 km) from the road.

While you're enjoying the scenery, don't forget to watch out for bears. Even if you're aware that Waterton hosts black bears and grizzlies, you probably wouldn't expect to encounter them on the prairie. Modern North Americans tend to think of bears as mountain dwellers. But grizzlies naturally range into grasslands. They're confined almost entirely to remote mountains nowadays only because humans have developed most of the lowlands and killed any bear that showed itself on the prairie.

Waterton Lakes National Park is one of the last places on the continent where grizzlies still frequent the plains, and you may be lucky enough to see one. But you're not likely to see any near the Red Rock Parkway. You will see black bears, though, and cinnamon-colored bears that are sometimes mistaken for grizzlies, but these, too, are black bears. In fact, most of Waterton's black bears are colored brown. So be alert for bears, even when you're walking just 50 feet (15 m) from your car to an overlook (see pp. 84–85).

After you soak up the prairie and navigate the bear jams (see sidebar opposite), you'll arrive at **Red Rock Canyon.** The Grand Canyon it's not—at its maximum, Red Rock is only about 100 feet (30 m) across and 70 feet (21 m) deep. But it's a beautiful miniature. Over the last 10,000 to 7,000 years **Red Rock Creek** has sliced into the iron-laced mudstone—the hardened sedimentary remnants of an ancient shallow sea. At times this sea dried up, exposing layers of the iron to the air. When it oxidized it formed the red mineral hematite, giving the canyon walls their broad, ruddy stripes. Narrow bands of white and pale green mark where the layers were not exposed to air.

A nearly flat, 0.4-mile (0.6 km) trail loops up and down the canyon, crossing it on bridges. As you gaze down into the canyon, you'll see mosses growing on the rock walls in the damp shade. The moss breaks the rock into soil, which filters into cracks and provides just enough nutrition for alpine firs and other plants to grow seemingly out of sheer stone. Near its mouth the canyon opens up and flattens out into an alluvial fan as Red Rock Creek enters Blakiston Creek. Prairie grasses and wildflowers adorn the fan's outer edges. Balsam poplars and cottonwoods thrust from wetter areas nearer the creek, favored by elk.

Around Town

Back on the entrance road heading toward town, the road rises into the mountains. Soon you pass the western edge of Middle Waterton Lake. A couple of minutes later, you'll hit Upper Waterton Lake and the Waterton Townsite. On the north end of town, stop in at the visitor center (*mid-May–early Oct.*). In addition to picking up the usual maps, trail guides, and schedules of interpretive programs, be sure to check for trail closures; it's not uncommon for bear activity to temporarily shut down a few hiking trails.

Just down the hill from the visitor center sits the town, a bustling bit of city during prime seasons. **Waterton Townsite** is a full-blown municipality comprising hundreds of houses, stores, restaurants, and other businesses. Yet nature is never far away. You'll often see bighorn sheep and deer resting in the shade of the buildings. Though people rarely see them, mountain lions sometimes prowl the town at night, hunting those sheep and deer. On occasion bears pass through town too, leaving wide-eyed tourists in their wake.

Waterton Township offers fine mountain scenery in all directions. Moreover, the town sits at the northern end of **Upper Waterton Lake,** an aqueous sliver 7 miles (11 km) long that runs south all

Bear Jams

In the late summer and fall, when roadside shrubs sag with ripe berries, the Red Rock Parkway becomes an outstanding location from which to enjoy a long, safe look at black bears. The most alluring habitat lies on the north side of the road just east of the Crandell Campground, about midway along the parkway. Bears prefer the cool of morning and evening.

Sometimes you have no choice but to do some bear-watching. While cruising the parkway, motorists commonly run up against a "bear jam." This traffic clot occurs when one driver spots a bear near the road and stops to look. Others join in, and soon cars are lined up along the parkway. Just remember to park on the shoulder and to watch the bears from the safety of your vehicle. Despite the warnings of park wardens, people sometimes walk up to bears to shoot close-up photos. Bad idea.

Bear jams happen so often during busy times of the year that the park deploys staffers nicknamed "bear jammers" to patrol the roads. In addition to managing the traffic, they protect bears and people from one another.

Middle Waterton Lake

the way into the United States. The deepest lake in the Canadian Rockies, Upper Waterton hits icy depths of some 500 feet (152 m).

Tour boats *(call Waterton Inter Nation Shoreline Cruise Co. 403-859-2362)* depart daily from the town's marina, treating passengers to two-hour cruises that loop around the lake's shoreline, passing close to waterfalls, sheer cliffs, and wildlife. Hikers can be dropped off at various points for rambles ranging from a couple of hours to several days. Most popular is the **Kootenai Lakes Trail** out of Goat Haunt, at the lake's southern end: It makes a climb of 2.5 miles (4 km) up to Kootenai Lakes. There's a fair chance you'll spot moose around the lakes. If you don't dawdle too long, you can take the morning boat to Goat Haunt, hike to Kootenai Lakes and back, then catch a return boat in the afternoon.

The High Country

If you feel the urge to venture into the high country, you can start at the south end of town with the **Bertha Lake Trail,** a 3.5-mile (5.6 km) path one way. Many people walk only the first 1.8 miles (3 km) of the trail, which climb gently through a montane forest of pine, aspen, and birch to **Lower Bertha Falls.** Take your time and smell the flowers, such as paintbrush, harebell, and the felicitously named pearly everlasting.

If you feel frisky and want to ascend steep switchbacks for another 1.7 miles (2.7 km), you'll pass through prime bear habitat, savor fine views down to Upper Waterton Lake and up to Vimy Peak, and see Upper Bertha Falls diving off a limestone cliff. At the northern tip of **Bertha Lake** is the lake's campground. Nearly a mile long (1.6 km) and as little as 150 feet (46 m) wide, the lake is fringed by spotty subalpine forest and lush meadows and backed by a stone wall more than 1,500 feet (457 m) high. Scan this cliff for mountain goats.

Even more ambitious hikers can tackle the park's classic high-country route: the **Carthew-Alderson Trail.** It runs about 12 miles (19 km) between the townsite and Cameron Lake. Because it's too long to hike out and back in one day, the best option is to take the shuttle bus *(403-627-5205)* 10 miles (16 km) out the Akamina Parkway to **Cameron Lake** and hike back from there. Spend some time at the lake, too. You may even want to rent a canoe, rowboat, or pedal boat and skim across this comely body of water to the south end of the lake, which lies across the border in Glacier National Park. Grizzlies commonly forage in the avalanche paths on the steep slopes there.

Don't linger too long before you hit the trail, however; it's best to get into the high country early so that you can start back by about noon. You don't want to get caught above tree line if an afternoon electrical storm rips through. The Carthew-Alderson Trail begins at the outlet of Cameron Lake amid the thick conifer subalpine forest. Long switchbacks make the steep grade tolerable, and the route flattens out after a couple of miles. You'll continue through meadows flocked with bear grass until you reach Summit Lake.

From there the trail climbs some 1,500 feet through gradually shrinking forest until it emerges into the alpine environment, affording broad views across some meadows. Admire the red rock (argillite) underfoot; it has been around for as long as 1.5 billion years. Some of the oldest exposed sedimentary rock in the Canadian Rockies, it predates almost all life on Earth and contains only fossils formed by primitive blue-green algae. More climbing leads to the payoff: **Carthew Summit.** From well over 7,000 feet (2,134 m), you see distant peaks, snowy ridges, glacial lakes, and, far to the northeast, the open plains of the prairie.

As you descend along the staircase lakes, watch for icy snow patches; though the trail typically is passable by mid-June, some snow lingers well into summer. Continue through the alpine environment until you once again descend into forest. From krummholz (the stunted trees near timberline), you'll pass into dense subalpine, and end up in drier Douglas-fir and lodgepole pine forest before reaching town in a poplar grove at Cameron Falls. ■

Mount Revelstoke National Park

■ 64,247 acres ■ Southeast British Columbia ■ Best season early July–late Sept. ■ Camping, hiking, mountain climbing, biking, cross-country skiing, snow-shoeing, bird-watching, wildlife viewing, wildflower viewing, scenic drive ■ Contact the park, Box 350, Revelstoke, BC V0E 2S0; phone 250-837-7500. parkscan.harbour.com/mtrev

THOUGH MOUNT REVELSTOKE NATIONAL PARK lies barely 50 miles (80 km) from the Canadian Rockies, it protects part of a distinct system within the Columbia Mountain Range. The Columbias—composed of the Purcell, Selkirk, Cariboo, and Monashee mountains—consist of older, harder rock, such as granite and marble; they feature sharper peaks and steeper valley walls than the Canadian Rockies.

The Columbias are also much wetter than the Rockies and are blanketed with the verdant vegetation of the "interior wet belt." Much of Mount Revelstoke National Park is temperate old-growth rain forest, an increasingly rare habitat in British Columbia because of widespread logging. Mount Revelstoke is famous for the wildflower extravaganzas that brighten its subalpine meadows during the summer.

What to See and Do

Apart from the Meadows in the Sky Parkway and environs, nearly all of Mount Revelstoke National Park is remote backcountry.

Meadows in the Sky Parkway

From a visitor's point of view, this 16-mile (26 km) route constitutes the heart of Mount Revelstoke National Park, and it is just as appealing as its lyrical name suggests. The road takes off from Trans-Canada 1 on the outskirts of the city of Revelstoke and climbs nearly a vertical mile in long, looping switchbacks to the parking lot at Balsam Lake, just below the summit of **Mount Revelstoke.**

During the busy summer season the lot gets jammed, so it's best to start early. If you're fit and ambitious, however, you can forget all about the parkway and your car and strike out on the **Summit Trail** instead. The Summit reaches Balsam Lake in a mere 6 miles (9.7 km)—but the price of this more direct line of ascent is some steep grades that will get your quadriceps quivering. (Remember that you're in bear country, and behave accordingly; see pp. 84–85.)

The parkway begins amid the big trees of the Columbia Mountains rain forest. Pullouts provide fine views of the forest and the city of Revelstoke. Just over halfway up the parkway, the **Snowforest Viewpoint** offers long vistas of the Selkirk and Monashee Mountains and the Columbia River Valley. At this point, some 4,000 feet above sea level, the cedar and hemlock of the rain forest begin abandoning the slopes to the spruce and fir of the subalpine or "snow" forest.

Western redcedars, Giant Cedars Trail

At the end of the drive you'll park next to **Balsam Lake,** which has a picnic area and other facilities. Short strolls on the **Eagle Knoll Trail** or to the **Panorama Viewpoint** yield the promised vistas. During the snow-free season, a shuttle can transport you the final 1.25 miles (2 km) to the summit or you can hike the last 0.7 mile (1.1 km) of the Summit Trail to the top. While you pause to catch your breath on the moderately steep ascent, appreciate the avalanche lilies.

Once in the summit area around **Heather Lake,** you'll be faced with several choices, all of them appealing. To start with the big picture, walk up the quarter-

Indian paintbrush

mile (0.4 km) **Firetower Trail** to the historic lookout tower and feast on the 360-degree visual smorgasbord. To the west and southwest jut the snowcapped peaks and glaciers of the Monashees. To the north and northwest, more sawtooth mountains form a ragged skyline; below sprawls the Columbia River and its broad basin. To the southeast you see a vast expanse of the Selkirks, which include Mount Revelstoke, crowned by 10,027-foot **Albert Peak.**

Back down around Heather Lake, switch your camera lens from macro to micro and amble the flower-filled half mile (0.8 km) of the **Meadows in the Sky Nature Trail.** At the trailhead, pick up one of the interpretive pamphlets; it will tell you whether you're admiring white mountain valerian, yellow arnica, purple lupine, or pink mountain daisies.

Three longer trails also strike out from Heather Lake: the **Eva Lake Trail** is 3.7 miles (6 km) one way; the **Miller Lake Trail** is 3.4 miles (5.5 km) one way, and branches off the Eva Lake Trail; and the **Jade Lakes Trail** is 5.6

miles (9 km) one way. The Eva Lake and Miller Lake Trails traverse gently rolling terrain showered with wildflowers and end at mountain lakes. The Jade Lakes Trail entails some steep climbs, but these uphill labors lift hikers above the trees into the alpine area, where they will be treated to superb vistas and may spot hoary marmots, golden eagles, and other high-country inhabitants.

Skunk Cabbage and Giant Cedars

The short and easy Skunk Cabbage and Giant Cedars Trails both start from picnic areas off Trans-Canada 1 near the eastern boundary of the park. Both are interpretive trails, peppered with signs that educate visitors about these fascinating habitats.

"Skunk cabbage is here indigenous and is found in acres of stinking perfection," wrote Canadian railroad engineer Sir Sandford Fleming more than a century ago. The aroma Fleming referred to hangs over the **Skunk Cabbage Trail** when the plant is blooming. But you won't need to wear a mask as you walk the 0.7-mile (1.1 km) boardwalk through the marshy lowlands along the **Illecillewaet River.** Skunk cabbage is a perennial herb that sends up 2- to 3-foot, clublike yellow flower spikes from late April to mid-May, with broad leaves that sometimes reach your chest. This trail also features excellent bird-watching in May and June.

The 0.3-mile (0.5 km) **Giant Cedars Trail** ushers you into a quiet sanctuary of imposing trees, abundant moisture, and dense, diverse undergrowth. You could walk this path in five minutes, but take 20 or 30 minutes (or more), read the informative signs, relish the serenity, and soak up the refreshing coolness—on a summer day it's 15 to 20 degrees cooler inside the forest than outside. These valley-bottom old-growth rain forests boast 5-foot-thick (1.5 m) western redcedars that form a canopy more than 200 feet (61 m) high.

Many of the interpretive signs explain why such old-growth has value that transcends the aesthetic. For example, moose survive the Columbia Mountains' winters by retreating to the old-growth. There the canopy intercepts much of the snow, enabling the moose to move about easily. Big, rotting trees also provide denning sites for wolverines, marten, and other animals; black bear dens have been found in the cavities of large cedars as high as 50 feet off the ground.

One sign beside a hulking cedar asks "Did this tree help grow the wheat in your bread?" The answer is yes. Like a giant pump, these trees pull in moisture and transpire it; a big cedar exhales as much as a hundred gallons a day. That moisture drifts east, where some of it falls as rain on prairie wheat fields. If these trees didn't pump water back into the air, it would quickly flow to the Pacific—and you'd go hungry. ■

Cow parsnip, Skunk Cabbage Trail

Glacier National Park

■ 333,590 acres ■ Southeast British Columbia, 10 miles (16 km) east of Mount Revelstoke National Park ■ Best months July-Sept. ■ Camping, hiking, mountain climbing, rock climbing, biking, cross-country skiing, snowshoeing, bird-watching, wildlife viewing, wildflower viewing ■ Contact the park, Box 350, Revelstoke, BC V0E 2S0; phone 250-837-7500. parkscan.harbour.com/glacier

WELCOME TO THE WORLD of the vertical. It seems as if everything in Canada's Glacier National Park is steep: the lofty mountains, the valley walls, the hiking trails, the highway grades, the stream gradients. Not surprisingly, most of the park consists of rugged backcountry, but Trans-Canada 1 provides a few points of easy access.

The park's angularity is typical of the Columbias, the mountain system just west of the Rockies that encompasses Glacier and its next-door neighbor, Mount Revelstoke National Park (see pp. 110-13). It's telling that mountain goats are the most common large mammal in the park.

The park's other defining trait is precipitation. Moisture-laden Pacific storms roll over the park, annually dumping almost 2 feet (60 cm) of rain and more than 30 feet (9 m) of snow on the visitor center at Rogers Pass. On the park's wet west side, Mount Fidelity gets 55 feet (16.8 m) of snow on average. Typically campgrounds and lower trails are free of snow only in July, August, and September, and higher trails only in August and September.

What to See and Do

Rogers Pass

Perched about midway along Trans-Canada 1 as it curves through Glacier National Park, Rogers Pass, elevation 4,534 feet (7,297 m), is home to the visitor center and a few hiking trails. The center resembles an 1890s railway snowshed, evoking the area's rich transportation history.

In fact, the gripping story of the construction of the railroad and highway through this rough, snow-smothered stretch of the Columbias has earned Rogers Pass the designation of national historic site. Given the size and frequency of the avalanches that roar down the mountains every winter and spring, keeping the railroad and highway open remains a challenge. In the winter, the Royal Canadian Horse Artillery sets up 105mm howitzers along the highway. When conditions are right and the Trans-Canada is closed, the Horse Artillery fires shells into trigger zones at the top of known avalanche chutes, which sends the waves of snow down the slopes.

Avalanches exert a year-round influence; those cleared runways constitute a fourth ecological zone in the park, along with the interior rain forest, the subalpine forest, and the alpine tundra. Look across

Illecillewaet River, Great Glacier Trail

the valley from the visitor center in summer and you'll see avalanche chutes thick with grasses, wildflowers, and shrubs. Grizzlies are fond of these steep, elongated meadows; they can sometimes be seen using their long front claws and powerful shoulders to plow up glacier lily bulbs or to dig madly in pursuit of plump ground squirrels.

The High Country

The most accessible high country in Glacier surrounds the **Illecille-waet Campground,** located on a spur road that goes east off Trans-Canada 1 a couple of miles southwest of Rogers Pass. Half a dozen major trails—the park's only cluster of trails—fan out from this campground. The campground's kiosk provides information on campfire programs and guided hikes and evening walks.

One of the most scenic hikes originating from the campground is the 2.6-mile (4 km) **Avalanche Crest Trail,** which entails plenty of dogged uphill work but largely avoids painfully steep pitches. The route begins in a mossy, old-growth forest amid the giant west-

Mountain Caribou

Only about 2,500 mountain caribou exist, and all of them inhabit southeastern British Columbia. Genetically speaking, the mountain caribou is the same subspecies as the woodland caribou that roams throughout boreal Canada. The mountain caribou's unusual method of dealing with the heavy snowfall of the Columbia Mountains, however, makes it a unique ecotype.

Unlike other caribou, the mountain caribou spends the late fall and early winter in old-growth forests at low elevations, where the big trees shield the forest floor from much of the snow and make foraging relatively easy. Then, as the snowpack deepens, the mountain caribou does something counterintuitive: It heads up into the mountains.

Unlike any other ungulate (hoofed mammal), the mountain caribou abandons its winter shelter and goes up where the snow is deeper—and where thick masses of edible lichens grow on high-elevation, old-growth trees (mainly Engelmann spruce and subalpine fir that are more than 200 years old).

Though little bigger than a deer, a mountain caribou has feet larger than those of a moose. This means the mountain caribou does not sink into the snow, so it spends less energy walking on snow than it would digging through it for food. By standing atop the snowpack, the mountain caribou can reach lichens growing higher up on the trees.

Old-growth trees are also more likely than young ones to be rotten—and, therefore, more likely to topple over or lose branches during winter storms. A downed tree or a fallen branch means more accessible lichen—and thus an easier winter for the caribou.

ern redcedars characteristic of the interior rain forest and the Engelmann spruce more typical of mid-elevation forest. The trees drip with lichens—classic winter fare for mountain caribou—and the verdant understory brims with dogwood, bunchberry, foam flower, and bog orchid.

Around the trail's midpoint the vegetation begins thinning and the views begin lengthening as you enter the subalpine. After a little more legwork you'll break into the land above the trees, where the trail ends at the base of an alpine basin

you want to get closer to one, try the demanding 2.5-mile (4 km) **Sir Donald Trail.** Plenty of hikers are happy to stroll just the first bit of the trail as it slips through lovely interior rain forest along the **Illecillewaet River.** At about the halfway point you'll cross the roiling stream formed by the meltwaters of the Vaux Glacier. A few hundred yards later you'll wheeze past the fork at which the **Perley Rock Trail** —an equally strenuous and somewhat dangerous hike—branches off. It's at this point that the hiking turns truly arduous.

Ferns and false hellebore

sandwiched between Eagle Peak on the right and Avalanche Crest to the left. If the weather allows and there isn't too much snow, intrepid hikers can pick their way up to the crest, nearly 1,000 vertical feet higher. The views are spectacular, but exercise caution if there is snow to cross: This is a starting block for avalanches, so the snow under your feet could be one in waiting.

The Avalanche Crest Trail provides fine views of glaciers, but if

When you sink gratefully to the ground at trail's end beneath the fierce brow of 10,814-foot (3,314 m) **Mount Sir Donald,** gaze up the alpine basin in front of you at the massive snout of the **Vaux Glacier.** Don't approach too closely; the steep snout sometimes disgorges rocks and chunks of ice. Just stay back and marvel at this landshaping mass of mobile ice—one of the more than 400 glaciers that gave the park its name. ■

Kootenay National Park

■ 347,400 acres ■ Southeast British Columbia, 20 miles (32 km) west of Banff
■ Best months June-Oct. ■ Camping, hiking, mountain climbing, fishing, mountain biking, cross-country skiing, snowshoeing, wildlife viewing, hot springs, scenic drive ■ Adm. fee ■ Contact the park, Box 220, Radium Hot Springs, BC V0A 1M0; phone 250-347-9615. www.parkscanada.gc.ca/kootenay

IT'S NO SURPRISE THAT A fantastic scenic drive runs through the middle of Kootenay National Park. This park was created around the Banff-Windermere Highway, which, when it was completed in 1922, was the first motor road to cross the Canadian Rockies. The deal included the designation of 5 miles (8 km) on each side of the highway for a park, and today the Banff-Windermere (Hwy. 93) remains Kootenay's backbone, providing access to hiking trails, campgrounds, and picnic areas. The 58-mile (93 km) drive passes through a remarkable diversity of habitats; Kootenay is the only national park in Canada in which you can see both cactuses and glaciers. Its semiarid southwestern corner, where prickly pear cactus grows along with Douglas-fir and ponderosa pine, provides important winter range for wildlife, especially bighorn sheep.

What to See and Do

Drop in at Kootenay's information center *(late May–early Sept.)* in the town of Radium Hot Springs. Hwy. 93 heads east from town and enters the park in half a mile. The striking scenery begins at once as you wind through **Sinclair Canyon;** scan the ruddy cliffs for bighorn sheep. A mile farther takes you to the **Radium Hot Springs Pools** *(fee),* where you have a choice of relaxing in 84°F or 102°F (29°C or 39°C) pools of mineral water. These bubbling springs form part of a pool complex complete with restaurant, locker rooms, swimsuit and towel rentals, and massage service.

When you're finished soaking, continue into the park along Sinclair Creek and up toward Sinclair Pass. Near kilometer marker 9 you will come to the trailhead for the Kindersley Pass and **Sinclair Creek Trail,** a 10.8-mile (17 km), loop that climbs halfway up Sinclair Creek to the alpine environment. At about kilometer 16, pull off at the **Kootenay Valley Viewpoint,** which delivers the promised panorama of the valley plus the surrounding mountains. From there the highway turns north and follows the Kootenay River, passing a number of picnic areas and trails.

If you've got strong legs, backcountry skills, several extra days, and a hankering to backpack through some of the most scenic wilderness in the Canadian Rockies, pull over just shy of kilometer 72, at the southern end of the **Rockwall Trail.** (The northern end of this semicircular route lies at the Paint Pots; hikers will need to do a two-vehicle shuttle, hitchhike, or hike down the road for the 8 miles/13 km between the trail-

Coyote

heads.) This 34-mile (55 km) trail alternately climbs into subalpine and alpine habitat and descends into lushly forested creekside valleys. Much of the hike takes place below the eponymous Rockwall—a sheer, imposing, limestone cliff that runs 33 miles (53 km) through Kootenay and Yoho National Parks, rising as much as 3,000 feet (914 m) above its base. In the valleys, notably along the north fork of Numa Creek, be alert for bears (see pp. 84–85).

At kilometer marker 85 you'll encounter the **Paint Pots.** Take time to observe the clay deposits stained yellow and red by iron-rich water bubbling up from several springs. Centuries ago, local Ktunaxa gathered here to collect the clay and mix it with animal fat for body paint.

Two miles (3.2 km) past the Paint Pots is **Marble Canyon,** a dizzyingly deep and narrow gouge in the gray limestone. Walk the 15-minute trail and stare down into the blue-green glacial meltwater coursing along the canyon bottom.

About 2 miles (3.2 km) past

the Marble Canyon you'll come to the trailhead for perhaps the finest day hike in the park: the **Stanley Glacier Trail.** This path of 3.4 miles (5.5 km) one way winds through the site of a 1968 forest fire called the **Vermilion Pass Burn,** where more than 7,290 acres (2,950 ha) of subalpine forest were devastated. Today a profusion of young lodgepole pines and a riot of wildflowers grow here.

The trail eases beneath 10,351-foot-high (3,155 m) **Stanley Peak.** You may spot moose in the lower elevations and hoary marmots and mountain goats up in the alpine area near the end of the hike. Finally, you'll top a knob and enjoy a magnificent view of Stanley Glacier.

The drive ends at **Vermilion Pass,** near the park's northeast boundary. At 5,415 feet, the pass marks the continental divide between water that flows to the Pacific and water that flows to the Atlantic. A 0.5-mile (0.8 km) interpretive path called the **Fireweed Trail** leads through another portion of the Vermilion Pass Burn. ∎

Yoho National Park

■ 323,706 acres ■ Southeast British Columbia, 120 miles (193 km) west of Calgary ■ Best months mid-June–mid-Oct. ■ Camping, hiking, mountain climbing, kayaking, canoeing, fishing, mountain biking, wildlife viewing, wildflower viewing, fossils ■ Adm. fee ■ Reserve up to a year ahead for summer stays at Lake O'Hara and Emerald Lake Lodges, and up to three months ahead for restricted access via bus for day use and camping at Lake O'Hara ■ Contact the park, P.O. Box 99, Field, BC V0A 1G0; phone 250-343-6783 or 250-343-6433 (reservations). www.parkscanada.gc.ca/yoho

A CREE WORD, *Yoho* roughly translates to "Wow!" This expression of awe and wonder perfectly sums up Yoho National Park, a flamboyantly scenic slice of the western side of the Canadian Rockies. The visual feast inludes dozens of 10,000-foot-plus mountains, turquoise lakes, lush conifer for-

Lefroy Lake and distant Ringrose Peaks

est, lofty waterfalls, creek-laced meadows colored by wildflowers, frothing rivers, sheer limestone and shale cliffs, and grinding glaciers whose cracks flash aqua in the sun.

Small-scale delights complement the glorious large-scale setting. Lower your gaze from the heights and you may see a beaver hauling an aspen branch to its lodge; red heather brightening the alpine tundra; a moose grazing in a bulrush-whiskered marsh; avalanche chutes thick with alder, willow, and cow parsnip; or a pileated woodpecker tattooing a Douglas-fir. Such variety stems from the park's extensive diversity of habitats, from marsh to meadow to mountaintop.

The vast majority of Yoho is wilderness, but casual explorers can gain access to the wilds via Trans-Canada 1, which cuts through the middle of the park, and via a handful of spur roads branching off it. An extensive network of trails—everything from short strolls to multiday treks—provides further opportunities to savor Yoho's beauty.

What to See and Do

Start at the visitor center in the tiny town of Field, in the middle of the park on Trans-Canada 1. To be more precise, start in the parking lot: Drink in the snow-topped mountains that surround you. Then go inside to learn more about this striking land and the ways to explore it.

A couple of miles northeast of Field, turn off the highway onto **Yoho Valley Road.** This 8-mile (13 km) spur includes some hairpin switchbacks that necessitate leaving trailers near the highway. But the serpentine slowness of the road is in direct proportion to the grandeur of the mountainous terrain. You'll follow the forested banks of the Yoho River north to **Takakkaw Falls,** at the road's end.

Takakkaw and the other waterfalls in the valley are a legacy of the Ice Age. Glaciers pushed through the existing valley and carved it into a deep trough. In the process, the glaciers left tributary valleys literally hanging in the balance, their streams spilling over the steepened sides of the main valley. Takakkaw was one of those valleys, and it is the highest; in fact, at 1,246 feet (380 m), including one 833-foot (254 m) free-fall drop, it's one of the highest falls in Canada.

A ten-minute stroll from the parking lot takes you across the Yoho River and through the forest to Takakkaw. The last part of the trail winds among stunted trees and ends at the base of the bare stone cliff, just a couple of hundred yards from the bottom of the falls. Be warned: The last stretch of trail lies within Takakkaw's blast zone. Wear rain gear or the blowing spray will soak you.

The Takakkaw Falls parking lot serves as the jump-off point for a web of trails in the park's subalpine zone. Hikers pass through thick forests of Engelmann spruce and subalpine fir—shady, cool, and lushly vegetated. You'll encounter avalanche chutes strewn with red osier dogwood and glacier lilies, willow-flanked creeks brimming with glacial meltwater, and meadows bedizened with false azalea, paintbrush, and pasqueflower. The trails in these dark, damp forests typically remain snowbound until mid-June.

Emerald Lake

Just a mile (1.6 km) southwest of Field, another spur road leads 5 miles (8 km) north to Emerald Lake, the largest body of water in the park (and one of the prettiest in the Rockies).

You can best enjoy the lake by hiking the 3.2-mile (5 km) loop called the **Emerald Lake Circuit.** This path begins in heavy forest punctuated by sunny avalanche chutes. Near the far shore, however, the trees dwindle in size and number until you emerge onto a gravelly, lightly vegetated alluvial fan. The material that has built this fan comes from the mountains above the lake, where ancient glaciers dropped their sediment loads.

As you skirt the lake, its surface may radiate the hue that inspired its name. However, the color changes according to the light, the season, the time of day, and the amount of glacial meltwater that's

Moon over Little Oderay Mountain

pouring down from the mountains. This meltwater carries "rock flour" (or glacial silt), which is dust-fine rock particles pulverized by glacial erosion. The particles take months to settle to the bottom; the smallest among them—and the last to settle—reflect the blue and green wavelengths of the light spectrum. Thus emerald green or turquoise dazzles us.

High above Emerald Lake lies an equally dazzling but less readily visible treasure, one that lay buried for some 515 million years. There, on a steep, scree-covered ridge, is the **Burgess Shale,** one of the most important fossil sites in the world. Discovered in 1909, the Burgess Shale has yielded tens of thousands of fossils, representing some 170 species from the beginning of the Cambrian period. Perhaps most remarkable, the fossils consist not only of hard body parts such as bones and shells, but also soft body parts such as muscle fiber and tissue. Scientists can tell what some of these creatures had for a last meal half a billion years ago (see p. 166).

Several other digs in the area, including the **Mount Stephen Trilobite Bed,** have unearthed thousands of additional fossils. To protect them, the Burgess Shale and the Mount Stephen Trilobite Bed are closed to the public except via hikes led by licensed guides. You can make reservations for the strenuous but worthwhile hikes through the Yoho-Burgess Shale Foundation *(800-343-3006).*

Lake O'Hara

The Lake O'Hara area is so appealing and fragile that access to it is tightly controlled. Anyone can hike the 8 miles (13 km) one way from the highway at any time, but you can't drive up the road on your own. Day hikers, overnight campers (a backcountry campground has 30 sites), and guests heading

Subalpine larches against Mount Huber

for Lake O'Hara Lodge must park near the highway and shuttle to the lake in a bus *(reservations required)*. The bus has a limited number of seats available each day, so reserve well in advance.

In general, competition for reservations at Lake O'Hara is fierce. Day hikers or campers can reserve three months in advance, and it helps if you are flexible with the dates of your visit. In part, the visitor restrictions serve to protect wildlife, particularly grizzly bears. But mostly Parks Canada is mainly endeavoring to conserve the sensitive alpine and high subalpine habitat for which the Lake O'Hara area is renowned.

The shuttle bus deposits passengers at an information hut a few minutes walk from Lake O'Hara, where most trails start. Scooped out by glaciers and fed by glacial meltwater, the lake reflects the encircling 10,000-foot (3,048 m) peaks on its luminous green-blue surface. Those who prefer level paths can take the **Lake O'Hara Shoreline Trail,** a 2-mile (3.2 km) loop around the lake. Most of the other trails head away from the lake, and that means climbing.

The **Lake Oesa Trail,** 1.7 miles (2.7 km) one way, is a fine example of the area's moderately pitched subalpine trails. It leads up from the northeast shore of Lake O'Hara, switchbacking through the subalpine forest and depositing you atop a cliff above the lake. From there you cross rocky slopes shorn of most vegetation by frequent avalanches. Before long you enter grassy subalpine meadows flagged by the silky plumes of pasqueflower and riddled with stone outcroppings. Often following the outlet creek from Lake Oesa—which at times tumbles precipitously enough to achieve waterfall status—the trail winds among copper-colored quartzite cliffs until topping out at **Lake Oesa** itself.

This small lake is a classic tarn: It pools in a bowl at the base of a rock amphitheater carved by glaciers. Steep headwalls splotched with snow and ice rise around the lake; dark, jagged peaks hover high above it.

Five routes lead into Lake O'Hara's storied alpine area, but only experienced hikers should tackle these strenuous and somewhat treacherous trails. Typical is the **Wiwaxy Gap/Huber Ledges Trail,** which starts at the northwest end of Lake O'Hara and tightropes 2.6 miles (4 km) through the high country to Lake Oesa. The climb begins with steep switchbacks for an hour or two; luckily, the view improves with each labored stride. You can gaze at turquoise Lake O'Hara below and Yoho's mountain bounty all around.

After topping out at about 8,300 feet (2,530 m) on a saddle some 2,300 feet (700 m) above Lake O'Hara, the trail edges southeast across the steep southern flank of 11,000-foot **Mount Huber.** The path here is nearly level, allowing you to catch your breath while savoring the spectacular open views. You may spot mountain goats grazing on the grassy patches that dot the bare rocks. We clumsy humans can only marvel as the powerful, sure-footed beasts negotiate their near-vertical world.

Following paint marks and cairns, you continue across the mountainside, descending slightly. Listen for the whistles of hoary marmots or the even higher-pitched squeaks of pikas as these alpine rodents scramble amid rock piles. Small explosions of moss campion, purple saxifrage, and other tundra-adapted wildflowers brighten the stern countenance of the stony slope. In several hours—assuming you have the good sense to take your time—you'll arrive at Lake Oesa. From there you can take the Lake Oesa Trail back to Lake O'Hara or go on through the alpine landscape for 1.5 miles (2.4 km) on the **Yukness Ledges Trail.** You'll end up at Opabin Plateau. ■

Mushroom and heather

Banff National Park

■ 1.6 million acres ■ Southwest Alberta, 60 miles (96 km) west of Calgary ■ Best months July-Sept. ■ Camping, hiking, boating, downhill skiing, cross-country skiing, snowshoeing, wildlife viewing, wildflower viewing, scenic drives, glacier tours ■ Adm. fee ■ Reserve months ahead for summer lodging in Banff or Lake Louise; arrive early for road-accessible campsites ■ Contact the park, Box 900, Banff, AB T1L 1K2; phone 403-762-1550. www.parkscanada.gc.ca/banff

VAST, WILD, AND CLASSICALLY SCENIC, Banff National Park lies at the heart of the Canadian Rockies system, bordered by three other national parks and several designated wildlands. Glaciers, grizzly bears, emerald green lakes, alpine tundra, wolves, old-growth conifer forests, subalpine mead-

Hiking Sentinel Pass above Minnestimma Lake

ows flashing with flowers, waterfalls, soaring peaks—Banff has it all.

The dramatic parapets of the eastern main range, which constitutes much of Banff's terrain, began forming about 140 million years ago. On the east side of the park, you'll see the front range—a soufflé of strikingly folded shale and limestone that the Earth whipped up about 85 million years ago. The park's geology then remained relatively static until 2 million years ago, when mighty Ice Age glaciers began molding the land. From 1200 to 1845, advancing glaciers of the little ice age continued to sculpt the peaks and valleys.

On this varied geological canvas, Mother Nature has painted a complex picture that includes diverse ecological communities. All these places are accessible to casual visitors via Banff's roads, tour boats, tramways, and especially its 1,000 miles (1,610 km) of hiking trails. The tourist infrastructure and development is particularly pronounced in the park's

What to See and Do

Begin your visit in the town of Banff. Fight your way through the summer traffic and the throngs of shoppers to the Banff National Park Information Centre, in the middle of town. If you leave there feeling the need for some elbow room, numerous drives and nearby hiking trails offer respite.

If you'd like to open your visit with an overview, take the 2.9-mile (4.7 km) round-trip hike to **Tunnel Mountain Summit.** Located about 1,000 feet (305 m) above the east side of town, it allows you to gaze down on Banff and across the Bow River Valley.

In the same vicinity you can get to other viewpoints via the **Tunnel Mountain Drive.** (For directions, pick up Parks Canada's "Day Hikes in Banff National Park" brochure.) On this route, stop at the parking lot on Tunnel Mountain Road, just east of the Tunnel Mountain Campground, and walk the 300 yards of the **Hoodoos Interpretive Trail.** Signs along the easy path explain the formation of the odd geologic features known as hoodoos; before you know it, you're at an overlook gazing down on a cluster of them. Gray-white-tan and dozens of feet high, these pillars of hardened mud and stone look like unfinished statues awaiting their final shape.

More ways to explore the area beckon on the south and west sides of town. Once again starting with the overview, take the **Sulphur Mountain Gondola** *(fee)* to the upper gondola terminal. There you can take in views from nearly 3,000 feet above Banff and the Bow River Valley. A half-mile (0.8 km) interpretive trail ascends to the summit of **Sanson Peak,** where you'll see a restored 1903 weather observatory and perhaps some bighorn sheep.

Just northwest of the peak sits the **Cave and Basin National Historic Site** *(403-762-1566),* which houses the springs that led to the establishment of the park in 1885. The site has displays about the history of Canada's national parks—Banff was the first—and a couple of short trails that wind through wetlands harboring orchids and numerous bird species.

A little farther northwest you can drive or hike along the **Vermilion Lakes**—three shallow, marsh-fringed oases. You might spot elk and coyotes. You'll probably see bald eagles, geese, and ospreys. And you're certain to notice the imposing presence of **Mount Rundle,** the town's signature mountain.

Sunshine Meadows

For a lot more elbow room, leave the town of Banff behind and head west 5 miles (8 km) on Trans-Canada 1 to Sunshine Road. This 6-mile (9.7 km) spur curves southwest along Healy Creek to the base of the Sunshine Village ski area gondola *(winter only).* For a price you can take a shuttle 3.3 miles (5.3 km) up the dirt road to the ski area (you can catch a shuttle from Banff, too) or you can walk or bike up the steep road.

From the ski area, labor upward another quarter mile (0.4 km) through scattered larch trees until you emerge above tree line

Canoeing on Lake Louise

into **Sunshine Meadows.** Mountain vistas unroll in every direction as you stroll easy trails that loop through the mountain heather, woolly everlasting, pasqueflower, valerian, and more than 300 other plant species—some quite rare—that populate this alpine meadow *(do not stray from the trails and trample the fragile vegetation).* Paying shuttle customers can join guides for half-day and full-day nature walks through the area.

Sunshine Meadows continues in a 9-mile (14.5 km) arc along the Continental Divide. To explore it further, leave the main trail network and go off for a few miles along the path toward Citadel Pass. After about half a mile (0.8 km) you'll cross into **Mount Assiniboine Provincial Park** *(250-422-4200)* in British Columbia.

Bow Valley Parkway

The Bow Valley Parkway (Hwy. 1A), about 2 miles (3.2 km) east of Sunshine Road on Trans-Canada 1, angles northwest about 40 miles (64 km) to Lake Louise. This road parallels the Trans-Canada; its lower speed limit allows you to enjoy the scenery and wildlife. The route goes through forest, flirts with the Bow River, passes meadows, offers numerous viewpoints and interpretive signs, and provides access to several hiking trails and campgrounds.

You're likely to spot wildlife, particularly elk, along the road or in the aspen groves. You may see cows and their gangly calves, a bachelor herd of young males, or an old bull elk brandishing an improbably huge rack. Sometimes you'll see black bears rooting around in the meadows. At river overlooks—notably the **Backswamp pullout** 2 miles (3.2 km) from the Trans-Canada—scan the expansive riparian wetlands and you may spy great blue herons, belted kingfishers, and ospreys bulleting into the water, their talons thrust downward in hopes of snatching a fish.

One of the most popular hikes in the Canadian Rockies branches north off the Bow Valley Parkway about 12 miles (19 km) from its southern junction with the Trans-Canada. An unusual trail leads you along **Johnston Canyon,** a limestone gash that at times is 100 feet deep and maybe a tenth of that

across. Peering into its depths to watch Johnston Creek thrash its way down to the Bow River is exciting enough, but for long stretches you can walk right up the creek, just a few feet above its surface, via a concrete-slab catwalk attached to the canyon wall. This rare perspective almost allows you to feel the geological forces at work as the water scours the rock. Run your fingers over the smooth, mossy stone and look closely at the half circles that the creek has neatly carved in the bedrock.

The length of the hike ranges from 0.7 mile (1.1 km) to 3.7 miles (6 km) one way, depending on your ambition. Many people stroll the shorter distance to **Lower Falls,** the first of seven cascades that vary in height from less than 10 feet to nearly 100. Watch for black swifts jetting through the canyon; this is one of only two places in Alberta where they nest. Proceed another mile (1.6 km) through a gradually widening and gradually less crowded canyon to **Upper Falls,** a 100-foot beauty. Near the plunge pool—where the falling water hammers into the bedrock at the bottom—the far wall is a glistening, golden travertine drape. The luminous colors come from the mixing of lime-

A snow blanket in Bow Valley

stone with microscopic algae. Many people turn back here, but continue for another five minutes: The trail winds up to an overlook on the canyon rim that yields excellent views from beside and above the cascade.

You can hike through lodgepole pine forest *(follow signs)* for another 2 miles (3.2 km) or so to the **Ink Pots**—a network of seven cold mineral springs in the open, mountain-lined valley of upper Johnston Creek.

Lake Louise

At the northern end of the Bow Valley Parkway you'll come to Lake Louise, the other hub of Banff National Park. The area boasts its own visitor center, located in the village near the highway, along with ample stores and hostelries. But despite these distractions, you'll be drawn a couple of miles west to the lake.

It is the definitive scene of the Canadian Rockies—a stunning, turquoise-green body of water framed by old-growth fir and spruce and backed by snow- and glacier-girded mountains. You definitely should admire it, shoot photos of it, canoe on it, and walk alongside it on the 1.8-mile (3 km) **Shoreline Trail,** but don't let the lake overwhelm you; some residual energy will be required to explore the area's other appealing sites.

Several outstanding (and often crowded) trails take in the lake's shoreline or provide views of Lake Louise; they also spotlight some of the region's assets. The 2.2-mile (3.5 km) ascent to **Lake Agnes** rewards hikers with the promised views and a teahouse at which to relax. (The respite will be mandatory, not optional; the trail is fairly steep.) The Canadian Pacific Railroad (CPR) first built a teahouse on this site in 1901 in a bid to lure people to the mountains. From the teahouse, walk east 0.8 mile (1.3 km) through a flowered avalanche slope to the summit of **Little Beehive,** whose view of the Bow Valley is so superb that a fire lookout tower once stood there.

Another CPR teahouse perches 3.4 miles (5.5 km) from Lake Louise along the dramatic **Plain of Six Glaciers Trail.** It follows the Shoreline Trail to the end of the lake, then continues toward **Mount Victoria.** Hoary marmots whistle from the avalanche slopes beside the trail, while mountain goats clamber about the steep rocks above. Below lie fields of

Scaling Quartzite Cliffs above Lake Louise

smashed rock—moraines left by the Victoria Glacier as it retreated. From the teahouse you can see the 260-foot-high (79 m) snout of Upper Victoria Glacier and, farther away, several other glaciers (but not all six that give the trail its name). To walk through an Ice Age landscape, continue southwest from the teahouse about a mile (1.6 km) to the end of the trail. You may hear the reverberating crashes of rockfalls as you pass beneath enormous cliffs frosted in glacial ice. The trail ends atop a lateral moraine above the Lower Victoria Glacier.

At the **Lake Louise Sightseeing Gondola** *(fee)*, you can ride the gondola, an open chair, or a bubble chair up to the 6,610-foot-tall (2,015 m) summit of **Mount Whitehorn.** From here you can see more than a dozen glaciers, the lofty peaks of the Continental Divide, fields of wildflowers, and, yes, Lake Louise.

Although entirely separate from Lake Louise, several nearby areas are considered to be within its orbit. Prominent among them is **Paradise Valley,** just a few miles to the south. The 11.2-mile (18 km) round-trip **Paradise Valley Trail** begins on Moraine Lake Road, 1.5 miles (2.4 km) from the Lake Louise townsite. The path cuts through forested valley bottom, past boggy areas replete with wildflowers, past slopes blanketed in mountain heather, across boulder fields favored by pikas, and under the looming wall of **Mount Temple,** whose massive north face rises to 11,626 feet, making it the tallest mountain near Lake Louise.

In the outer orbit of Lake Louise you'll find **Moraine Lake,** 8 miles (13 km) south of the townsite and reachable by road. This lake is headed by what some authorities consider the greatest cliff in the Canadian Rockies: The wall, made uneven by the spikes of ten peaks, towers more than 3,300 feet above the lake and stretches for nearly 10 miles (16 km).

Several trails crisscross the area. They include the interpretive **Rockpile Trail,** a half-mile (0.8 km) jaunt that deposits you atop a huge debris pile offering grand views of the lake and peaks. ∎

Following pages: Rainbow over Mount Rundle

Icefields Parkway Scenic Drive

■ 143 miles (230 km) long ■ Between Lake Louise village and Jasper townsite ■ Best months June-Sept. ■ Camping, hiking, biking, wildlife viewing, wildflower viewing, scenic drive, waterfalls, glacier tours ■ Adm. fee for Banff and Jasper National Parks ■ Contact Banff National Park, Box 900, Banff, AB T1L 1K2, phone 403-762-1550, www.parkscanada.gc.ca/banff; or Jasper National Park, Box 10, Jasper, AB T0E 1E0; phone 780-852-6176. www.parkscanada.gc.ca/jasper

IT'S TIME FOR THE SUPERLATIVES: The Icefields Parkway is the finest scenic drive in the Canadian Rockies. This 143-mile (230 km) road takes motorists and cyclists through the unspoiled high country of northern Banff and southern Jasper National Parks. This is a land of broad rivers, bighorn sheep, proud mountains, waterfalls, bears, lakes, mountain goats, and more than a hundred glaciers, some so close to the road that you can feel their chill. And you can see all these things because much of the parkway lies in high subalpine, where trees are short and sparse and don't obstruct the views.

You could complete this drive in a few hours, but you should savor every mile. Tarry at some of the dozens of viewpoints. Hike some of the trails that branch off the parkway. Tour the Columbia Icefield. And to give yourself plenty of time and miss some of the crowds, start early; it's

What to See and Do

Starting at the parkway's southern end, where it forks off Trans-Canada 1 near Lake Louise village, you're immediately in the company of big mountains, setting the scenic tone for the drive. Soon you pass a picnic site, a viewpoint, a trailhead, and a campground. But don't pull over yet. Wait until 20 miles (32 km) along, when you can't restrain yourself any longer, then stop at the viewpoint for **Crowfoot Glacier.** This ice cliff is a must-see, a mass of slow-motion ice flopping over the wall of stone above the lake.

Across the parkway is the **Dolomite Pass Trail,** a fairly steep 5.5-mile (8.9 km) ascent. If it's

mid- to late July, you may want to hike at least the first 3.7 miles (6 km) to **Helen Lake.** The trail winds through upper subalpine meadows thick with Indian paintbrush, glacier lilies, and other wildflowers hurriedly blooming to take advantage of the fleeting high-country summer. Keep an eye out for two seldom-seen species: wolves and mountain caribou (see sidebar p. 116).

Now that you've broken the ice (so to speak), three areas within the next 4 miles (6.4 km) deserve stops. First comes **Bow Lake,** where a picnic site overlooks the radiant glacial waters. Second is the Bow Glacier Viewpoint and

Crevasse climbing, Athabasca Glacier

the start of the **Bow Glacier Falls Trail.** This 2.7-mile (4.3 km) path skirts part of the lake and then edges up a narrow gorge (dangerously slippery when wet or snowy) to the crest of a glacial moraine. From there, finesse the rocks for half a mile (0.8 km) to the bottom of Bow Glacier Falls.

Third comes Bow Summit (6,849 feet/2,088 m). From the lower parking lot off the parkway, some 27 miles (43.5 km) north of Lake Louise, you can take the half-mile (0.8 km) **Bow Summit Trail** to the platform over **Peyto Lake.** After savoring vistas of the lake, Peyto Glacier above it, and the Mistaya Valley, and watching marmots and pikas skittering about the rocks, return the half mile (0.8 km) to the parking lot via the **Timberline Trail.** It wades through subalpine forest and meadows blooming with fleabane, pearly everlasting, and white, pink, and yellow heather.

Snow-coach tour of Athabasca Glacier

Next, pull over at the Waterfowl Lakes Campground. Two excellent trails depart from the Mistaya River Bridge in the campground: They stay together for the first 0.8 mile (1.3 km), then head left 2.1 miles (3.4 km) to **Cirque Lake** or right 1.7 miles (2.7 km) to **Chephren Lake.** Chephren is especially striking given its backdrop of Howse Peak and Mount Chephren.

If you'd like another short stroll, drive 9 miles (14.5 km) farther north to the small parking lot from which the quarter-mile (0.4 km) **Mistaya Canyon Trail** starts. Its name suggests mystery and the canyon makes good on that promise. You emerge from a thick forest to encounter a 50-foot-deep, 10- to 20-foot wide slash in the gray limestone with a waterfall spilling over the top and tumbling into white water below. This is the river you saw being born in Peyto Lake. Note the partial potholes along the water's edge, where water has spun gravel in circles, grinding out and polishing these perfect curves. There are no railings or other protections along the rim, so enjoy the canyon

from the bridge that crosses it.

Head on up the parkway another 29 miles (46.7 km) to the parking lot for the **Parker Ridge Trail.** This 1.5-mile (2.4 km), moderately inclined trail leads you through stunted, high-elevation forest to wildflower meadows and on up to the crest of the alpine ridge that gives the trail its name *(stay on the path to protect the fragile vegetation).*

Note the orange, black, and green rock lichens; they produce an acid that hastens the breakdown of rock and the creation of soil. At the top of Parker Ridge turn left (southeast) and follow the path to a vantage point high above **Saskatchewan Glacier.** At 6 miles (9.7 km) long, this is the largest of the glaciers that grind down from the Columbia Icefield.

That ice field is the driving force behind your next stop, 6 miles (9.7 km) up the road, just across the boundary into Jasper National Park (see pp. 144-151). If you only get out of your car once on the Icefields Parkway, get out here. Park at the **Columbia Icefield Centre** *(780-852-6288,*

May–mid-Oct.), which provides museum-like displays about the Columbia Icefield and serves as the base for tours of the **Athabasca Glacier**—the gigantic mass of ice on the slope across the road.

An ice field forms when snow accumulates over many years. The pressure resulting from the packed snow causes ice to form, and with enough pressure—at a snow depth of about 100 feet—a denser ice, called glacial ice, forms. Snow keeps falling, the ice thickens, and the ice field expands. When it reaches downward sloping valleys, the leading edge flows downhill, creating a glacier. At about 125 square miles (325 square km), the Columbia Icefield is the largest in the region.

To introduce yourself to the Columbia Icefield, take the **Toe of the Athabasca Glacier Trail.** Go across the parkway from the Columbia Icefield Centre and up a short spur road to the parking lot. From there a half-mile (0.8 km) path bridges a meltwater stream and crosses over limestone smoothed by the passage of the glacier, which reached this far as late as the 1950s.

The trail ascends fairly steeply over some rough rock to the top of a flattish area near the toe of the glacier. You can safely walk up and caress this glacier; its toe isn't a vertical wall that might drop chunks of ice onto your head. But don't step anywhere that looks wet, or you could plunge up to your shins in mud. More important, don't venture onto the glacier unless you go on one of the

Peyto Lake

guided "ice walks." Several people have died after falling into hidden crevasses.

For another perspective of the Athabasca Glacier, take a snowcoach tour *(call Brewster Snocoach Tours 877-423-7433)*. These massive vehicles, carrying several dozen passengers and a guide, rumble well out onto the glacier's surface. Above the glacier lies a rare (one of only two in the world) triple continental divide: Here, waters split off to the Pacific, Atlantic, and Arctic Oceans.

The guide lets everyone out onto a large, safe area. Take a sip of glacier meltwater while you're there, and think about the fact that it may have come from ice that fell as snow as long as 150 years ago.

From the Columbia Icefield Centre keep driving north through Jasper. Tempting pullouts include the **Tangle Falls Viewpoint** (look for bighorn sheep), the **Stutfield Glacier Viewpoint,** and the trail that heads up Beauty Creek to **Stanley Falls.** Soon you'll draw alongside the Sunwapta River, whose spectacular demise you can witness if you turn off the parkway 30 miles (48 km) north of the center and drive the quarter-mile (0.4 km) access road to **Sunwapta Falls.** Walk across the footbridge and look down into the canyon, where the Sunwapta roars around the bend and ends its life by diving into the Athabasca River. Continue along the drive into Jasper National Park (see pp. 144-151). ■

Following pages: Ascending north side Athabasca Glacier above Athabasca Valley

Jasper National Park

■ 2.7 million acres ■ 180 miles (290 km) west of Edmonton, borders Banff National Park on north ■ Best months June-Sept. ■ Camping, hiking, rafting, canoeing, fishing, horseback riding, downhill skiing, cross-country skiing, snow-shoeing, wildlife viewing, wildflower viewing, boat tour, scenic drives, hot springs ■ Adm. fee ■ Contact the park, Box 10, Jasper, AB T0E 1E0; phone 780-852-6176. www.parkscanada.gc.ca/jasper

ARGUABLY, JASPER IS THE WILDEST PARK in the Canadian Rockies. Though ample parts of it are developed and easily accessible, it is so vast—it's the largest park in the Rockies—that it includes huge tracts of pristine land. Because the wilderness hovers so near, visitors can quickly shift from the

Cavell Lake

civilized to the untamed. A few minutes down most of the trails—there are more than 600 miles (966 km) of maintained trails—and you're in a realm where nature rules. The majority of these paths began as game trails, trampled down over time by elk, deer, moose, caribou, and some of the other large mammals for which Jasper is known.

Jasper also is a rugged, mountainous place. The peaks of the eastern front range and eastern main range of the Rockies form the snowcapped skyline. More than 40 percent of the park lies above tree line, in the alpine area. But in some places these heights can be easily reached with a few hours of hiking, or, in one case, by riding seven minutes on a tramway.

This entry describes areas of Jasper not covered in the preceding entry on the Icefields Parkway (see pp. 136-143), which includes a sizable strip of southern Jasper National Park.

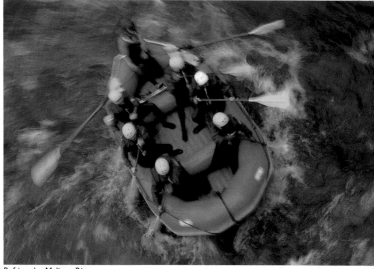

Rafting the Maligne River

What to See and Do

After you stock up on pamphlets and maps at the helpful Jasper Park Information Centre in downtown Jasper, stick around a while to explore. Many outdoor attractions are located close by, most notably a network of easy and rewarding trails.

Pyramid Bench

This lake-blessed terrace to the west and north of Jasper is so close to town you can stroll there.

Clear signage helps guide visitors through the web of trails available here, but you still may want to carry the Parks Canada "Summer Trails Guide," which has visitor information as well as maps and route descriptions for these and many of the park's other relatively short trails. (There is also a "Winter Trails Guide.") Visitors are allowed to take horseback rides on some of these trails—fun for those who like to ride horses, but if you're hiking be sure to watch your step.

Another option is to drive 3 or 4 miles (4.8 or 6.4 km) up Pyramid Lake Road to the north part of Pyramid Bench, to Patricia and Pyramid Lakes. These beautiful glacial lakes sit in an area of mixed forest inhabited by deer, moose, and a variety of birds.

The Whistlers Trail

Less than 3 miles (4.8 km) southwest of Jasper is The Whistlers Trail, which gets its name from the whistling sound made by marmots. The 4.9-mile (7.9 km) trail ascends nearly 4,000 feet (1,219 m) to the 8,104-foot (2,470 m) summit of **The Whistlers.** Diligent switchbacking has kept the trail's grade from being impossibly steep, but any way you look at it, a gain of 4,000 feet at this altitude will leave you gasping for air.

There is an alternate route to the summit that takes less of a physical toll. You can drive just over half a mile (0.8 km) beyond the trailhead to the Jasper Tramway *(780-852-3093)* and pay to take a tram to a point near the summit. The tram lines are long during the summer, but this is by far the easiest way to get to the alpine environment that is centrally located in the park.

You're in that alpine environment as soon as you step off the tram. Walk around the viewing deck and you'll see in the foreground low-lying vegetation and rocks characteristic of alpine tundra. The fantastic backdrop to this scene is half a dozen mountain ranges, sprawling river valleys, and crystal-clear spring-fed lakes winking in the sun.

Just past the deck a short boardwalk trail leads visitors through rocky alpine terrain. From here, you can hike to the summit on the tail end of The Whistlers Trail. The 650 vertical foot ascent of the trail's last 0.7-mile (1.1 km) at this altitude challenges most visitors, so take it easy and enjoy the views. Many people only go as far as a prominent knoll about halfway up.

Typically you'll be sharing the flat, several-acre summit with only a handful of other people. Even so, years of careless footsteps have scoured the area of plants; you'll have to walk over to the sides of the summit area and look down the slopes to see healthy vegetation *(be sure not to trample the plants while trying to get a closer look at them).*

During the brief, midsummer bloom look for white dryas, alpine anemone, alpine forget-me-not, and alpine poppy. If you watch the rock piles, you'll likely spot pikas and marmots scurrying about, and a binocular scan of the surrounding mountainsides may turn up bighorn sheep. Golden eagles and northern harriers may glide overhead while ptarmigan cluck about on the ground. A sundial-style peak finder is absolutely packed with lines pointing to dozens of mountaintops that crowd the panorama, including **Mount Robson,** at 12,972 feet (3,954 m) the tallest mountain in the Canadian Rockies.

Mount Edith Cavell Area

Take the Icefields Parkway south 4.6 miles (7.4 km) to Hwy. 93A. Continue on 93A for 7.25 miles (11.7 km) to the Mount Edith Cavell area, home to surpassingly beautiful subalpine meadows, an old-growth forest, and Angel Glacier. This area draws admiring crowds, so park the car and try to get on the trail before midmorning. Actually, there are two trails, the **Path of the Glacier Loop** and the **Cavell Meadows Loop,** but they neatly combine into a 5-mile (8 km) double loop with a short connecting path.

The two trails start out together beside the rubble left by a past advance of Cavell Glacier; watch for golden-mantled ground squirrels and pikas amid the quartzite boulders. After about 600 yards (183 m) take a hard left and go up a lateral moraine; you'll suddenly find yourself in a lush subalpine forest. Some of the old trees at the forest's edge bear the marks made by the glacier as it ground down the valley 150 years ago.

You're now on the Cavell Meadows Loop. As the trail angles up along the crest of the moraine, gaze across the narrow valley for outstanding views of **Angel Glacier,**

its enormous front of ragged, split-
ting ice draped over a steep slope
of Mount Edith Cavell. If you wait
and watch you may see a chunk of
ice, perhaps as big as a house, snap
off the face of the glacier with a
sound like a gunshot, followed by
the sights and sounds of the chunk
cartwheeling to the valley floor.

After you ascend on a reasona-
ble grade for maybe half an hour
through old-growth spruce and fir,
the forest starts to thin. Soon the
trees, much smaller now, huddle in
little clusters and a sea of subalpine meadow fills the mountain-

side. In summer (which starts
around mid-July up here), the
meadow is ablaze with the red of
Indian paintbrush, the yellow of
arnica, and the pink of mountain
heather. When the ground is wet,
the alpine meadows are most vulnerable to trampling and erosion.
Watch for voluntary or temporary
closure on portions of this trail
in springtime.

The trail may get a little con-
fusing due to all the illicit paths
people have created by walking
across the sensitive vegetation, but
you can't get lost if you stick with

Mount Unwin (left) and Mount Charlton (right) beyond Maligne Lake

the largest trail and carry a map and directions *(do not venture on the illicit trail that leads below the glacier—you could be hit by a stray chunk of ice)*. Essentially, you loop through subalpine meadows and some alpine meadows (watch for mountain caribou and stay alert for grizzly bears) and come back down to where you first emerged from the forest.

Take the trail back down to the moraine, and about 600 yards (183 m) from the parking lot, turn left away from the lot to complete the Path of the Glacier Loop. You descend through boulder fields to the little lake at the base of **Cavell Glacier.** Here icebergs shed by the glacier float around, shining aqua-white in the sunlight. From this point the trail follows the glacier's meltwater creek back to the lot.

Maligne Lake Road

Several sites stretch from Maligne Canyon, 7 miles (11.3 km) northeast of the town of Jasper, to the northern tip of Maligne Lake, 30 miles (48 km) southeast of Jasper. Pick up Maligne Lake Road off Trans-Canada 16, approximately

Bull elk sparring during fall rut, Bankhead Meadow

3 miles (4.8 km) east of Jasper. **Maligne Canyon** is a classic Canadian Rockies canyon: a deep, narrow, limestone slash, with spruce trees growing along its rim and mosses and ferns greening its dark, dank interior. A 2.3-mile (3.7 km) round-trip **interpretive trail** eases along the canyon's edges and lets you peer 160 feet (49 m) down to the frothy **Maligne River.** Fresh water flows from springs along the trail, evidence of subterranean connections to Medicine Lake, 9 miles (14.5 km) away.

Back on Maligne Lake Road, **Medicine Lake** is the next destination, though you may pull off along the way to watch elk or black bears—from your car, parked safely off the road, of course.

As you cruise alongside this lovely lake on a sunny July morning, it appears to be perfectly normal—sparkling water, conifer fringe, an osprey flapping overhead grasping a freshly caught fish.

But if you were cruising by on a sunny October morning the lake not only wouldn't look normal, it wouldn't be there at all. Water is constantly draining from the lake by means of a vast underground cave system (remember the springs along the trail through Maligne Canyon?). By fall, the flow of water into the lake dwindles; eventually the water drains away and the lake disappears.

Maligne Lake, 15 miles (24.1 km) farther down the road, pulls no such disappearing acts. The largest lake in the Canadian Rockies, it curves gently southeast deep into the wilderness. This lake is long and slender: It stretches 17 miles (27.4 km) and often is only a few hundred yards across. A gantlet of 10,000-foot (3,048 m) peaks line its shores, and you can run it in a 90-minute guided boat tour that motors down to Spirit Island and back. You also can rent canoes or kayaks and explore the lake on your own *(call Maligne Tours 780-852-3370)*.

Back on dry land, you might consider the several day hikes that start from the small developed area at the end of the road. Two in particular—the **Opal Hills Loop** (5.1 miles/8.2 km round-trip) and the **Bald Hills Trail** (6.4 miles/10.3 km round-trip)—merit the effort that these medium-difficult routes demand. Both provide grand views of Maligne Lake, subalpine meadows festooned in wildflowers from late June through late August, and the opportunity to see plenty of wildlife. Maligne Tours offers horseback rides in this area, and guided hikes can be arranged through local outfitters in the town of Jasper.

Miette Hot Springs

Many visitors to the park drive north from Banff along the Icefields Parkway and then exit Jasper by heading east on Trans-Canada 16 toward Edmonton. But just a few miles before leaving the park, turn south and drive down an 11-mile (17.7 km) spur road to one last hot spot—literally, in this case: Miette Hot Springs.

As tempting as they are, don't rush to the hot springs pools at the end of the road right away; you'll want to enjoy narrow, winding, and scenic **Miette Hot Springs Road.** About halfway to the pools, pull over at **Ashlar Ridge Viewpoint** to behold the 1,000-foot limestone cliff that juts up amid the mountains of the front range.

Visitors frequently spot black bears along this road; if you see one, watch but don't feed. Not only could you get hurt, but bears

that develop a taste for human food become problem bears and frequently must be killed. Remember the adage, "A fed bear is a dead bear."

When you arrive at the hot springs, you also have arrived at the trailheads for two fine hikes: Sulphur Pass by way of the **Fiddle River Trail** (3.2 miles/5 km round-trip) and **Sulphur Skyline Trail** (6 miles/9.7 km round-trip). The path to Sulphur Pass takes you through the ruins of the old pool building, where interpretive signs explain how the hot springs work, and on up to wildflower meadows and long views.

The Sulphur Skyline Trail gains more than 2,000 feet (610 m) in elevation and has some memorably steep sections. It deposits you on a summit above tree line that presents fantastic vistas of the front ranges and even the foothills of the Rockies. This summit has a reputation for afternoon thunderstorms, so you'd best get up there early and head back down below tree line if the weather starts turning ominous.

Now, at last, it's time to relax in the hottest mineral springs in the Canadian Rockies, which bubble out of the earth at 129°F (54°C). Don't worry, though; that scalding water is cooled down to 104°F (40°C) in the two main pools, so you can ease aching muscles in blissful comfort. If you can tolerate bliss for only so long, there's also a 59°F (15°C) cold plunge. Around the pool area are plenty of places to picnic, as well as frequent glimpses of bighorn sheep; even here, the wildness of Jasper National Park asserts itself. ∎

The Prairie

View of sunset from 70 Mile Butte, Grasslands National Park

LIKE A DOG ROLLING IN CLOVER, a 1,500-pound bison bull flops on its back in the dust wallow and thrashes back and forth. Around it the herd of 50 bison goes on about its business—grazing, suckling orange-brown calves, swatting at flies with their tails.

Warm sand trickles between your toes as you climb to the top of a dune. All around, islands and peninsulas of grass and blooming wildflowers bring color to this undulating sandy sea.

A small piece of dinosaur bone preserved over the ages in the hot, dry badlands—a whisper from 75 million years ago, a glimmer of a lost world—lies by your hiking boot, ready to be touched, picked up, wondered about.

Twenty feet ahead of you, in the cattails, a beaver clutching a willow branch in its mouth swims toward its lodge.

Tens of thousands of squirming snakes packed into a few dens instill onlookers with a sense of dread and a sense of awe—and a paranoid need to continually check around their feet for strays.

Which of the above scenarios can the Canadian prairie lay claim to? All of them.

Of course, the prairie also offers the classic scene of rolling hills carpeted with grasses swaying in the wind, where the coyote's mournful howl slices the night and the swift pronghorn trots along a distant ridge. But this classic core is supplemented by a diverse array of other landscapes and wildlife.

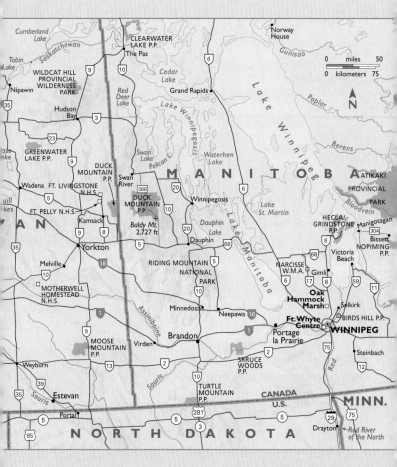

The Canadian prairie is part of the Great Plains of North America, most of which lie in the midwestern and western United States. It is the land that lies between forest and desert, though it contains bits of both. In Canada, the prairie stretches across the southern sections of Manitoba, Saskatchewan, and Alberta. Strongly influenced by distance from the Pacific Ocean and its moisture-bearing winds, the prairie shifts from fescue in the west to mixed-grass in the middle to tallgrass in the east.

The prairie is a tremendously fecund place, especially in its wetter areas, but this circumstance has contributed to its downfall. Capitalizing on the rich soil, farmers and ranchers have plowed and grazed the vast majority of the Canadian prairie, transforming it into a domesticated shadow of its former self. Oil and gas development and dambuilding have further degraded the natural bounty of the region, as have the invasive, non-native plants that have spread across much of the land in the wake of the plow and the cow. More than 20 species of prairie mammals, birds, and plants appear on Canada's endangered species list.

Black-tailed prairie dog, Grasslands National Park

Fortunately, wild pockets still remain, inviting you to get a sense—albeit incomplete—of the pre-European prairie. Some of these isolated fragments lack certain elements that would be present if the landscape was still largely undeveloped; despite the widespread habitat fragmentation, however, most species of native prairie wildlife and plant life are prevalent. Many of these oases have been protected as national parks, provincial parks, wildlife management areas, and the like. Roam these remnant prairielands and discover for yourself the beauty and diversity of the plains.

Incorporating three distinct life zones, Riding Mountain National Park is the all-around champion when it comes to wildlife, which includes thriving populations of elk, moose, beaver, and black bear, plus white-tailed deer, lynx, coyote, river otter, pine marten, wolf, and even a small herd of plains bison. Though much smaller and more heavily managed (a fence surrounds the entire park), Elk Island National Park protects tracts of exquisite open aspen parkland—the transitional zone between the prairie and the boreal forest—and is home to sizable herds of both plains and wood bison.

A few prairie sites are renowned for the unique wildlife they offer: Narcisse Wildlife Management Area features the aforementioned snakes, while the badlands of Dinosaur Provincial Park play host to the skeletal remains of long-dead animals.

If you travel deep into these sanctuaries, with the grass underfoot and the warm breeze tugging at your hair, you can still feel the essence of the prairie that inspired Wallace Stegner to describe it as "a distance without limits, a horizon that did not bound the world but only suggested endless space beyond." ■

Spray Lake, Duck Mountain Provincial Park

View of Astotin Lake from Living Waters Boardwalk

Elk Island National Park

- 47,938 acres ■ North-central Alberta, 28 miles (45 km) east of Edmonton
- Best months May-Oct. ■ Camping, hiking, kayaking, canoeing, biking, cross-country skiing, snowshoeing, bird-watching, wildlife viewing, scenic drive
- Adm. fee ■ Contact the park, R.R. 1, Site 4, Fort Saskatchewan, AB T8L 2N7; phone 780-992-2950. www.parkscanada.gc.ca/elk

AN ISLAND, INDEED. Elk Island National Park began, in 1906, as a home for a dwindling local population of elk, a slice of wildness in a rapidly filling ocean of agriculture. The park remains such an sanctuary, but it also provides a haven for a bit of the lower boreal mixed forest and aspen parkland ecosystem. Farming, ranching, oil and gas exploration, and forestry have severely altered more than 75 percent of Canada's aspen parklands—a transition between the prairie and the boreal forest—making this one of the country's most imperiled landscapes.

Elk Island is a lovely mosaic of open aspen parklands, denser conifer forests, grassy meadows, and wetlands. Famous for its wildlife—abundant and exceptionally visible—Elk Island has one of the greatest concentrations of large mammals in North America in a wild area, including sizable numbers of bison, moose, deer, and, appropriately, elk. The park generally is snow free May through October, and the wildlife viewing is exceptional throughout this fair-weather period.

What to See and Do

Branching north off Yellowhead Hwy. (Trans-Canada 16), which runs east to west through the southern part of Elk Island, the 13-mile (21 km) paved **Elk Island Parkway** slips through the middle of the park to the north entrance. Nearly all that the park has to offer can be reached via the parkway and a few side roads. The drive is quite scenic and typically sprinkled with wildlife; the animals are more active in early morning or evening. You'll likely see a bison trotting across the road or a moose standing in one of the wetlands.

The parkway starts in classic aspen parkland—groves of trembling aspen interspersed with grasslands. In half a mile (0.8 km) you'll come to the information center *(May-Sept.),* where you can get maps, look at natural history displays, and ask about wildlife-viewing opportunities.

Bison Loop Road

After 1.5 miles (2.4 km) turn east onto Bison Loop Road, a short (0.6 mile/1 km) dirt road that circles through an area where dozens of plains bison often hang out in summer. Elk Island has the rare honor of hosting both bison subspecies: the plains and the wood bison. The park straddles the rough boundary of the historic ranges of these subspecies. In Elk Island the plains bison are kept north of Yellowhead Hwy. and

the wood bison to the south of the highway. (To look for wood bison, take the 11.5-mile/18.5-km **Wood Bison Trail,** which loops out from Yellowhead Hwy., across from the start of the parkway; or watch for them as you drive along the highway.)

The two subspecies look similar, but you can learn to tell them apart. The plains bison has a shorter neck, a more rounded hump, and a larger "beard." Furthermore, the plains bison bull averages a measly 11 feet long and 1,600 pounds, whereas the wood bison bull averages around 13 feet long and 1,850 pounds—the largest land mammal native to North America. Whichever you may encounter, that's a big hairy beast.

Bison are fast and temperamental, so stay at least 100 yards (90 m) away from them unless you're in your car. Sometimes you'll get a safe, close look from your car while driving this road or Elk Island Parkway; you may even

A young coyote in search of mice

get to, or have to, drive right through the herd. If the bison are blocking the road, wait for them to move off. If you can't wait, proceed very slowly. Don't honk, or your car may need some bodywork—and not all insurance policies cover bison damage.

Ponds and Lakes

Half a mile north of Bison Loop Road, Elk Island Parkway winds through a cluster of ponds—part of the vast prairie pothole network of ponds, lakes, and marshes. In the summer you'll likely spot loons, grebes, and Canada geese paddling the waters. During spring and fall lucky visitors may sight trumpeter swans—a species reintroduced to Elk Island.

A minute's drive past the last pond brings you to the turnoff to **Tawayik Lake,** a mile's drive to the west. A variety of birds draws visitors to the lake, as do the three hiking loops that start from the picnic area in the aspen parkland. The 7.8-mile (12.5 km) **Shirley Lake Trail** skirts shallow ponds and lakes favored by nesting waterfowl. At dawn and dusk you may see elk in the meadows. Return to the picnic area via about a mile (1.6 km) of the **Simmons Trail.**

For another nice hike, drive 1.5 miles (2.4 km) past the Tawayik turnoff to the 7.5-mile (12 km) **Hayburger Trail.** Along this varied walk look for moose in the black spruce bogs and for plains bison in the meadows and aspen parklands. In the meadows near the trailhead you'll see places where bison have trampled and eaten young aspen; not only do they get a meal, but this helps keep the aspen from overrunning the open grasslands, which are important bison habitat.

Astotin Lake Area

Four miles (6.4 km) up the parkway, numerous recreational possibilities await at the Astotin Lake Area. You may explore lovely Astotin Lake by canoe, kayak, or sailboat *(no rentals; no motorized craft allowed).* The **Lakeview Trail** curves 2 miles (3.2 km) along the northeast shore of the lake, passing through aspen forest and some black spruce bogs. Look for the two beaver ponds. The **Shoreline Trail** follows the lake's southern edge for 1.8 miles (2.9 km). Check the coves for red-necked grebe and the enormous American white pelican.

On the east side of the recreation area, away from Astotin Lake, lies the **Amisk Wuche Trail.** Of all the trails in Elk Island, this one delivers the most bang for the buck. Only 1.5 miles (2.4 km) long, this interpretive loop winds through a mixed aspen, birch, and spruce forest and crosses several beaver ponds and kettle lakes on floating boardwalks. ∎

The Relocation Shuffle

Elk Island requires active management. The 7-foot (2 m) fence encircling Elk Island keeps predators out—no bears or wolves inhabit the park—and keeps resident wildlife in. With the absence of major predators, the bison and elk proliferate beyond the carrying capacity of the land, so the park oversees the capture and relocation of the excess animals beyond the park.

Cottonwood trees in autumn, Cottonwood Flats Trail

Dinosaur Provincial Park

■ 18,039 acres ■ Southeast Alberta, 88 miles (142 km) southeast of Drumheller ■ Best months late May–early Oct.; summer temperatures often exceed 90°F (32°C) ■ Camping, hiking, scenic drive, interpretive tours, fossils, badlands ■ Reservations required July–Aug. for campground and interpretive tours; reservation desk opens May 1 ■ Contact the park, P.O. Box 60, Patricia, AB T0J 2K0; phone 403-378-4342. www.gov.ab.ca/env/parks/prov_parks/dinosaur

FORGET "JURASSIC PARK" AND BARNEY. If you love dinosaurs—real dinosaurs—head for Dinosaur Provincial Park in southeastern Alberta's badlands, one of the richest dinosaur fossil reservoirs in the world. Some 75 million years ago, during the late Cretaceous period, this parched, rocky, eroded land looked dramatically different: It was a coastal plain covered by a lush subtropical forest peppered with swamps and rivers—excellent dinosaur habitat.

When the dinosaurs died, their bodies became encased in layers of mud, silt, and sand, which built up over the ages and eventually turned into sedimentary rock. Subsequently, more layers of sediment buried the layers entombing the dinosaurs. But ice age glaciers stripped away much of the overlying sediments, and rushing meltwater at the end of the last ice age gouged deep into the landscape, cutting down to the layers sheltering the dinosaur fossils. Erosion hasn't stopped since then, and fossilized dinosaur bones now lie just beneath the surface in many places; sometimes they even can be found lying in the open on dry streambeds or sticking out of the wall of a ravine.

Dinosaur Provincial Park's badlands are visually stunning in a minimalist sort of way. The erosive forces have carved hoodoos (rock pillars), sinkholes, narrow gullies, and multicolored, deeply grooved hillsides. In addition, a green strip—the riparian corridor created by the Red Deer

River—runs through the park. This elongated oasis of life is rare in the prairie badlands, as are its old cottonwoods and many of the plant and animal species found within. For this reason, as well as the exceptional fossil beds and the park's location in Canada's most extensive tract of badlands, the United Nations bestowed upon Dinosaur the much coveted designation of World Heritage site.

What to See and Do

The best way to glimpse the long-gone world of the dinosaurs is to go on one of the interpretive tours offered by the field station of the Royal Tyrrell Museum—considered by many to be the finest paleontology museum in the world (see sidebar p. 165). Better yet, go on two or three. Park personnel encourage visitors to stay at least two days, saying "a place that's been 75 million years in the making is worth a couple days of your time to enjoy!" On your own, you can wander down one of the park's five established hiking trails (found in three different habitats) and take a scenic drive through the badlands on the Public Loop Road.

Eroded badlands of Coulee Viewpoint Trail

Begin by stopping just as you enter the park to stroll the easy **Prairie Trail.** This 300-yard path circles through a sample of the grasslands that characterize the fringe of the park. Most compelling, the trail leads to viewpoints from which you can look across the badlands that constitute the heart of Dinosaur. Once you've drunk your fill of the panorama, continue half a mile (0.8 km) down the road to the Royal Tyrrell Museum Field Station.

Royal Tyrrell Museum Field Station

The museum's field station acts as a de facto visitor center; you can load up on park literature and get oriented to the park. The displays include fossils of species that aren't the usual suspects, such as the Quetzalcoatlus, a flying reptile with a 40-foot (12 m) wingspan. A horrifying scene that the kids are sure to love shows four dromaeosaurs staging a packlike attack on a duckbill. You'll even learn some things, such as the fact that dinosaur remains are much more likely to be preserved if they're buried quickly, as they were by riverborne sediments in these badlands.

Assuming you have reservations or good luck getting tickets, you can attend a 30- to 45-minute talk in the field station's **Prep Lab.**

Styracosaurus model outside Royal Tyrrell Museum Field Station

Inside the wonderfully disheveled, warehouselike lab, its shelves heaped with fossils in plaster jackets, technicians labor at long tables, brushing and picking at discovered specimens.

Interpretive Tours

Fossils require more interpretation than do mountains, waterfalls, and charismatic megafauna, so more than in most parks, the interpretive tours here are essential to fully understand and enjoy the park. Some of the tours will take you into the 70 percent of the park that is a natural preserve—and off-limits without a park guide.

For an easy, general overview of the park, with an emphasis on dinosaurs, take the **Badlands Bus Tour.** This two-hour trip *(fee)* takes you onto a gravel road that winds through the natural preserve. The bus stops at several intervals so you can get off for a

closer look at things. Though the pace of erosion has slowed from the great Ice Age meltdown, the soft badlands sediments still erode 500 times faster than do the Rockies, so new fossils are constantly being exposed. At this rate, the guides joke, they'll be out jobs in 30,000 years because the badlands will be gone.

Two guided hikes, each 2.5 hours long, take you to fossil sites. On the easy to moderately strenuous **Fossil Safari** you'll head to a known fossil site in the natural preserve, where you'll see fossils and learn about the creatures that once fleshed out those bones. The **Centrosaurus Bone Bed Hike** (1.5 mile/2.4 km round-trip) leads to one of the world's most renowned dinosaur excavations, though it's now inactive. In the 1980s, this bone bed—the size of two tennis courts—yielded a tremendous number of fossils and extensive knowledge about the way the *Centrosaurus* dinosaurs lived.

The Badlands

If you can curb your dinosaur lust for a moment, drive the 2.25-mile (3.6 km) **Public Loop Road** to sample the badlands scenery. Although the gravel road is only a couple of miles long, it curves along the perimeter of the natural preserve, showcasing some of the badlands' beautiful erosion patterns and formations.

Three trails branch off the road. The 0.8-mile (1.3 km) **Badlands Trail** will take you through a slice of the badlands. Though seemingly barren, tough animals and plants have adapted

Royal Tyrrell Museum

The world-class Royal Tyrrell *(4 miles/6.4 km NW of Drumheller, in Midland Provincial Park. 888-440-4240. www.tyrrellmuseum.com. Closed Mon. early Oct.–mid-May; adm. fee)* displays more than 35 dinosaur skeletons and hundreds of fossils, the most under one roof anywhere. Its imaginative presentations and interactive learning opportunities are a perfect blend of the engaging and the educational.

The museum covers the breadth of life on Earth, beginning with the first evidence of slimy life about 3.5 billion years ago up to the last ice age, some 12,000 years ago; however, the dinosaurs of the late Cretaceous occupy center stage.

Hands-on exhibits make learning fun. A crank at the "Clamming Up" display opens and closes giant clam shells, demonstrating the different ligament-muscle solutions for such an operation. Similarly, a crank controls the jaws of big dinosaurs, showing that the muscle-driven levers suited a dinosaur's needs: A plant-eater's jaws move slowly and powerfully, whereas a fish-eater's jaws move quickly but weakly.

Scare yourself by following the "Caution, Danger Ahead" signs into the Theropod Hall; "theropod" means "beast foot" and includes all the carnivores. In another part of the museum, you can play a video game where you try to avoid being eaten by carnivorous dinosaurs.

You'll reach the zenith of dino-mania in a series of warehouse-size halls where whole skeletons are displayed in action scenes. You'll see old favorites, such as triceratops and *Stegosaurus,* as well as the less familiar, including a *Parasaurolophus,* a duckbill found in Dinosaur Provincial Park. One vast exhibit depicts a community of dinosaurs complete with skin, as true to life as can be determined. And in the ever popular attack scene, an *Allosaurus* rips at the throat of a *Camptosaurus.*

During summer and early autumn, the museum conducts a full menu of programs in the surrounding badlands. These range from a 90-minute tour of a dig site to multiweek "field experience" opportunities, where volunteers shovel and sweat alongside crews digging for dinosaurs. A popular compromise is the day dig; participants work with excavators at a dig and even learn to map and jacket fossils.

to the rigors of this habitat. Sage-brush and cactuses manage to get by. Occasionally you'll spot a white-tailed deer nibbling at some grass. Watch overhead for golden eagles and prairie falcons. (The half-mile/0.8 km **Coulee View-point Trail** beginning at the field station travels through similar landscape, but avoid it during wet weather because the rock surfaces get slippery.)

Follow the **Trail of the Fossil Hunters** half a mile (0.8 km) to a quarry marker. It is here that Barnum Brown—perhaps the greatest dinosaur hunter of the 20th century—conducted excavations for the American Museum of Natural History in New York.

The 1-mile (1.6 km) **Cotton-wood Flats Trail** loops through the Red Deer River riparian zone —the hotbed for plant and animal life. Riparian woodland areas make up only about one percent of the Alberta prairie, so they provide a rare sanctuary for eastern king-birds, orioles, mountain bluebirds, great blue herons, porcupines, bobcats, deer, and more. Above it all spread the big old cottonwood trees, some anchored by gnarly, deeply incised trunks a hefty 3 to 4 feet (0.9 to 1.2 m) in diameter. Sadly, the cottonwoods are not regenerating: Dams upriver have stopped the big floods that provide the conditions required by cotton-wood seeds to germinate. ∎

The Burgess Shale

Can trilobites match the appeal of dinosaurs? Well, no, but that doesn't mean they should be ignored. They and their brethren played a key role in the evolution of life on Earth. These unassuming little crustaceans and other ancient marine creatures are the stars of the Royal Tyrrell Museum's latest major display: the Burgess Shale.

The Burgess Shale is the remnant of a 515-million-year-old Cambrian period ocean floor that now forms part of a mountainside in British Columbia. It is one of the world's great fossil sites for trilobites and other marine organisms. Tens of thousands have been excavated, and more remain to be discovered.

Representing as many as 170 species, the fossils are remarkable not only for their variety but for the presence of well-preserved soft body parts, even entire soft-bodied organisms. The Burgess Shale has provided an extraordinarily clear and extensive view of the Cambrian period, a crucial time when multi-cellular life blossomed. Study and restudy of these famous fossils has challenged our thinking about major evolutionary issues. For instance, recent research on the fossils indi-cates that mutation and natural selection are not the only evolu-tionary forces at work—rapid diversification and random extinc-tions also play critical roles.

The Burgess Shale exhibit pulls visitors into a dark room, as if underwater, where they stand on a clear floor surrounded by clear windows. This convincing illusion will have you holding your breath. Enlarged models of some of the Burgess Shale creatures are sus-pended all around you.

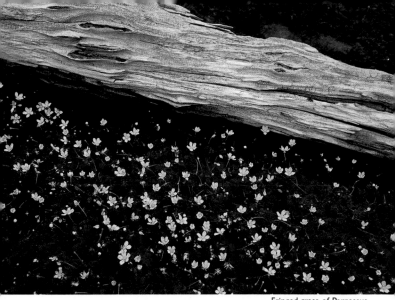

Fringed grass-of-Parnassus

Cypress Hills Interprovincial Park

■ 89,771 acres ■ Southwest Saskatchewan and southeast Alberta, 40 miles (64 km) southeast of Medicine Hat ■ Best months April-Oct. ■ Camping, hiking, canoeing, fishing, biking, downhill skiing, cross-country skiing, snowshoeing, wildlife viewing, auto tours ■ Adm. fee ■ Contact the park, P.O. Box 850, Maple Creek, SK S0N 1N0, phone 306-662-5411 (Saskatchewan); or P.O. Box 12, Elkwater, AB T0J 1C0, phone, 403-893-3777 (Alberta). www.cypresshills.com

FROM A DISTANCE, the Cypress Hills must have looked like a mirage to early pioneers. Imagine slowly making your way across the prairie on horseback or foot, the flat, dry grasslands stretching away to the curve of the Earth. Suddenly, far ahead on the horizon, this 1,000-square-mile plateau—an oasis of conifer forest and aspen groves—rears from the flatness, 2,000 feet above the prairie that encircles it. At 4,810 feet above sea level, it is the highest point between Labrador and the Rockies. Maybe you, too, would have been disoriented enough to mistake a lodgepole pine for a "cypres" (as jack pines were often called in eastern Canada) and so misname this geologic phenomenon.

The Cypress Hills were once part of a much larger plateau, but the preglacial ancestors of the Milk and South Saskatchewan Rivers eroded away most of it. They left only the part in the middle that lay beyond the reach of either river—the Cypress Hills. Elevated as they are, the Cypress Hills get more precipitation and less heat, so the vegetation differs in many ways from that of the prairie below. In addition to those lodgepole pines, you'll find white spruce, aspen, buffaloberry, twinflower, and other plants characteristic of the Rocky Mountain foothills. But you'll also find some grasses and shrubs typical of the prairie—which, added to the montane flora, make this one very diverse place. The fauna is diverse as well, though less so than it was before the area's bison, wolves, grizzlies, and black bears were hunted out.

Aspen stand near Reesor Lake

What to See and Do

Once two parks, the interprovincial park was created in 1989. The Saskatchewan portion is made up of two areas—the Centre Block and the West Block (there is no East Block)—separated by a 10-mile-wide (16 km) tract of private land known as the Gap. The West Block adjoins the Alberta Block.

Centre Block

The park's busiest hub lies in the Centre Block. During the summer this 17-square-mile piece of plateau teems with visitors. They stay at more than a dozen campgrounds and lodges and throng the pool, the golf course, the ball fields, and the café. Wilderness this is not, but you can still see some of the Cypress Hills as nature made them.

Begin with the **Centre Block Auto Tour,** a 15-mile (24 km) drive that covers many features of this tract of the park. *(Be advised: This gravel road can be slippery*

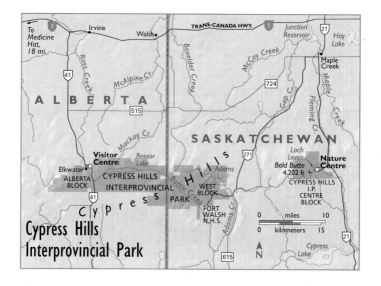

when wet.) Start at the nature center, where you can pick up an interpretive brochure to the drive.

Within a minute you'll be skirting **Loch** (as in "lake") **Leven,** popular with anglers and canoeists. Occasionally you'll see American white pelicans sweeping their bills through the water in hopes of netting some fish. These huge birds (5 feet tall with a wingspan of 9 feet) nest in the Cypress Hills and visit many of the park's waters to feed. However, they're not nearly as common on Loch Leven as they used to be because they're scared off by the alligators. Don't worry, these are fake gators, placed expressly to scare off pelicans—the voracious birds had been eating too many of the grass carp released into the lake to control aquatic weeds.

After you leave Loch Leven you ascend into some hills covered by a lodgepole pine forest. The **Cypress Hills** are the only place in Saskatchewan where these tall, straight trees grow. During spring and

summer the understory blooms with bunchberry, twinflower, and other wildflowers. A little farther up, the road pulls alongside the upper reach of **Boiler Creek,** which beavers have transformed into a series of ponds much favored by wildlife. White-tailed deer graze on the grassy margins; chickadees jitter through the aspens and willows while a great blue heron flaps ponderously overhead.

After the ponds the road winds up to **Lookout Point,** which offers grand views across the prairie. To the north you can see 40 miles (64 km) to the Great Sand Hills and beyond. For an equally fine view to the west, continue a few hundred yards down the road, park, and take the short walk to the top of 4,202-foot (1,281 m) **Bald Butte,** Centre Block's highest point. Just more than a mile past Bald Butte the road curves through grasslands mixed with stands of aspen and occasional lodgepole pine. Watch for deer, coyotes, hawks, and, during

July and August, a bright wild-flower show. From the grasslands the road loops back through the forest to Loch Leven.

If you want to explore the Centre Block on foot you can follow 15 miles (24 km) of cross-country ski routes that double as hiking paths. In addition, two interpretive trails offer pleasant walking. From its trailhead near the Lone Pine group campground, the **Highland Trail** loops 1.2 miles (1.9 km) through the Loch Lomond Valley. Early on you see the classic vegetation profile of such a valley: a pond in the bot-

tomland, cattails and sedges at its edge, willows upslope from there, then a band of aspen, and finally the white spruce and lodgepole forest on the highest parts of the slope. As the trail eases down and follows the bank of the pond, watch for moose high-stepping through the cattails and leopard frogs flutter-kicking through the grass or leaping for the water. Along the pond's far shore, you'll cross many beaver trails, which link the water and the aspens up the hill. Check out the sunny slope above for three-flowered aven, goldenrod, and other wildflowers.

Spruce bog near Reesor Lake

West Block

To visit the West Block, pick up a guide to the 50-mile (80 km) round-trip West Block Auto Tour, which includes directions as well as interpretive material, at the Centre Block's nature center. Then head out along the Centre Block Auto Tour. Up on the plateau turn west and drive across the **Gap.** Don't attempt this road when it's wet. Note the "knob and kettle" topography of the Gap. The kettles, many now ponds, are depressions created from the weight of great blocks of ice left behind by retreating glaciers; when the blocks melted a hollow appeared. The knobs are heaps of glacial till deposited by the retreating glaciers. Watch for pronghorn, North America's swiftest land mammal, in this open sagebrush country.

The West Block is basically undeveloped. As the road climbs to the top of the plateau, it passes through an expanse of thriving rough fescue grassland. Named for its dominant plant, this native grassland is an endangered ecosystem in Canada—less than 10 percent remains. In July and August this is a gorgeous drive, with the blue sky embracing the plateau and the grassland brilliant with yellow prairie coneflowers, purple low larkspur, white geranium, and the bright blue of beardtongue.

The West Block's most famed attraction is the **Conglomerate Cliffs,** located just over halfway along the tour. They were formed by water passing through the thick layers of sand, gravel, and cobblestone that cap the Cypress Hills uplands. When the water evaporated it left a residue of calcium carbonate that cemented the rocks together, creating relatively solid sedimentary rock. The cliffs' edge offers a big, 180-degree view to the east. The cliffs drop steeply about 150 feet (46 m) to **Adams Lake,** where you might see American white pelicans and a pair of nesting trumpeter swans.

Alberta Block

Bumping along gravel roads, you can cross from the West Block into the Alberta Block. The countryside is a scenic blend of conifer forest, aspen grove, and grassy meadows as you make your way west to **Reesor Lake,** where the road turns to pavement. The route traces the north shore, then climbs to a high plateau that was never glaciated; the land was just high enough to escape the ice sheets that flowed all around. Keep an eye out for coyotes, elk, and, more commonly, 13-lined ground squirrels as you drive another 10 miles (16 km) or so to the town of Elkwater, this block's hub.

At the Elkwater Lake Visitor Centre *(mid-May–early Sept.)* you can find out about the several gravel roads and 11 established hiking trails that enable visitors to easily explore the Alberta Block. Three trails are right in town, down by Elkwater Lake. The 1.8-mile (2.9 km) **Shoreline Trail,** and the 0.6-mile (1 km) loop **Soggy Bottom Trail** at its end, is a boardwalk and asphalt path that takes walkers, cyclists, and Rollerbladers along the lake's scenic south shore. The loop trail traverses forest, field, and marsh. The trailhead for the wilder 0.6-mile (1 km) **Sunset Trail** that winds through some prime waterfowl habitat lies across the road from the east side of Soggy Bottom.

Arguably you'll derive the most pleasure from the first half mile (0.8 km) or so of the 1.8-mile (2.9 km) **Beaver Creek Trail.** Starting from Beaver Creek Campground, at the southwest edge of town, this easy path leads through spruce and poplar forest. After maybe ten minutes you'll emerge into the open as you encounter a series of about half a dozen beaver ponds. At dawn and dusk, and sometimes during the day, you'll see beavers hauling aspen limbs through the water or slapping mud onto their lodges.

Linger around these ponds and you may see everything from a moose to a muskrat. Often hairy woodpeckers scuttle up and down the aspens, prying off pieces of bark in search of delectable bugs. Dragonflies hover in the meadows, their wings rasping on the dry blades of grass. Sometimes a flock of dozens of black-masked cedar waxwings descends on a pond. These birds station themselves on the bare branches of fallen trees to make sudden sorties to capture flying insects. ■

Reesor Lake fringed by fescue grassland

70 Mile Butte

Grasslands National Park

■ 115,000 acres ■ Southern Saskatchewan, 80 miles (129 km) south of Swift Current ■ Best months April-Oct.; July-Aug. can be extremely hot and dry ■ Camping, hiking, horseback riding, bird-watching, wildlife viewing, scenic drive ■ Contact the park, P.O. Box 150, Val Marie, SK S0N 2T0; phone 306-298-2257. www.parkscanada.gc.ca/grasslands

THE SUBTLE REALM OF THE MIXED GRASSLAND PRAIRIE isn't for everyone, but many people—if they give it some time—respond profoundly. The spaciousness feels like freedom. Instead of emptiness, they see eternity. Grasslands National Park stretches across the low, rolling hills along the Saskatchewan-Montana border. One of Canada's newer national parks, it consists of two separate areas: the West Block and the East Block, with the more remote East Block consisting of badlands and uplands.

What to See and Do

Stop at the visitor center, in the town of Val Marie, just outside the northwest corner of the West Block. If you'd like to start with a grand overview, ask the park staff for directions to **70 Mile Butte.** You can drive nearly to its base and then strike out cross-country—there are almost no established trails in this largely wilderness park. A round-trip hike of a couple of hours will give you the pleasure of gazing east across the park from atop this long, 100-yard-high (91 m) tabletop. You'll see the **Frenchman River Valley**—the West Block's dominant feature—and the veins of the coulees that feed into it. This network of waterways, contemporary and ancient, has carved the plateau before you into the deeply grooved terrain you see today.

For a closer look at the heart of the West Block, pick up a brochure or audiotape at the visitor center and take the **Frenchman River Valley Ecotour,** an interpretive drive along a decent gravel road.

Decent unless it rains, that is: When wet, the clays under the gravel get extremely slick, and vehicles—even those with 4WD—simply can't get traction. You could be stranded for hours, even longer, so stay off this road if you see rain brewing—and remember that summer thunderstorms do occur.

Head 12 miles (19 km), on paved roads, east to the northern entrance to the West Block, where the 17-mile (27 km) round-trip ecotour begins; numbered posts mark stops discussed in the brochure. You'll drive south through the mixed-grass prairie, characterized by foot-high blue grama grass, spear grass, and wheat grass. Here and there crocus, golden bean, locoweed, and other wildflowers fleck the prairie. Watch for pronghorn out in the flats and ferruginous hawks riding the thermals.

At stop number two, walk out to the big reddish rock to the east. This is a rubbing stone, smoothed over the ages by itchy bison scratching themselves on it. Bison no longer inhabit the park, but they are part of future management plans.

At the last marked stop, pull over and enjoy the **prairie dog town.** The Frenchman River Valley area is the only place in Canada inhabited by black-tailed prairie dogs. Watch the complex social lives of these charming critters as they groom each other, bark, and whistle. In addition, you might see a burrowing owl, a rare and imperiled bird in this area that makes its home in abandoned prairie dog burrows. ▪

Above: Sharp-tailed grouse. Below: Golden bean. *Following pages:* View from the yellow locoweed-speckled flank of 70 Mile Butte

Duck Mountain Provincial Park

■ 351,945 acres ■ Southwest Manitoba, 40 miles (64 km) northwest of Dauphin ■ Best months May-Oct. ■ Camping, hiking, canoeing, wildlife viewing ■ Contact Manitoba Conservation, Box 640, Swan River, MB R0L 1Z0; phone 204-734-3429 or 800-214-6497. www.gov.mb.ca/natres/parks/regions/western /duck.html

POISED ATOP A HIGH PLATEAU at the northern edge of the prairie, a southern thrust of the boreal forest—white spruce, jack pine, and balsam fir—cloaks the higher portions of this park. The lower portions feature aspen, birch, and willow, species typical of the park's prairie lands. Mostly undeveloped, the park is a scenic sanctuary for wildlife such as black bear, red fox, coyote, bald eagle, wood duck, wolf, white-tailed deer, and moose.

What to See and Do

Duck Mountain does not have a visitor center, but local information is available at several lakes where recreational development has clustered. You can explore Duck Mountain via a couple of easy canoe routes or three roads that cut through the park, but the best way is to hike some of the many trails.

Wellman Lake

In the extreme southeast corner of the park you can start hiking at Manitoba's highest point: **Baldy Mountain.** Drive up to the summit, at 2,727 feet, then climb an additional 40 feet up a tower, from which you can see south all the way to Riding Mountain. The viewing tower stands along the sometimes steep 1.9-mile (3 km) **Baldy Mountain Trail,** which starts at the summit's picnic area.

About 10 miles (16 km) northwest of Baldy Mountain on PR 366, just before it intersects PR 367, lies the **Wapiti Trail.** "Wapiti" is the proper name for "elk." Nearly 1,500 of these regal creatures call Duck Mountain home. You'll often see some at dawn or dusk, especially in the meadows about 0.7 mile (1.1 km) from the trailhead, if you hike the trail's 2.8-mile (4.5 km) loop or 1.4-mile (2.3 km) loop .

The 2.8-mile (4.5 km) **Shell River Valley Trail,** close to Childs Lake, loops through mixed forest, a meadow, past the Shell River, and through a calcium bog. Hikers are rewarded with a spectacular panorama of the river valley once they reach the viewpoint.

Finish your visit to the park with a flourish: Hike the 0.7-mile (1.1 km) loop to the top of **Copernicus Hill.** There's a plaque honoring the Polish astronomer near the summit, but the sights from the 30-foot (9 m) viewing tower are the real prize. You can enjoy a 180-degree view to the north, looking across the treetops. When the aspens turn to gold in the fall, the scene is dazzling . ■

Riding Mountain National Park

■ 735,360 acres ■ Southwest Manitoba, 10 miles (16 km) south of Dauphin
■ Best months May-Oct. ■ Camping, hiking, boating, canoeing, fishing, mountain
biking, cross-country skiing, snowshoeing, bird-watching, wildlife viewing, scenic
drives ■ Adm. fee ■ Contact the park, Wasagaming, MB R0J 2H0; phone 204-
848-7275 or 800-707-8480. www.parkscanada.gc.ca/riding

A CUT ABOVE. The literal truth of this statement strikes visitors with
forceful clarity as they approach Riding Mountain National Park from
the east. Driving through the flat fields and pastures of the Manitoba
lowlands, motorists see to the west a sudden rise in the land, a looming
shale cliff that stands like a rampart. This is the Manitoba Escarpment,
which divides the lowlands from the Saskatchewan Plain. Eleven thousand years ago this escarpment was the western shoreline of the enormous glacial Lake Agassiz. Today it puts Riding Mountain on a pedestal
some 1,400 feet (427 m) above the prairie that laps against its base.

The geographical location of the escarpment further enhances the exceptional nature of Riding Mountain. It sits at an uncommon confluence
of three life zones and features tracts of fescue grassland, aspen-oak, and
mixed-forest ecosystems. It also lies near the center of the continent; as
a result, this prime location contains a tremendous diversity of flora
and fauna. Supported in huge numbers by this lush park, those animals
include some 4,000 elk, 4,000 moose, 1,000 black bears, and six or seven
packs of wolves.

What to See and Do

The town of Wasagaming, on
Clear Lake just inside the park's
southern boundary, serves as Riding Mountain's staging ground.
You'll find groceries, gas, lodging,
and, most important, the **Parks
Canada visitor center** (*mid-
May–mid-Oct.*). Before heeding
the call of the wild you can watch
videos, browse displays, pick up
trail guides and maps, and check
out interpretive activities.

Wasagaming Area

You can start your exploration of
the wild simply by strolling five
minutes south from the visitor
center to **Ominnik Marsh.**

Typical of the prairie pothole
lakes and ponds that dot the park,
Ominnik Marsh was created by
melting glaciers at the end of the
last ice age. A 1.2-mile (1.9 km)
trail, most of it floating boardwalk, loops through this lively
marsh. Step softly and you'll likely
see blue-winged teal, pintail, and
northern shovelers paddling amid
the willows; red-winged blackbirds
and sedge wrens flitting about the
reeds; and black terns hovering
over open water scanning for min-
nows. Rent a "Marsh Kit" at the
visitor center if you'd like to in-
vestigate some of the underwater
insect life.

Sunset reflected in pond along Lake Audy Road

Not all the marsh denizens sport feathers and wings. Riding Mountain is famous for its beavers, which number about 20,000; no wonder they're a staple for the park's wolves. Keep a close eye on the channels that crisscross the reeds and you may spy a beaver sculling quietly along. Often you can hear them chewing

times. Fire creates a dynamic and healthy shifting balance between the fire-dependent grassland and the fire-vulnerable forest (see sidebar p. 187). Note the horsetails, fungi, and mosses that grow in the shade of the spruce trees and the rough fescue, buttercup, aster, and black-eyed Susans that thrive in the sunlit grasslands. When you

View of Manitoba Escarpment

on willow branches or slapping the water with their tails. You'll see several lodges, some within 10 to 20 feet (3 to 6 m) of the path. Watch quietly and you may see a beaver drag an aspen branch on top of the lodge, press it into the roof, and caulk it with mud.

Half a dozen miles northeast of Wasagaming you can stretch your legs on one of several trails. Try the **Brûlé Trail,** a 2.6-mile (4.2 km) loop that comes alive via an excellent interpretive brochure (available at visitor center or trailhead). *Brûlé* translates to "burnt" and expresses the major theme of this trail, which passes through an area that has burned many

reach Kinosao Lake, look for ospreys and loons.

Highway 19

The 21-mile (34 km) gravel Hwy. 19 explores the deciduous forest that typifies Riding Mountain's east side. It heads east from Clear Lake to a point just outside the park's eastern boundary.

Go north on the short spur road off Hwy. 19 to **Whirlpool Lake,** which offers a campground, a picnic area, and good opportunities to see bald eagles and, in the evening, great gray owls.

Farther east along Hwy. 19 the moderately challenging **Gorge Creek Trail** runs 4 miles (6.4 km) one way between Dead Ox Creek picnic site to the west and Birches picnic site to the east. If possible, hike east and downhill—the route descends about 1,000 vertical feet—to Birches picnic site. To avoid the steep return, climb park a second car here. For the most part the path curves through sun-dappled hardwoods at the bottom

greater variety of fruit bushes than any other part of the park; saskatoons and pin cherry ripen in July, chokecherry and nannyberry in August, and wild plum, hazelnut, and cranberry in September. Consequently, bears frequent this area. Stay alert (see pp. 84-85).

Back on the highway, drive through the historic East Gate and

Grazing bison, Bison Range

of the gorge, 200 feet (61 m) deep in places, that the two creeks have slashed through the shale of the Manitoba Escarpment. At times the trail edges along the rim of the gorge, providing some fine views.

Just a few hundred yards from the park's east entrance, a narrow dirt road branches north off Hwy. 19 and leads to the self-guided 1.4-mile (2.3 km) **Burls and Bittersweet Nature Trail.** The path circles through an eastern hardwood forest of bur oak, green ash, and white elm. Look for burls—the round growths on poplar trees—and bittersweet, a woody vine that wraps itself around trees. This fertile area brims with a

continue perhaps half a mile (0.8 km) into the hay and wheat fields outside the park. Turn around and behold the steep uplift of the escarpment—and the looming splendor of Riding Mountain.

Highway 10

Seeing the northern part of the park is easy. Beginning at the southern entrance, near Wasagaming, Hwy. 10 runs 33 miles (53 km) up to the northern entrance. This memorably scenic —and paved—road is lined by a robust forest of spruce and aspen, grassy meadows, several lakes, and a multitude of ponds and wetlands. But above all, this

route is known for its wildlife. If you go in the early morning or at dusk, you're nearly guaranteed to see some animals. Park interpreters lead wildlife-viewing caravans up this road *(for reservations and information call 204-848-7228)*. When you do sight an animal, remember not to get too close, to pull off onto the shoulder, and to stay in your vehicle.

You may see elk grazing on the highway margin. During the fall rut you may hear a bull elk bugling as it tries to impress females or warn off another bull trying to invade its harem, which can number as many as 30 cows. If the invading bull is about the same size as the dominant bull and sports a roughly equal rack, the two may rush each other and bash their heads together. Two or three collisions usually decide the

matter, though occasionally the belligerents' antlers lock and they both starve to death or get taken down by predators.

Black bears show up on the roadside at times, especially in July and August. If you're really lucky you may see a lynx slink across the road at night, probably hunting a snowshoe hare, its favorite prey. Long-legged, big-footed, and thickly furred, lynx appear much larger than their actual size of perhaps 2 feet at the shoulder and 15 to 20 pounds. It's not uncommon to spot moose in the willow-fringed wetlands and small lakes.

If your thirst for wildlife and scenery isn't slaked, hike one of the several trails that branch off Hwy. 10. About 17 miles (27 km) north of Wasagaming is the **Bead Lakes Trail,** a 2.5-mile (4 km) loop that passes by the third and

Clear Lake

fourth members of the Bead Lakes chain. It starts in a mature forest of birch, spruce, and poplar, where you often hear the drumming of woodpeckers, and gently descends to the lakes. Look for signs of wildlife: the track of a wolf in the mud, a snowshoe hare carcass left behind by a lynx, or matted grass where an elk bedded down to chew its cud. After half an hour, the path hits the first lake and follows its wetland-fringed shore. In the soggy quarter mile (0.4 km) between this lake and the next you will sometimes see moose and frequently see moose prints, which are unmistakably huge.

During the middle of the day you are more likely to encounter moose up in the forest, where they seek hideaways in which to ruminate. As you walk along, it's not uncommon for a moose to sud-

denly rise to its feet from a quiet rumination near the trail. Don't panic, but don't think of it as a friendly Bullwinkle, either; moose are fast and powerful, and they occasionally attack people. Particularly dangerous are cows that have calves to protect and bulls during the autumn rut, when they will charge pretty much anything that moves. They've even been known to assault cars and trains.

About 4 miles (6.4 km) farther up the highway from the Bead Lakes Trail is the **Boreal Island Trail.** This half-mile (0.8 km) interpretive loop introduces hikers to the boreal forest, which covers the region north of the prairies and south of the Arctic tundra. As you hike the trail you'll learn how water shapes this forest. Black spruce and tamarack, trees that thrive in wet soils, grow in the

Aspen in fall color, Clear Lake

boggy areas. Look for orchids around the margins of these wet spots. Higher up the slope, white spruce and balsam fir grow taller in the drier, well-drained soil. Jack pine predominates in the highest and driest areas.

Just before Hwy. 10 crosses the park's northern boundary, stop and take the short walk to the **Agassiz Tower.** This 40-foot (12 m) aerie perches among the treetops of a flourishing forest of aspen and spruce. Ridges limit the southern views, but to the north you can see far across the prairie.

Bison Range

As you head west on Lake Audy Road *(off Hwy. 10 NW of Wasagaming)*, the forest gradually dwindles and the landscape opens up; patches of grassland become more frequent and larger. And you encounter bison.

A century and a half ago some 60 million plains bison ranged across North America. But by 1889 fewer than a hundred remained in the wild, and none at all in Riding Mountain. Slowly, conservation-minded people coaxed bison numbers back from the brink. In

1931, a few of them were brought to Riding Mountain from a park in Alberta to establish a small herd. That herd, which today averages about 35 members, still inhabits the park. They live in the Bison Range: two expansive (1,600 acres/648 ha altogether) enclosures about a 15-mile (24 km) drive northwest of Wasagaming. To simulate their natural movement between fescue grassland and aspen parkland, the bison are moved back and forth seasonally between the enclosures.

To visit the Bison Range, pick up a brochure and take the two-hour **Bison Range Driving Tour.**

During the summer the bison herd resides in the south range, the fescue grassland portion of its habitat. The bison fatten up on the energy-rich fescue after it has set seed.

A vital resource to bison and many other animals and plants, fescue grasslands are one of the most endangered ecosystems in Canada. The prairie provinces once harbored more than 60 million acres (24.3 million ha), but today only about 3 million acres (1.2 million ha) remain in a natural state, approximately 4,500 acres (1,821 ha) in Riding Mountain.

Flame and Fortune

Fire plays an essential role in keeping the park's ecosystems healthy. Both the forests and the grasslands depend on fire to recycle nutrients, help plants reproduce, and create a diverse array of vegetation, which in turn produces habitat for a variety of animals. For example, moose, deer, bear, and other species that require some open areas suffer when the forest, unchecked by fire, takes over meadows and grasslands.

For many decades park staffers labored vigorously to suppress all fire in Riding Mountain, just as other people suppressed fire throughout North America. But by the 1970s scientists had realized their mistake, and they began looking for ways to restore fire to the park.

That's easier said than done in a location that is surrounded by development, including homes and towns. Unlike remote parks, in which managers can let naturally ignited fires burn, Riding Mountain must plan its fires carefully and keep them from spreading beyond the intended burn sites.

Despite its intricacies, prescribed fire has become a valuable tool for park managers. Visitors sometimes will encounter prescribed burns in the park, generally in May and June when environmental conditions are good. This may cause some inconvenience, but bear in mind that it must be done if Riding Mountain is to live up to Canada's 1930 National Parks Act: "Parks shall be maintained and made use of so as to leave them unimpaired for future generations."

If those visitors come back to the site of that fire in subsequent years, they'll see grasses, fireweed, willow, thistle, three-flowered aven, and other plants thriving in the wake of the flames, fed by the the warm sunlight and the minerals in the ashes, no longer obscured by the trees. They'll see elk and deer nibbling on those plants. And they'll see why fire is necessary.

As you drive into the enclosure, the herd may be close to the road. Pull over and quietly watch, but don't get out of the car. Bison are big (bulls can exceed 2,000 pounds/ 907 kg), fast (they can gallop 35 mph/56 kmph), and sometimes aggressive toward humans.

The best place from which to watch the animals is the **Bison and Grasslands Exhibit,** an interpretive shelter that overlooks the south range's main expanse of fescue grassland. You can frequently spot the herd from here, and you can learn about them from the extensive interpretive displays. The shelter also is a safe spot to be if the bison wander close; signs warn you to look around before you leave your vehicle and walk the 100 yards (91 m) from the parking lot to the shelter.

If you observe the herd for a while, you may see all sorts of behavior. Perhaps an orange-cinnamon calf will nurse from its mother. Maybe an adult will wallow in the dust or mud, flopping back and forth on its back and sides to get rid of bothersome insects. During the mating season, in July and August, visitors may witness bulls knocking heads.

The Rest of the West

Beyond the Bison Range, the rest of Riding Mountain's west side is largely backcountry. By driving outside the park on farm roads you can reenter in the far west and drive to **Deep Lake, Bob Hill Lake,** and the **Birdtail Bench** area. Long trails lead through this open country blend of grassland, forest, and lakes. Squint up at the sky and you may spy red-tailed hawks and other raptors prowling for rodents. Elk, deer, and moose congregate here between mid-September and mid-October, so scan the **Birdtail River Valley** with your binoculars. You also may spot wolves and bears, though more likely you'll just stumble across their tracks and other signs. ■

Wetland reclamation of old farmland

Spruce Woods Provincial Park

■ 66,593 acres ■ Southern Manitoba, 40 miles (64 km) southeast of Brandon
■ Best months May-Oct. ■ Camping, hiking, canoeing, fishing, mountain biking,
horseback riding, wildlife viewing, sand dunes ■ Adm. fee ■ Contact Manitoba
Conservation, Box 900, Carberry, MB R0K 0H0; phone 204-834-8800 or 800-
214-6497. www.gov.mb.ca/natres/parks/regions/western/spruce_woods.html

THERE ARE INDEED SPRUCE WOODS in this lovely provincial park, as well as
river bottom forest along the Assiniboine River, mixed-grass prairie, and
upland deciduous forest. But despite its name, Spruce Woods is best
known as the home of the Spirit Sands. Named for its religious signifi-
cance to local aboriginal people, these expansive and largely unvegetated
dune fields are absent in the rest of Manitoba and rare throughout Canada.

The dunes formed at the end of the last ice age. Today the Assiniboine
River is a meandering waterway narrow enough to throw a rock across,
but 12,000 years ago it was a mile-wide rush of glacial meltwater pouring
into ancient glacial Lake Agassiz. When this vast lake dried up, a 1.6-mil-
lion-acre (647,500 ha) delta of sand and other sediments was revealed.
Of this, only the 1,000 acres (405 ha) of the Spirit Sands remain as living
dunes that shift with the prevailing winds; the rest has been blown away
or overrun by vegetation.

What to See and Do

The eastern three-quarters of the
park is somewhat inaccessible
backcountry, but the western
swath along Hwy. 5 can easily be
explored via a few gravel roads,
several established hiking (and
some biking) trails, and the Assiniboine River canoe route (rentals
available in season; call Up the
Creek Outfitters 204-526-7145
or 877-331-3326).

Most of the easily accessible
features of Spruce Woods, including the interpretive center and the
Kiche Manitou Campground, lie in
the southwest corner of the park,
just off Hwy. 5. The campground is
bordered by a wetlands area in the
shape of a horseshoe with its ends
pinched almost together; it's a
former oxbow bend of the Assiniboine River that got cut off from

the main channel. Bird-watchers
can indulge themselves by walking
around the edge of this wetland—
great blue herons, belted kingfishers, Canada geese, and myriad
ducks abound.

Just east of the campground
you can walk the 0.9-mile (1.4 km)
Isputinaw Trail, an interpretive
loop that passes through a surprising number of habitats in such a
short distance. The trail begins on
a boardwalk that snakes through a
swamp thick with willows. After
about 100 yards (91 m), it hits the
hillside of the valley created by the
ancient Assiniboine River.

On the ascent, notice how the
vegetation profile changes as the
soil gets drier farther upslope. From
the river bottom woods of elm,
maple, and dogwood, punctuated

Moonrise over the Spirit Sands

by boggy areas redolent with marsh marigolds, the path rises through a hazelnut grove and a tract of bur oaks, then emerges onto the ridge top, where white spruce hold sway. A bench overlooks the Assiniboine River Valley; use binoculars to scan the many ponds for beavers and ducks.

The **Spirit Sands** to the northwest of Kiche Manitou Campground can be explored on numerous trails. All start at the interpretive kiosk in the parking area off Hwy. 5; look at the map and devise a loop of your own. You'll begin in dunes overgrown by a verdant blend of white spruce, ground juniper, grasses, aspen, oak, and other greenery. Observation platforms beckon atop some of the high points.

Near the heart of the Spirit Sands the vegetation thins and you finally emerge onto the open dunes, a sea of sand in which the waves move very slowly—the dunes travel southeast about 10 inches (25.4 cm) a year. In the far southwest sits the **Devil's Punch Bowl,** a depression where subterranean streams undercut the sand hills and caused a collapse. This sunken oasis features beaver ponds inhabited by muskrat, weasels, and painted turtles. If slogging through the soft sand sounds unappealing, consider a covered wagon tour run by a private operator *(call Nadine and Larry Robinson 204-827-2800 or 204-379-2007).*

Another oxbow lake sparkles in the sun about a mile (1.6 km) north on Hwy. 5 from the Spirit Sands parking lot. **Marshs Lake** can be enjoyed from a pleasant 1-mile (1.6 km) interpretive trail that loops along the inside of the oxbow. The path goes through one of the continent's northwestern-most outposts of eastern deciduous forest, a comely place of green ash, elm, wild grape, and ostrich ferns. The lake gets its name from a pioneer family, but marshy areas do line the trail; look for beavers, muskrat, ducks, and kingfishers.

Five miles (8 km) north of Marshs Lake, take a short road east

Sunflower

to the parking lot for the **Epinette Creek Trails.** This extensive network leads deep into the park and draws overnight backcountry hikers, as well as mountain bikers looking for challenging rides. If you lack the time or inclination for that, you can experience Epinette's variety and beauty in a half-day out-and-back walk. In just the first few miles you'll see a meandering creek interrupted by beaver dams; open grasslands favored by hawks; a dense forest of maple, ash, balsam poplar, and elm; and a 1997 burn site where blackened trees contrast with the lush fireweed and young aspens that are starting the next forest. ■

Ducks, Oak Hammock Marsh

Winnipeg Area Parks

Birds Hill Provincial Park: ■ 8,673 acres ■ Southern Manitoba ■ Best seasons spring-fall ■ Camping, hiking, biking, fishing, cross-country skiing, wild-life viewing, wildflower viewing, scenic drive ■ Adm. fee ■ Contact Manitoba Conservation, Birds Hill District Office, Box 183, R.R. 2, Dugald, MB R0E 0K0; phone 800-214-6497. www.gov.mb.ca/natres/parks/regions/central/birdshill.html

Fort Whyte Centre: ■ 450 acres ■ Southern Manitoba ■ Year-round ■ Adm. fee ■ Hiking, canoeing, fishing, bird-watching ■ Contact the center, 1961 McCreary Rd., Winnipeg, MB R3P 2K9; phone 204-989-8355. www.fortwhyte.org

Oak Hammock Marsh: ■ 8,896 acres ■ Southern Manitoba ■ Best seasons spring and fall ■ Adm. fee ■ Hiking, canoeing, bird-watching, wildlife viewing ■ Contact Oak Hammock Marsh Interpretive Centre, Box 1160, Oak Ham-mock Marsh, MB R0C 2Z0; phone 204-467-3300. www.ducks.ca/ohmic

ALTHOUGH WINNIPEG—Manitoba's provincial capital—is by far the province's largest city, several appealing natural areas are located within it or close by. Four rivers and numerous creeks run through Winnipeg, creating lush riparian habitat for many animals. Tallgrass prairie, marshes, wet meadows, oak woodlands, aspen and spruce forests, and cedar bogs round out the diverse landscapes in the vicinity.

What to See and Do

Birds Hill Provincial Park

Birds Hill Provincial Park is lo-cated about a dozen miles north-east of Winnipeg. Given its paved in-line skating paths and tennis courts, parts of Birds Hill feel like a city park. But numerous hiking, biking, and horse trails quickly take you into wilder places.

The 0.6-mile (1 km) **Bur Oak**

Trail gets its name from those stunted, wonderfully gnarled trees, home to vesper sparrows, spotted towhees, and decidedly indigo-colored indigo buntings. The **Cedar Bog Trail** also passes through some bur oaks, but this 2.2-mile (3.5 km) path adds grasslands, a splendid stand of eastern white cedar, and the mucky delights of a bog to its mix. The 0.9-mile (1.45 km) **White-tailed Deer Trail** leads through woodlands and meadows favored by these graceful deer.

Fort Whyte Centre

Fort Whyte Centre—a combination of natural history museum and natural area—sprawls on the southwest edge of Winnipeg. As you drive up to the center, note the three dozen or so bison in the 70-acre **Bison Prairie.**

Inside the interpretive center you can learn more about bison and the tallgrass prairie they once roamed. One display, for example, shows a soil profile of the prairie, so you can see that half the mass of most prairie plants lies below ground, out of harm's way. A related exhibit tells the tale of how large-scale industrial agriculture has caused the loss of about half of the prairie's topsoil and the degradation of much of the soil that remains. Outside, a maze of paths and boardwalks lead through stands of aspen and willow and past wetlands home to squawking ducks and geese.

Oak Hammock Marsh

The fact that Ducks Unlimited Canada has its national headquarters at Oak Hammock Marsh should clue you in on what to expect. This vast wetland area 20 miles (32 km) north of Winnipeg is one of the finest places in North America in which to view migrating waterfowl. During the spring and fall, some half a million assorted ducks and

Canada geese in flight, Birds Hill Provincial Park

Biking through Birds Hill Provincial Park

geese stop here to feed and rest.

As you stroll along the **dikes** that vein the marsh, you sometimes must shout to your companions to make yourself heard over the cacophony of feeding and nesting ducks and geese. Boardwalks and viewing mounds provide additional vantage points from which to watch the unfolding social scene. You may also see avocets, grebes, phalaropes, snowy owls, and others of the more than 280 bird species that have been sighted here. Save an hour or two for the sprawling and informative **Conservation Centre,** which features many interactive and educational displays. ▪

Narcisse Wildlife Management Area Snake Dens

■ 320 acres ■ Southern Manitoba, 60 miles (97 km) north of Winnipeg
■ Best months late April, first 3 weeks of May, and early Sept. ■ Hiking, snakes
■ Contact Manitoba Conservation, Box 22, 200 Saulteaux Crescent, Winnipeg,
MB R3J 3W3; phone 800-214-6497. www.gov.mb.ca/natres/wildlife/managing
/snakes_narcisse.html

THOUSANDS AND THOUSANDS of red-sided garter snakes. Wriggling in great masses. Congregating into squirming, tumbling "mating balls." Crawling over your shoes if you stand in the grass. If all this sounds fascinating (bear in mind that garter snakes are harmless), head to the Narcisse Wildlife Management Area (NWMA) Snake Dens.

As you near the NWMA Snake Dens on Hwy. 17, signs say "Reduce Speed—Respect Nature." What they're telling you is don't run over the snakes migrating across the highway. A recently installed tunnel and fence system diverts thousands of snakes to safety, but hundreds could still be crushed by heedless drivers. Once at NWMA Snake Dens, a 1.8-mile (2.9 km) **trail** loops through aspen parklands to four big, active snake dens outfitted with observation platforms and interpretive signs. You may also see red-tailed hawks, white-tailed deer, sharp-tailed grouse, and...but nobody much cares: The red-sided garter snakes are king.

It's no coincidence that they (and a few western plains garter snakes) gather in this place. Much of the region is underlain by limestone riddled with sinkholes and underground caves. In most places these cavities lie deep beneath the ground, but here they're close to the surface and, where the roofs have fallen, the snakes can descend into these havens to hibernate. Only by massing in dens below the frost line but above the water table can they survive Manitoba's brutal winters—they are cold-blooded and must avoid extreme temperatures. And, once winter has passed, the nearby wetlands teem with tasty frogs and toads.

Activity peaks during the first hot, sunny days of spring after the snow has melted, typically during late April or the first three weeks of May. The snakes emerge into the sunlight, where you can admire their 2- to 3-foot-long yellow-and-black bodies with red blotches along both sides—hence the name. You may see their red, black-tipped forked tongues flick out to sense you—unless they're in mating mode, in which case they won't care. When an attractive (large, thick) female appears, dozens or even hundreds of males will pursue her until they intertwine in a mating ball that rolls along the ground. After the mating season ends, the snakes disperse up to 10 miles (16 km) to their summer feeding grounds.

Fall, typically early September, brings the snakes slithering back to their dens. They remain active and visible near the den mouths until wet, cool weather drives them below. ■

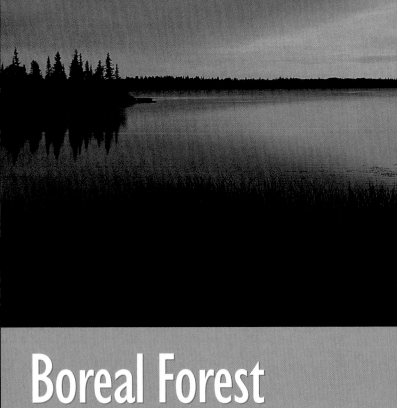

Boreal Forest

Sunset over Rocky Lake, Manitoba

As you're hiking up a hill in Whiteshell Provincial Park among the spruce and jack pine, stop at a rocky outcrop and settle down for a rest. Before you pull out your water bottle, take a moment to appreciate that rock beneath you. When you run your hand across the gray-white granite and pink feldspar, you're touching bedrock that formed between 3.5 billion and 2.5 billion years ago.

This rock, which underlies the region's boreal forest and crops up above the ground in many places, is called

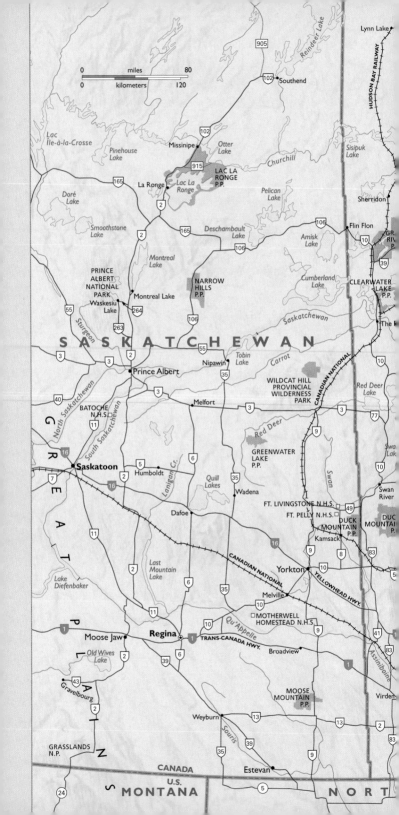

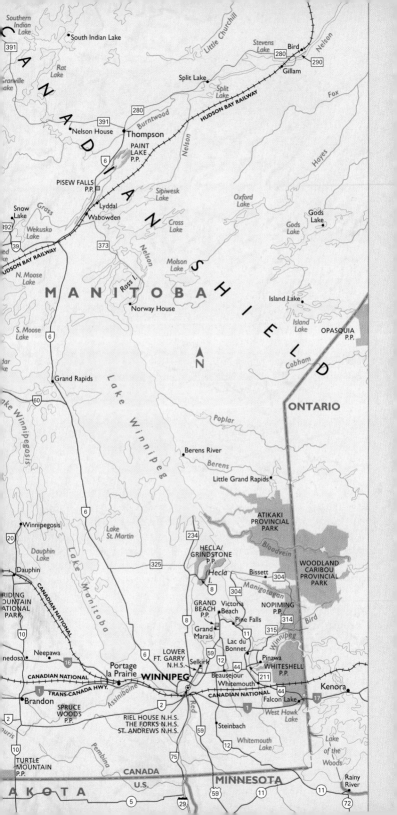

Canada geese, Alfred Hole Goose Sanctuary, Whiteshell Provincial Park

the Canadian Shield. A few parts of it date back a mere 1.7 billion years, but most of the Canadian Shield is much older. This Precambrian rock (the term "Precambrian" refers to the geologic period from 4.5 billion to 540 million years ago) is the oldest rock in North America; it is also some of the oldest rock on the planet. Back in its youth, it formed soaring peaks and jagged canyons. Billions of years of erosion can wear down anything, however, with the result that today's shield is only a nub of its former self.

Much of the bedrock is covered by deposits of glacial till, left behind when the ice sheets retreated some 10,000 years ago. In many places both the bedrock and the till are covered by water—look at a map of the region and you'll see an awful lot of blue. As you drive, hike, or canoe through the region you'll typically encounter a mosaic of lakes and wetlands, bedrock outcroppings, and boreal forest.

"Boreal" derives from Boreas, the god of the north wind in Greek mythology, and refers broadly to things pertaining to the north. In less poetic terms, the boreal forest is a region in the Northern Hemisphere where the coldest months are long and the warmest months are short, the precipitation is low, and the growing season is brief. The boreal forest is

an immense band of trees that runs between the treeless tundra to the north and the temperate forests and prairie to the south.

Compared with the even more northern portion of the boreal forest called the taiga—a mix of small trees and scrub—this area is relatively robust. Yet its mature trees may average only about a foot in diameter and perhaps 50 feet in height—squirts by the standards of the old-growth forests found along the British Columbia coast.

The long, cold winters of the boreal forest have much to do with the size of its trees. But the animals grow just as large as their southern counterparts, and there are plenty of them, especially large mammals. The region is well populated by moose, wolves, woodland caribou, black bears, lynx, and white-tailed deer.

In Western Canada, the boreal forest forms a thick crescent that begins in southeast Manitoba and arcs northwest across central Manitoba and the northern half of Saskatchewan. Few people inhabit the region, especially northern Saskatchewan. Only a handful of roads cross this remote, watery terrain, but some of those lead to provincial and national parks that allow visitors to sample the haunting beauty and wildness of the forest. ■

Whiteshell Provincial Park

■ 672,371 acres ■ Southeast Manitoba, 80 miles (129 km) east of Winnipeg
■ Best months May-Oct. ■ Camping, hiking, rock climbing, boating, canoeing,
swimming, fishing, mountain biking, snowmobiling, cross-country skiing, wildlife
viewing, scenic drives ■ Adm. fee ■ Contact Manitoba Conservation, Box 22,
200 Saulteaux Crescent, Winnipeg, MB R3J 3W3; phone 204-945-6784 or 800-
214-6497. www.gov.mb.ca/natres/parks/regions/eastern/whiteshell.html

FOR AN INTRODUCTION TO Canadian Shield country and a lesson in its
virtues, Whiteshell Provincial Park is the place to go. On Whiteshell's numerous trails, you'll walk across low domes of ancient stone and wander
through a forest of white spruce (Manitoba's official provincial tree), jack
pine, and balsam fir, with a sprinkling of aspen, balsam poplar, and birch.
In many places you will encounter bogs and fens where black spruce and

Whiteshell River

tamarack are the only trees that can survive. Other bodies of water abound, including wetlands, ponds, and more than 200 lakes.

Outdoor enthusiasts of all sorts flock to Whiteshell. Big and beautiful and only a 90-minute drive from Winnipeg, the park attracts well over a million visitors a year. Within Whiteshell's boundaries you will find 11 campgrounds, about 3,300 cottages, and more than 70 businesses. There are resorts, tennis courts, marinas, riding stables, and a golf course. Even at the busy townsites and heavily developed lakes, you'll see river otters sliding through the water and hear loons calling. If you want to escape the crowds and plunge deeper into the natural world, it doesn't take much time—just a few minutes' driving and half an hour's hiking. Most of the park is wilderness, so if you go backpacking or take one of the backcountry canoe routes you can find abundant wildlife, unspoiled nature, and solitude . The northern end of the park also features some remote lodges that can be reached by small plane or boat.

What to See and Do

Travelers can obtain information at any of four park offices scattered about Whiteshell Provincial Park. People taking Trans-Canada 1 from Winnipeg to the park often start at the office at **Falcon Lake,** in the far south of Whiteshell. The Falcon Lake townsite is one of the most developed places in the park. Cottages line the shores of this 8-mile-long (13 km) lake, but roads on the north and south shores yield pleasant scenery and occasional sightings of river otters, mergansers, red foxes, loons, and other wildlife. If you spot an otter, watch a while, especially if it's in a feeding frenzy. These agile animals will dive to the bottom, surface 15 or 20 seconds later, gobble their prize in about ten seconds, and dive again.

West Hawk Lake

West Hawk Lake, located on Hwy. 44 half a mile (0.8 km) north of the Trans-Canada and a couple of miles north of Falcon Lake, is unusually round, unlike the park's other, amoeba-shaped bodies of water. At 377 feet, West Hawk is Manitoba's deepest lake. The atypical shape and depth and other evidence tell scientists that a crashing meteor created the lake long ago, perhaps 100 million years.

West Hawk Lake is almost completely undeveloped on its east side, where the only land access is via the **Hunt Lake Trail.** Starting about a mile from the border with Ontario, this fairly demanding 7.8-mile (12.6 km) out-and-back path skirts Hunt Lake's east end and soon joins West Hawk Lake's eastern shore. For about the last 2 miles, the trail hugs that shoreline as it passes through a splendid forest of cedar and eastern white pine—the westernmost range of eastern white pine in Canada. As

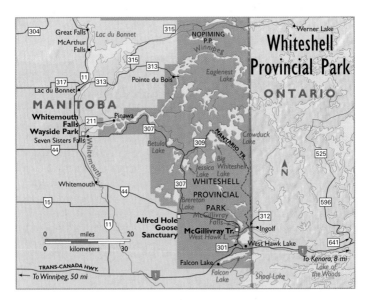

Bannock Point petroforms

the trail climbs up and down the hilly landscape, you'll sometimes get expansive views across the lake.

McGillivray Falls

Some six miles north of West Hawk on Hwy. 44 you can visit a classic example of nature's derangement. The **McGillivray Falls Trail** explores a drainage system, typical of Whiteshell, in which erosion-resistant bedrock outcroppings disrupt the normal dendritic pattern (like a branching tree) of the water to create a pattern in which water flows every which way but uphill. You can make this easy-to-moderate trail into a 1.7-mile (2.7 km) or 2.8-mile (4.5 km) loop.

You'll come to McGillivray Falls about five minutes after leaving the parking lot. It's more a tumbling rapid than a true waterfall, but it tumbles through a lovely wooded glade. As you ascend moss-coated rocks beside the falls, watch your step—it can be very slippery when wet. Note that the rock face along the creek shows no sign of erosion. That's because glaciers cut this channel during the ice ages and water found it later. At the top of the falls sprawl a beaver pond and meadows. In the early morning or evening you may see white-tailed deer or moose here.

Near the far end of the trail's oval loop lies **McGillivray Lake.** Characteristic of Canadian Shield lakes, it is shallow—about 10 feet (3 m) maximum—and tea colored, thanks to its load of nutrients, algae, and humic acid. Watch for bald eagles and ospreys fishing on the lake. The trail returns to the parking lot on higher ground among the aspen, birch, white spruce, and jack pine.

Near the McGillivray Falls Trailhead, Hwy. 44 turns west and traverses typical Whiteshell terrain of wooded hills, exposed bedrock, and various bodies of water. A couple of miles past McGillivray, stop at the **Lily Pond pullout.** About a quarter mile (0.4 km) long, the pond is underlain and walled in by cliffs of 2.5-billion-year-old Canadian Shield rock, though it was only thousands of years ago that glaciers scooped out the depression in which the pond

water rests. Both yellow and white lilies grow here. The yellow species blooms in May, the white in June, and both blossom into September. Scan the pond for muskrat (their ratlike tails distinguish them from beavers), ducks, and, on the lily pads, mink frogs, generally rare but often seen here in the summer.

Alfred Hole Goose Sanctuary

It's not often that a bet over whiskey engenders a goose sanctuary. In 1939 mink rancher Alfred Hole bet a crock of whiskey that he could keep four abandoned Cana-da goose goslings alive for six weeks. He did, raising them to adulthood and releasing them on this pond. The original four began migrating with wild geese, but they always returned home. After a while, hundreds of migrating Can-ada geese regularly stopped over at the pond, which now forms the heart of the Alfred Hole Goose Sanctuary and Visitor Centre.

Located beside Hwy. 44 on the park's western edge, the sanctuary is home to about 100 geese in the summer, among them five or six nesting pairs at the main pond.

White Lake

Black ducks, hybrid mallard, and wood ducks also raise families here. The **visitor center** includes an observation room that has floor-to-ceiling windows overlooking the pond. A spotting scope allows you to watch the geese closely, though often they waddle about within a few feet of the windows. Be patient and you'll observe all sorts of behavior—including almost nonstop hissing, squabbling, preening, bathing, and feeding. Maybe you'll see a riled goose chasing another, flying low across the water, neck outstretched, mouth agape, and honking madly. Sometimes you'll even witness a gosling's first flight.

From the visitor center a 1.6-mile (2.6 km) trail follows the pond's north and west banks. Along the trail you'll find other wildlife, such as beavers, snapping turtles (known to eat goslings at times), and many duck species. Sometimes in late July and early August, hikers will see moose with their stilt-legged calves.

About a mile (1.6 km) east of Alfred Hole, Rte. 307 heads due north into the central area of

Sunset over White Lake

Whiteshell. Scattered along the 15-mile (24 km) road between here and the junction with Rte. 309 are trails, campgrounds, swimming beaches, picnic grounds, waterfalls, and lakes. And those are just the recognized sites. You may make an impromptu stop to watch a black bear pawing through a rotted log in pursuit of tasty ants. Or perhaps you'll pull over by an inviting granite outcrop and turn it into a picnic area. You could spend a week covering this stretch of road.

The Backcountry

Once you reach Rte. 309, take it to the north shore of **Big Whiteshell Lake** and vicinity. The area offers hiking, a bike trail, two public beaches, and some developed amenities, but it's also one of the best jump-off points to explore the backcountry. For many visitors a canoe is the vehicle of choice in this watery world. Whiteshell boasts some 200 miles of connected rivers, lakes, and streams and routes that will suit everyone from novice to rabid adventurer. From the marina on the north or south shores of Big Whiteshell

Lake you can paddle deep into the park to the north or south. Gliding along you'll pass feeding moose, looming granite cliffs, and regal bald eagles. At any of the many campsites you'll fall asleep to the cries of loons and possibly, in the fall, the howls of wolves.

If you prefer terra firma for your backcountry expedition, at the north shore of Big Whiteshell Lake you'll find the northern trailhead for the **Mantario Trail.** At 37 miles (60 km) one way, it is the longest trail in the park. Mantario Trail is difficult and remote, so make sure you're prepared before tackling this three- to six-day wilderness trek.

The trail winds through a great diversity of habitats, including orchid-fringed spruce-and-tamarack bogs, rocky ridges topped with jack pines, and dense white spruce forests. Wildlife is plentiful in this wild backcountry. Try to hike the Mantario Trail between late August and late September, when the ground is dry, the horseflies and mosquitoes have abated, and the temperatures are cool enough to make backpacking comfortable.

Pine Point Rapids

Returning on Rte. 309 from Big Whiteshell Lake, continue north on Rte. 307, heading northwest out of the park. Stop just north of Betula Lake and stroll the **Pine Point Rapids Trail,** Whiteshell's most scenic day hike. The route consists of two joined loops, the first leading to the second, so you can go 3.2 miles (5 km) or 4.9 miles (7.9 km). For 1.5 miles (2.4 km) the path runs through boreal forest, pine and spruce spreading a canopy over an understory enlivened by bluebead lily, wild lily of the valley, and moccasin flower, a showy pink orchid. Bedrock erupts in places, creating openings where little grows except yellow, red, black, and green lichens.

Near the far curve of the first loop, the trail picks up the White-shell River and threads its north shore to a vantage point overlooking Pine Point Rapids. The second loop continues along the bank of the Whiteshell, passing Acorn Falls and Viburnum Falls. In the river's quieter stretches, watch for ducks and geese. At Viburnum Falls the trail swings through the forest to the first loop, which leads back to the trailhead. ∎

Whitemouth Falls

As you exit Whiteshell Provincial Park on Rte. 307, don't be in a hurry to leave the area. About 3 miles (5 km) west of the park boundary, just after you pass through the town of Seven Sisters Falls, turn north on a short gravel road *(watch for sign)* to **Whitemouth Falls Wayside Park.** This is an appealing picnic site, its tables scattered among oak, aspen, spruce, ash, and birch. The understory of blueberries, chokecherries, raspberries, and other fruiting bushes attracts black bears in July and August. White-tailed deer and red foxes are also common.

After eating, stroll down past the blue flag and harebells to the falls that give this wayside its name. More horizontal than vertical, Whitemouth Falls nonetheless manages an impressive rush of water as the Whitemouth River thunders down an incline riddled with massive outcrops of Canadian Shield bedrock. The Whitemouth goes with a bang, not a whimper, as it empties into the Winnipeg River. River otters patrol this stretch of river, and muskrat and beavers swim in the calmer spots.

Birders come to the Seven Sisters area to look for boreal forest species, such as great gray owls, northern hawk owls, black-backed woodpeckers, chestnut-sided warblers, pileated woodpeckers, bay-breasted warblers, and American redstarts. Other feathered crowd pleasers that frequent the area include ospreys, bald eagles, and American white pelicans. During the spring and fall migrating ducks paddle about, and terns dive into the water seeking a succulent fish dinner. Birders also go a stone's throw away to Natalie Lake, created by the Seven Sisters dam, to look for oldsquaws, common loons, grebes, and all three species of North American scoters.

Nopiming Provincial Park

■ 353,112 acres ■ Southeast Manitoba, 90 miles (145 km) northeast of Winnipeg ■ Year-round ■ Camping, hiking, canoeing, fishing, mountain biking, skiing, wildlife viewing ■ Adm. fee ■ Contact Manitoba Conservation, Box 22, 200 Saulteaux Crescent, Winnipeg, MB R3J 3W3; phone 800-214-6497. www.gov.mb .ca/natres/parks/regions/eastern/nopiming.html

LIVING UP TO ITS NAME (*nopiming* is Anishinable for "entrance to the wilderness"), Nopiming Provincial Park serves as a transition between the settled country to the south and the trackless wilderness to the north. A mix of civilization and nature, the park has several lodges and cottages on its southern end. It permits logging and mining in some areas, but most of the land is development free, a home to wolves, bears, and lynx.

Nopiming is classic shield country: ancient rock mixed with boreal forest and bodies of water. For a closer look, hike the **Ancient Mountains Trail,** just off Rte. 314 (which runs through the park), east of Tooth Lake. This moderately difficult 1.1-mile (1.8 km) round-trip walk passes through an area swept by a 1983 fire that exposed the bedrock. Use the brochure *(available at trailhead or Black Lake Campground office)* as you examine light gray and brown layers of sedimentary rock and white pegmatite, flecked with pink feldspar, black tourmaline, and other crystals.

The **Fire of 'Eighty-Three Trail** also enters an area hit by fire during that fateful year. Short but fairly strenuous, the trail starts from Rte. 314 at the park's northern end. Get the interpretive brochure at the trailhead or the Beresford Lake Campground office; it explains how the forest is recovering and the vital role played by the burned landscape. Jack pine, which thrive here, are born of fire; sealed by a tough resin, the cones won't scatter their seeds until the ferocious heat bursts them open.

You'll also see many snags—dead trees that are still standing. These charred skeletons are essential to life here. Insects prosper in snags and other wildlife, such as three-toed woodpeckers, in turn jackhammer into the snags and feed on the insects. Tall snags also make good nesting sites and perches for birds such as northern hawk owls (which hunt during the day, so watch for them), ospreys, and bald eagles.

Birds of many sorts—some 190 species—flock to Nopiming, yet the most popular flier here is a bat. Bats of a few different species live in the park, some in large colonies. At dusk these famously nocturnal feeders pour from their daytime chambers in a fluttering stream. To witness this phenomenon, go to the **Tulabi Falls Campground,** located off Rte. 315 in the southern part of the park, at dusk.

Many visitors explore Nopiming by canoe. A map of distances, portages, and backcountry camping is available at the district offices in Lac du Bonnet and Bissett. The popular **Manigotagan Canoe Route** has rapids from Class II to Class V. For a 7-day trip, access the Manigotagan River at Long Lake via Rte. 304. For a 4-day trip, reach Quesnel Lake via the road south to Caribou Lake Landing from Rte. 304 just west of Bissett. ■

Hecla Village, Hecla Island

Hecla/Grindstone Provincial Park

■ 267,861 acres ■ Southeast Manitoba, 90 miles (145 km) north of Winnipeg
■ Best months May-Oct. ■ Camping, hiking, boating, sailing, fishing, cross-country skiing, bird-watching, wildlife viewing, scenic drive ■ Adm. fee ■ Contact Manitoba Conservation, Box 22, 200 Saulteaux Crescent, Winnipeg, MB R3J 3W3; phone 800-214-6497. www.gov.mb.ca/natres/parks/regions/central/hecla.html

THOUGH IT LIES MIDWAY between the Pacific and Atlantic Oceans, Hecla/Grindstone feels like a seaside park. That's because it's located in the middle of the southern lobe of Lake Winnipeg, one of the largest freshwater lakes in the world. In fact, the park encompasses more water than land. The terrestrial elements include three large islands, a number of small islands, and the Grindstone Peninsula. The largest island, Hecla, is 16 miles (25.7 km) long and 4 miles (6.4 km) wide. Connected to the mainland by a mile-long causeway (part of Hwy. 8), Hecla Island is the most accessible and developed area of Hecla/Grindstone Provincial Park.

If you visit Hecla Island in May or early June, your wildlife viewing may begin as soon as you're on the causeway. Western grebes favor the water between the mainland and the island as a stage for their elaborate courtship rituals. Whether you catch this display or not, there's plenty to see, spring through fall, the minute you reach Hecla Island itself. On this end of the island lies **Grassy Narrows Marsh,** one of Manitoba's finest wetlands and the best natural area in Hecla/Grindstone Provincial Park. Wetlands are among the most biologically productive communities in the world, and Grassy Narrows Marsh clearly demonstrates that fecundity.

You can explore the marsh via five trails and boardwalks, all of them easy walking, that range in length from 0.3 to 6.6 miles (0.5 to 10.6 km).

Fishing boat, Hecla Village, Hecla Island

Two also allow mountain bikes. From the main parking lot, many people begin their explorations by heading west on the 0.8-mile (1.3 km) **Chorus Frog Trail.** The trail wanders through patchy aspen groves before emerging into the open marsh, which is characterized by cattails, giant reed grass, and lots of water. The last few hundred yards of the trail lead out into the water on a boardwalk. An observation blind at the boardwalk's end allows you to watch mallard, green-winged teal, buffleheads, rare northern shovelers, and the many other duck species that stop here during spring and fall migration. You may also see a northern harrier searching for rodents or a tern rocketing into the water after fish.

At the start of the boardwalk, the **Turtle Trail** crosses the Chorus Frog Trail. This 4.7-mile (7.5 km) loop runs through marsh and along the shore of Lake Winnipeg. You'll probably find more frogs on Turtle Trail than on the one bearing their name—sometimes as many as one leaper every 10 yards (9 m). You may also spot red-sided garter snakes and signs of river otter, including scat, tunnels through the cattails, and bones from fish or other prey. Don't forget to look up as well as down, or you'll miss all the waterfowl, herons, blackbirds, and American bitterns here. Along the lakeshore, an observation tower offers great views west across the lake and east across the marsh.

Continuing into the park on Hwy. 8, about half a mile (0.8 km) past the park entrance gate, the **Wildlife Viewing Tower Trail** *(ten minutes one way)* leads you through mixed woods to a 25-foot viewing tower that

Limestone cliffs of Quarry Beach, Hecla Island

overlooks a blend of forest, marsh, and scrubby meadow. As the interpretive signs suggest, this is a wonderful place from which to spot one of the approximately 50 moose that inhabit the island. Wolves also make this end of Hecla Island their home, though they're seldom seen.

The north end of Hecla Island is a developed recreational area, with a campground, a golf course, a posh resort, a marina, bike paths, and picnic sites, but the call of the wild can still be heard there in certain places. The **Hecla Village Scenic Drive,** which begins just south of the village off Hwy. 8, winds along a beautiful shoreline, where you may see pelicans, Canada geese, or the occasional bald eagle. The **Lighthouse Trail** *(1.9 miles/3 km round-trip),* which starts at the Gull Harbour resort, likewise yields bird sightings—as well as stirring views of the lake from the tip of the slender peninsula guarded by the lighthouse. ▦

Paint Lake & Pisew Falls Provincial Parks

▦ 56,091 acres ▦ Northern Manitoba: Paint Lake, 20 miles (32 km) south of Thompson; Pisew Falls, 50 miles (80.5 km) south of Thompson ▦ Best months June-Sept. ▦ Camping, hiking, boating, canoeing, swimming, fishing, birdwatching, wildlife viewing ▦ Adm. fee ▦ Contact Manitoba Conservation, Box 22, 200 Saulteaux Crescent, Winnipeg, MB R3J 3W3; phone 800-214-6497. www.gov.mb.ca/natres/parks/regions/northern/paint_lake.html

PAINT LAKE AND PISEW FALLS PROVINCIAL PARKS generally are lumped together because they're close to each other and share an intimate connection—the **Grass River.** However, though the river anchors both parks, its nature differs radically from one to the other.

At Pisew Falls, the Grass River narrows to 200 feet (61 m) and drops more than 40 feet (12 m) over a fault in the Thompson Nickel Belt. Then it changes direction and thrashes down a stony gorge. **Observation platforms** by the falls and a suspension bridge just downriver provide fantastic views. Across the bridge, one trail leads to the top of the cascades; another, the **Upper Track Hiking Trail,** ranges downriver 6.8 miles (11 km) one way to **Kwasitchewan Falls**—at 46 feet (14 m), Manitoba's highest falls.

At Paint Lake, the Grass River widens into a maze of lakes, channels, and islands nearly 10 miles (16 km) across. A couple of campgrounds and a lodge allow visitors to stick around for an in-depth exploration of this watery labyrinth. You can find some hikes, but try to get out in a canoe or boat. Meander among the islands and along the rugged shoreline of this slice of northern Canadian Shield country. Take in the ancient bedrock, the boreal forest of spruce and pine, and sightings of black bear, river otter, and moose. ▦

Following pages: Pisew Falls

Grass River Provincial Park

■ 563,133 acres ■ Central Manitoba, 35 miles (56 km) southeast of Flin Flon
■ Best months mid-May–Sept. ■ Camping, hiking, boating, canoeing, fishing, wildlife viewing ■ Adm. fee ■ Contact Manitoba Conservation, Box 130, Cranberry Portage, MB R0B 0H0, phone 204-472-3331. www.gov.mb.ca/natres/parks/regions/northern/grass_river.html; or Grass River Corridor Tourism Assn., 228-35 Main St., Flin Flon, MB R8A 1J7, phone 204-687-6967. www.grassriver.mb.ca

WATER COVERS ABOUT 35 PERCENT of Grass River Provincial Park. Everywhere you turn there's a lake, a marsh, a river, a fen, or some other body of water. Though you can glimpse the area's scenic beauty from land, in order to experience the park's essence you must venture into those liquid realms. The park's name conjures an image of a channel of water, but as the Grass River snakes through the park it repeatedly balloons to form lakes. If you take the 80-mile (129 km) canoe route that follows the river the length of the Grass River Provincial Park, you'll be paddling across lakes most of the time.

Whether lake or river, the water is remarkably clear and clean; in fact, this area was designated a park, in part, to protect the superb water quality. The largely undeveloped park also protects an ark of wildlife, notably a population of rare woodland caribou. The woodlands in which these caribou prosper consist of black spruce, jack pine, assorted hardwoods, and other boreal forest trees underlain by the granite of the Canadian Shield, which characterizes the majority of the park. However, the southern portion lies in the boggy Manitoba lowlands, whose fens and bogs contain only stunted spruce and tamarack trees. Well-drained glacial features, such as moraines, and limestone outcrops support lush pine and white spruce forests. This geologic divide between north and south clearly reveals itself to visitors passing through the park on Hwy. 39.

What to See and Do

There are two ways to see Grass River Provincial Park: by water or on land. Hiking the trails requires less in the way of preparation and equipment, but exploring the park by boat can be worth all the effort. If you decide on water travel, contact the park or the tourism association for advice on routes and safety precautions. You can also hire a guide for canoe trips and motorboat tours. If you go on your own, you'll have to rent a canoe or gain access to one through a lodge in or near the park. Be cautious if you're a novice: Some of the lakes are large enough to whip up 5-foot waves during a big blow, and you'll want to stay away from the rapids.

By Water

A representative example of an easy day trip is the 3-mile (4.8 km) one-way section of the **trans-park canoe route** that begins at Iskwasum Campground and ends at

Iskwasum Lake at sunset

Landing a lake trout on Reed Lake

Loucks Falls. Push off from the little campground launch, preferably on a sunny and windless day, and paddle east along the south shore of Loucks Lake. As your canoe whispers through the water, you may see some mergansers or loons likewise paddling quietly along. Bald eagles often soar overhead, scanning the lake for fish. In various places you can take short side trips, such as easing into a shoreside pond to examine a beaver lodge and dam.

As you glide along keep an eye on the forest of 50-foot (15 m) spruce and pine. You may spot a moose plunging its face into the shallows to feed on vegetation or a river otter sliding down the well-worn runways that stripe the north bank not far from the campground.

If you're really fortunate, you may even spy a caribou. Hundreds occupy the park (the range of one herd includes Loucks Lake), yet people so seldom see these elusive beasts that they've been nicknamed "gray ghosts." Your best chance of being one of the lucky few is during May and June, when the females retreat to the islands in the lakes to calve. And yes, they do swim, so you could sight a rack of antlers cruising through the water.

Like the caribou—though obviously for different reasons—you may want to stop at one of the many islands. For an hour or two you can claim one for your own. Would a 5-acre wooded estate suit your fancy? Or are you more in the mood for an unfurnished, living-room-size granite knob? Both make great picnic sites.

So does **Loucks Falls,** the turn-around point for this day trip. Beach your canoe at the well-marked portage, then hike through the woods above the falls, thankful that you're not lugging a canoe. (You could portage your canoe and gear around the falls and paddle down the Grass River, if you wish.) Anywhere along the 200-yard (183 m) portage you can step a few yards off the trail and settle yourself on a granite slab above the rushing water—the falls is actually a cascading series of big rapids, not a vertical waterfall.

Many similar canoe routes await. And for voyageurs who want to linger in this watery wilderness, there are dozens of backcountry campgrounds designed for canoeists. (Three backcountry lodges beckon as well, if you prefer the amenities of civilization with your wilderness.)

As you sit around the evening campfire, the calls of loons—perhaps even some wolf howls—will pierce the deep silence. From shoreside marshes, frogs croak relentlessly, a sound like a thumb running down the stiff teeth of a comb, but hugely amplified. As the sun dissolves into a purple-pink cloud bank, the water turns iridescent blue and the white bark of

Autumn colors of red osier dogwood, Four Mile Island

the aspen and birch shine with a peachy alpenglow, like snow in the mountains. Then comes the dark, the stars, and, if you're lucky, the northern lights.

On Land

Though water dominates Grass River Provincial Park, earthy pleasures can be had. Hwy. 39, which traverses the southern portion of the park, isn't necessarily one of them—motorists are faced mostly with a wall of trees on either side. However, you will see the occasional black bear or deer by the road. And road cuts reveal pancaked slabs of dolomite, a sedimentary rock that lets you know you're in the Manitoba lowlands—even if you can throw a chunk of that dolomite north and hit the granite of the Canadian Shield.

Hwy. 39 leads to more scenic vistas. From the road you can enter three campgrounds, each of which provides access to a handsome lake and some informal hiking.

The **Karst Spring Trail**—an easy, 2-mile (3.2-km) loop that starts from the northwest end of

the Iskwasum Campground—is the park's only established path. Grab a brochure at the trailhead, and read the interpretive signs along the way. The trail starts amid forest carpeted by moss that springs underfoot; in places the bed of moss is 10 or 20 inches (25 or 50 cm) thick. After 15 minutes the trail pulls alongside a narrow channel of the Grass River and paces it for some time. Tarry at the overlook and watch terns diving for fish or a muskrat sculling through the reeds. Back on the trail, if it's between mid-May and mid-June, look for the nodding pink heads of calypso orchids sprouting from the green moss beds.

Halfway through the loop you'll see how the trail got its name. After bridging a creek near its confluence with the Grass River, the path turns upslope and follows the tumbling water about 100 yards (30.5 m) to its source: a hillside of sedimentary rock—hence "karst" (an area filled with sinkholes, caverns, and subterranean flowing water) "spring" trail. ∎

Lac La Ronge Provincial Park

■ 830,731 acres ■ Northern Saskatchewan, 100 miles (160 km) north of Prince Albert National Park ■ Camping, hiking, boating, canoeing, swimming, fishing, flight-seeing ■ Prepare for summer insects ■ Contact the park, Box 5000, La Ronge, SK S0J 1L0; phone 306-425-4234. www.serm.gov.sk.ca/parks /laclaronge

LAC LA RONGE PROVINCIAL PARK lies in northern Saskatchewan. Residents of the area continually fight the image that Saskatchewan is nothing but wheat fields. That's the south, they're quick to note, the prairie. Up north, in places such as this park, it's a different world of lakes, boreal forest, and the rugged granite of the Canadian Shield.

Mackay Lake

Water defines the park, as its name suggests. The lake is enormous, covering hundreds of square miles and containing some 1,300 islands. More than 100 smaller lakes hydrate the area, and the Churchill River marks the park's northern boundary. The largest provincial park in Saskatchewan, Lac La Ronge offers a wide variety of wildlife and habitats.

What to See and Do

Like other parks in the area, Lac La Ronge can be explored via hiking trails or waterways. Whichever way you decide to go, stop at the Saskatchewan Environment and Re-source Management office in the town of La Ronge or at the tourism booth (sporadically staffed) along Hwy. 2 in Air Ronge. The staff can help you decide where to go and whom to contact for help in getting there.

On Land

At the north end of Nut Point Campground *(0.5 mile/0.8 km N of La Ronge)*, you'll find the trailhead for the park's premier terrestrial outing: the **Nut Point Hiking Trail.** Though it's a land-based excursion, this hike derives much of its appeal from water, running the length of a narrow peninsula that extends into Lac La Ronge and offering some fine views of the surrounding waterscape. At several points, you can take side trails to the lake to swim or fish. On boardwalks the path passes through numerous muskegs (boggy depressions that are underlain by decaying plant matter).

The trail runs 9.3 miles (15 km) one way and takes about eight hours at a stop-to-smell-the-flowers pace. If you plan to traverse the entire trail, take camping gear or arrange for a boat to drop

you off at Nut Point (trail's end) so you can walk to the campground. Pick up a trail map/brochure at either the office in La Ronge or the tourism booth in Air Ronge, and watch for bears.

To see more of the park, head north from La Ronge on Hwy. 102. Within the first 20 miles (32 km) you'll come to three lakeside campgrounds and some other hiking trails. The last of these is the Nemeiben Lake Campground, where you'll find the trailhead for the 0.9-mile (1.5 km) **Nemeiben Lake Trail.** The trail meanders through a forest of pine and spruce and past outcroppings of Precambrian rock and muskegs. At trail's end a rocky point invites you to relax and look out over the water.

By Water

To see the park by water, start just outside La Ronge at Eagle Point Resort *(888-332-4536),* nestled on McGibbon Bay, an arm of Lac La Ronge. Though not a rustic getaway—as evidenced by the presence of a golf course—the resort does rent houseboats. In these self-contained craft you can venture out among the lake's islands and hidden coves for a day or a week.

The hub for exploring the Churchill River wilderness is the village of Missinipe, situated in the northwest corner of the park. Missinipe, 50 miles (80 km) north of La Ronge on Hwy. 102 (the last 30 miles/48 km are on gravel), sits on the banks of Otter Lake, part of the **Churchill River** system.

For an overview of this area, take a sight-seeing flight in a floatplane (flight-seeing). You'll observe how the Churchill broadens

Winter Lodging

The only place you'll see a beaver in a northern winter is on the Canadian nickel. But beavers don't hibernate. So how do they survive when their ponds freeze over?

Their lodges are the key. From the outside, a beaver lodge resembles a heap of sticks. Inside it's a tidy, cozy haven that shelters a family of beavers in comfort (interior temperatures can hit 60°F even when it's zero outside). Tunnels leading beneath the pond ice allow the beavers to reach their submerged stashes of food.

Horsetail ferns along Nemeiben Lake Trail

into lakes, then contracts into narrow white-water channels as it flows toward Hudson Bay. For a look around from the water, Thompson's Camps *(800-667-5554)* runs a 30- to 45-minute jet boat tour that goes up the river/lake system, blasting through rapids.

Horizons Unlimited/Churchill River Canoe Outfitters *(877-511-2726)* offers a slower, more intimate experience on canoe trips that last from a few hours to a few weeks. If you want to head out on your own, they'll outfit you with a canoe and arm you with maps and information. Unless you're a savvy veteran, though, it's best to go with a guide: He or she won't get lost in the maze of islands, channels, and broken shoreline. If you're a novice canoeist, guides offer on-the-spot lessons as you're traveling, or you can take a multiday course devoted to instruction.

Within hours of paddling away from the dock in Missinipe, you'll be deep into **Otter Lake.** Head southeast to slip into a thicket of forested islands thronging that end of the lake. Watch for bald eagles circling overhead or American white pelicans swimming across the water in synchronization as they sway and dip in search of fish. If you head north, you'll pass a shoreline of spruce punctuated by silver outcroppings of granite and come to famed **Otter Rapids,** a quarter-mile stretch of white water where the Churchill funnels into a narrow channel.

Experienced canoeists and kayakers come from all over to play in this white water, but novices can portage around it. Beyond Otter Rapids lie more islands and lakes, coves and waterfalls. After a day of paddling you can pick a campsite along the bank. ■

Prince Albert National Park

■ 957,529 acres ■ Central Saskatchewan, 40 miles (60 km) north of Prince Albert ■ Best weather mid-May–Oct.; some winter use ■ Camping, hiking, boating, canoeing, swimming, fishing, cycling, winter sports, wildlife viewing, scenic drives ■ Contact the park, Box 100, Waskesiu Lake, SK S0J 2Y0; phone 877-255-7267, ext. 0124. www.parkscanada.gc.ca/albert

TEN THOUSAND YEARS AGO the glaciers of the last ice age retreated from the area that is now Prince Albert National Park. The landscape must have looked pretty bleak, but it formed a sound foundation upon which nature has built the comely park that visitors see today. Spruce, birch, aspen, ferns, moss, and other plants now green the terrain, and the park sparkles with ponds, bogs, marshes, and at least 1,500 lakes and streams.

View of aspen parkland from Shady Lake Viewing Tower

Wildlife—including wolves, bald eagles, moose, black bears, bison, lynx, elk, beavers, and caribou—is abundant here.

The park's rich variety of plants and animals stems not only from its size and wildness but also from its diversity of habitat. Prince Albert National Park lies within a southern mixed-wood region that shifts from aspen parkland to boreal forest. And don't forget the southwest corner and a few other southern pockets, where rare untouched fescue grasslands add a whisper of the prairie.

Prince Albert is an easy park to visit. Parks Canada provides assistance in many forms: an information center, a nature center, interpretive programs, well-maintained hiking trails, and established canoe routes. The presence of the little town of Waskesiu—headquarters for the Prince Albert National Park staff and an outpost of amenities in the midst of this sprawling wilderness—also smooths the way for visitors.

What to See and Do

After you enter the park, stop first at the Parks Canada Information Centre, in Waskesiu, located on the eastern shore of **Waskesiu Lake** in the east-central part of the park. From there walk down the lake-shore a block to the nature center, which offers natural history information, interactive displays, videos of the park, and many activities for kids. You'll be well prepared for your visit.

After learning about the park, stroll about 200 yards (185 m) southeast from the information center to the **beaver ponds.** There you'll see beaver lodges, dams, and, if you're patient, even the 50-pound rodents themselves hauling willow branches and troweling mud onto their lodges, and otherwise being as busy as—well, you know. Ducks, kingfishers, and elk also frequent the area, though the elk are more likely to show during the early morning or evening. (Don't crowd these sometimes aggressive and up-to-800-pound critters; though it doesn't happen often, people have been injured by elk.) During the winter even the wolves sometimes come close to town; occasionally they run down an elk on the frozen lake just a stone's throw from Waskesiu's main drag.

Scenic Drives

Though the town clearly has its wild side, you need to venture more than a couple of hundred yards from the restaurants and souvenir shops to fully appreciate Prince Albert. You can begin exploring in your car. Visitors who approach the park from the south—as a large number do—shouldn't rocket up Hwy. 2 to Hwy. 264. This route may be faster, but it lies almost entirely outside the park. Instead, about 20 miles (32 km) north of the city of Prince Albert, turn west from Hwy. 2 onto Hwy. 263. This paved road, known as the **Scenic Route,** enters the park near its southeast corner about 10 miles (16 km) later. Then, after a couple of miles the road turns north and runs for some 30 miles (48 km) through the park to Waskesiu.

At first Hwy. 263 curves over rolling hills vegetated by trembling aspen and an occasional patch of prairie grassland. The light green leaves and white trunks of the aspen are easy on the eye in spring and summer, but the trees are positively radiant in autumn when the leaves turn gold. About 5 miles (8 km) into the park you'll come to Sandy Lake, which features a campground and picnic area. Another 6 miles (10 km) brings you to the trailhead for the **Spruce River Highlands.** This 5.3-mile (8.5 km) loop is strenuous, but go up the path less than half a mile and you come to a lookout point topped by a 30-foot (9 m) tower, which offers a grand view of the meandering Spruce River.

By the time you've reached the Spruce River Highlands, the transition to boreal forest has begun; as you continue north on Hwy. 263, you'll see more conifers and fewer aspen and other southern trees. By the time you reach the lookout point near **Shady Lake,** about 13 miles (21 km) north of

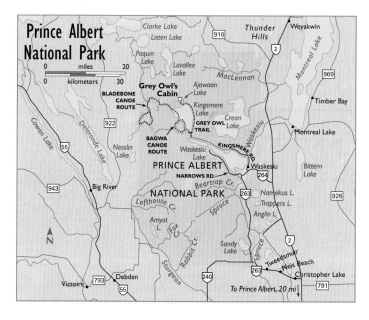

the highlands, you're in the North Woods—the boreal forest. Approximately 4 miles (6.4 km) from Shady Lake the road meets Waskesiu Lake and skirts its southeastern shore for a couple of miles to the town of Waskesiu.

Hwy. 263 is the most popular scenic drive, but two others merit a mention: **Narrows Road,** which branches off Hwy. 263 just south of Waskesiu and follows Waskesiu Lake's southern shore for 11 miles (18 km), and **Kingsmere Road,** which departs from Hwy. 264 north of Waskesiu and traces the lake's northern shore for 20 miles (32 km) to the Kingsmere River.

In addition to the scenery, these drives offer opportunities to see wildlife, especially if you roll along slowly early in the morning or at evening. In the aspen parklands you're likely to see elk and deer grazing on the grass, a black bear traveling through the woods, or a

beaver carving a wake through its glassy pond. Plenty of beavers occupy the boreal forest, and in the ponds in the north you might spot a moose munching aquatic plants. Sometimes you'll see spruce grouse blithely clucking along the roadside, seemingly fearless. A few fortunate visitors will glimpse wolves in the northern reaches of the park; occasionally someone even spies a white wolf.

By Water

Because nearly 10 percent of the park's surface is underwater, it comes as no surprise that many park activities revolve around the park's bodies of water. Some visitors are content to rent motorboats, canoes, or kayaks at one of the three marinas and just wander around a portion of the most convenient lake. Other visitors think of a boat as a place to sit while fishing. But many people use wa-

tercraft, particularly canoes, to explore the park, to slip into nooks and crannies that can't be reached any other way. (Any rental outfit will transport your canoe or other craft to almost any body of water you select.)

The opportunities for canoeing are essentially infinite; ask for suggestions at the information center. Then, early some morning, you can put in at a roadside complex of ponds, paddle a few hundred yards into the labyrinth, and watch the forest come to life. Canoe one of the slow, winding rivers, such as the Spruce, taking in the green tremors of the aspen and watching for deer and elk drinking at the river's edge.

You might paddle onto one of several large lakes *(novices should avoid crossing wide expanses of open water; sudden winds can render lakes dangerously choppy).* As you cruise along the shore, watch for bald eagles and ospreys in the treetops; perhaps you'll see the adults bringing fish to the voracious young in the nest.

Kingsmere Lake is the hub for some of the park's finest canoeing.

Autumnal beauty of Mud Creek

About 6 miles (9.5 km) long and nearly as wide, the lake offers plenty of shoreline to explore and campgrounds in which to stay; you'll have time for a thorough exploration. Many people canoe the lovely eastern shore, where four campgrounds dot the banks and paddlers can visit **Grey Owl's Cabin** (see sidebar p. 231). To reach the cabin and gravesite of this complex and fascinating man, leave your canoe at the Northend picnic site, a quarter mile from the Northend Campground, and take the 1.8-mile (2.9 km) trail.

Visitors can also get to the cabin via a 12-mile (20 km) hiking trail that begins at the Kingsmere River parking lot and follows the lake's eastern shore.

Kingsmere Lake is also the jumping-off point for the park's two main designated canoe routes. ("Designated" means route markers and established portages, but visitors of all skill levels should register at the information center.) Paddlers will find that the rewards of the **Bladebone Canoe Route** offset its tough portages. This four- to seven-day journey starts near the Bladebone Bay Campground at the northwest tip of Kingsmere Lake or at Nova Lake, across the park's western boundary. It passes through half a dozen smaller lakes in the park's hinterland, exposing paddlers to solitude, scenery, and abundant wildlife.

Don't be surprised to encounter American white pelicans. Less

Hawthorn tree berries

than 10 miles (16 km) north of the Bladebone route, some 15,000 of these birds nest on **Lavallée Lake,** making it one of the largest white pelican breeding colonies in Canada. Access to Lavallée is restricted to protect the birds, but since they forage widely—sometimes traveling 100 miles (160 km) a day in search of food—they show up on lakes throughout the park. These graceful, 5-foot-tall (1.5 m) birds with 9-foot (2.7 m) wingspans net fish in their pouches by sweeping their bills through the water, sometimes in synchronized groups.

Canoeists of all levels can manage the **Bagwa Canoe Route,** which loops out from the west shore of Kingsmere Lake. When you slide through diminutive **Clare Lake,** watch for herons mincing through the shallow water on their stilt legs, primed to spear small fish with their slender bills. You can paddle through this necklace of small lakes in one long day, but why move so fast? Linger at one of the campgrounds, watching the ospreys plunge into the water with outstretched talons and listening to the haunting cries of the common loon. If you prefer to keep moving, you could go around the loop twice.

Hiking

The park's trails come in many shapes and sizes. Lengths range from 300 yards (274 m) to 24 miles (38.6 km). Some trails run straight and flat; others twist and turn, rise and fall. You can take routes that run through the aspen parklands, trails that slip through the boreal forest, pathways that take you through the grasslands, and still others that pass through a variety of habitats.

In particular, Prince Albert offers numerous short, easy trails—which, taken together, showcase the park's diversity. You can start just 4 miles (6.4 km) north of town at the **Waskesiu River Trail,** a 1.2-mile (2 km) loop that begins where Kingsmere Road crosses the river.

For the first 0.3 mile (0.5 km) you'll be on a wheelchair-accessible boardwalk that closely follows the southeast bank of the river. Move out onto the lookout platforms and you're likely to see great blue herons stalking through the marsh or mergansers drifting with the gentle current. At the 0.3-mile (0.5 km) mark the path bridges the river, providing a great vantage point from which to view the riverscape and scan it for wildlife; don't forget to look down into the water for spawning suckers and other aquatic denizens. Across the bridge the trail loops through spruce and aspen forests, then back to the parking lot.

Another 10 miles (16 km) up Kingsmere Road, on the north shore of Waskesiu Lake, try the **Narrows Peninsula Trail.** This 1.9-mile (3 km) path threads along the perimeter of a finger of land that juts into the lake, nearly cutting off the lake's slender northwest end.

The route passes through a fairly open forest where in the spring you may hear the low throbbing of male ruffed grouse drumming and see foot-deep squirrel middens—mounds of the bits and pieces of conifer cones these chattering creatures have dropped from their feeding perches. At times you'll cross boardwalks that lead through reedy marshes, and at one point you'll encounter a luxuriant garden of ferns. Some of the time the trail goes along a 30-foot bluff, offering fine views of the lake and surrounding forest.

On the southern side of Lake Waskesiu, near the end of the Narrows Road, the **Treebeard Trail** takes you on a 0.7-mile (1.2 km) jaunt through the *Mi sis a kaw,* as the Woods Cree call it, which translates roughly as "Big Forest." (For the full experience, pick up one of the excellent trail guides at the trailhead and travel counter-clockwise.) Fittingly, the Big Forest harbors some of Saskatchewan's largest balsam poplar, white spruce, and balsam fir in the province, their size the result of an exceptionally high and nutrient-laden water table—and the fact that they've avoided fire since

False Feathers

Grey Owl, a wilderness champion who claimed to be a Canadian Indian, lived in rustic style with his First Nations wife on Ajawaan Lake. During the 1930s, Grey Owl traveled the world lecturing and writing about conservation. The press celebrated his efforts. Royalty honored him.

After his death in 1938, however, the truth emerged: Grey Owl was an Englishman named Archibald Belaney. Despite his ersatz origins, his devotion to nature was real—and his eloquence on its behalf endures.

about 1830. Many of these venerable trees are draped with a long, wispy lichen known as old-man's beard—hence the trail's name.

Consulting the trail guide and peering closely at the forest's features, you can learn a world of wonders about the North Woods. For example, the trail first passes through a mature forest that burned in 1890, resetting the forest regeneration clock.

Just as fire plays a key role in shaping northern forests, so do fearsome winters. Survey the understory for young balsam fir that are "layering." This process begins

Heading down to Narrows Peninsula Trail

when snow weighs down a branch close to the ground, partially burying it. The branch then often grows roots, whereupon its tip becomes the main stem of a new balsam fir growing up a few feet from the original.

The Treebeard forest shelters many animals. One of the first sounds hikers are likely to hear is the lilting whistle of the white-throated sparrow, which some field guides describe as sounding like *pure sweet Canada Canada Canada*. Another common sound is the rat-a-tat of a pileated woodpecker jackhammering a snag; it may be seeking carpenter ants or drilling a nesting cavity, later to be occupied by goldeneye ducks, flying squirrels, and other critters.

Summer brings an influx of warblers and other songbirds that winter in Central and South America. If you watch closely, you may notice that these songbirds tend to divvy up living space in the trees along a vertical axis. Blackburnian warblers, for instance, usually rule the treetops, while magnolia warblers live in the bottom branches. You may see a fisher, a member of the weasel family, whose numbers are in decline. Despite their name, these 3-foot-long predators don't fish; they prefer snowshoe hare and porcupines, which fishers skillfully flip over to expose the quill-less bellies.

If you're willing to drive a couple of hours west from Hwy. 263 on Hwy. 240, about half in the farmlands outside the park, you can reach the southwest section of Prince Albert, where the buffalo roam. About 200 of these prairie icons inhabit the fescue grasslands, the sedge meadows, and the aspen parklands—the only free-ranging herd of plains bison in Canada that occupies its historic range.

You stand a fair chance of seeing bison if you take the **Amyot Lake Trail,** a 9.6-mile (15.5 km) trek starting from the Westside picnic area (across the Sturgeon River bridge) that goes out to Amyot Lake and then loops back to the picnic area on the **Westside Boundary Trail.**

And then there's the bog. Many people think of bogs as drab, lifeless mosquito factories. They do produce mosquitoes, but those first two adjectives are unwarranted, as you'll see if you hike the 1.2-mile (2 km) loop of the **Boundary Bog Trail,** which starts just inside the Hwy. 264 park entrance.

If you want to understand the Canadian outdoors, you'd better get acquainted with wetlands: Bogs, fens, marshes, swamps, and muskegs cover about 14 percent of the nation, an area roughly one-third the size of western Europe. Take one of the Boundary Bog trail guides found at the trailhead on your hike.

For the first few hundred yards of the Boundary Bog Trail you'll be in mixed forest uplands, encir-cled by white spruce, jack pine, aspen, and black spruce. As you pass along the boardwalk, look around your feet at the profusion of feather mosses, such as knight's plume and stair step moss. After about half a mile (0.8 km) of gentle descent, you'll leave the forest and follow the boardwalk into the bog.

Like some of its brethren, Boundary Bog began as a big block of ice, separated from its mother glacier 100 centuries ago. Over time, debris carried in the meltwater of the retreating glacier buried the ice block. As the block melted, the soils on top slumped, leaving a rounded crater called a kettle. With its drainage blocked, the kettle slowly filled with water and sediments. Some of the vegetation at the edge then grew into a floating mat that extended over the water.

Due to the cold climate and their waterlogged condition, these plants didn't fully decompose when they died; eventually they turned into peat. The process continued, and goes on today, so the

Birch bark detail

mass of peat grows thicker and thicker. Kneel down and push the "ground" with your hand. It feels like a soggy sponge. The trail runs over a mat of peat 10 yards (9 m) thick and 3,000 years old.

After crossing several knolls serving as islands, you enter the heart of the bog. Kneel again and introduce yourself to sphagnum moss, boss of the bog; it creates the acidic environment in which it thrives. For most other plants, this is a tough place to grow, especially since the sphagnum gobbles a large share of the nutrients in the

water. Those scrawny, 10-foot-tall (3 m) tamarack trees, for example, may be 150 years old.

While you're down there on your knees, note the drooping pink flowers of the bog rosemary and the tiny white flowers of Labrador tea. Look closer and you may spot one of the four carnivorous plants that inhabit the bog; these include the pitcher plant, rendered vaguely sinister by its hooded leaves. The pitcher plant's red hue and the nectar-smeared lips of its leaves lure insects into the plant's maw. Once inside, their

Waskesiu Lake

escape is thwarted by downward pointed hairs and a slippery interior surface. Certain clever spiders have learned to spin their webs across the openings of pitcher plants, snaring flying insects.

Park interpreters leading walks through the bog occasionally let their charges do the Bog Dance: Hikers shuck their shoes, step off the boardwalk onto the cold, squishy moss, then jump up and down, making the peat mat jiggle. Trees quake 20 feet (6 m) away.

Continuing down the boardwalk brings you to the eye of the bog: a small lake in the center of the kettle. The stained water appears lifeless, but if you were to sweep a net through it you'd come up with dragonfly nymphs, little amphipods called sideswimmers, and perhaps even a leech. In time —call it a few thousand years—the sphagnum and peat will overrun this eye, completing the conquest begun so long ago.

From the eye the trail heads back to the parking lot, giving you time to reflect on the rare experience of going into a black spruce bog and coming out alive. ■

The Far North

Caribou Hills ablaze with fall color, Mackenzie River Delta area

THE FAR NORTH may surprise you.

During its long winter, Canada's northwest—particularly the three territories of Nunavut, Northwest Territories, and Yukon Territory—can certainly live up to its reputation as a land of ice and darkness. But summer brings out another, less familiar aspect of the far north. In June, July, and August, wildflowers blanket the ground. At high latitudes, the summer sun doesn't set for weeks on end. Daytime temperatures can top 70°F.

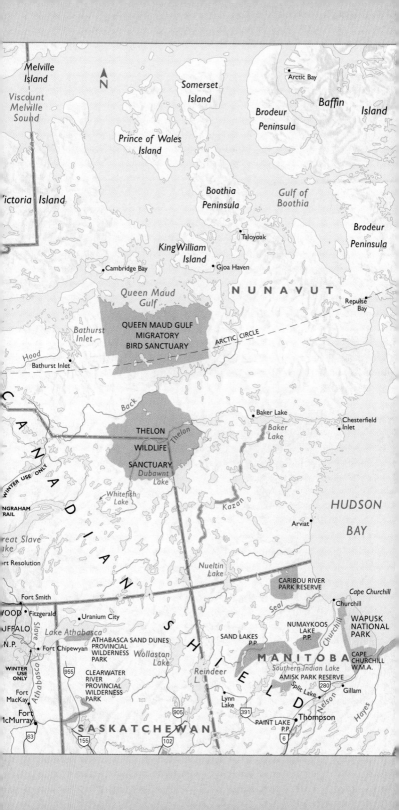

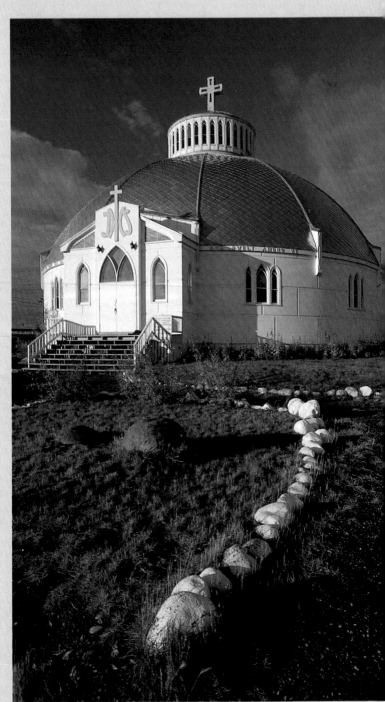

"Igloo church"—Our Lady of Victory Catholic Church, Inuvik

Bison skull amid sedges, Wood Buffalo National Park

Perhaps the biggest surprise of all is the scenic and biological richness that awaits the traveler to the far north. A journey can take you past mountain passes, waterfalls, forests, and river valleys. You'll see herds of caribou stretching to the horizon, hear wolves calling across the tundra, and meet rowdy congregations of beluga whales in river mouths. This remote region offers a grand wildness unmatched on this continent.

Canada's far north stretches from the Yukon Plateau and the Rocky Mountains in the west to the Hudson Bay in the east. Running across it in a rough diagonal from northwest to southeast is the tree line: the cold, invisible boundary above which trees cannot grow. Taiga—the northern portion of the boreal forest, featuring scraggly stands of smallish conifers interspersed with lakes and wetlands—characterizes the southern areas of the region. As you move north, the taiga becomes tundra, a treeless land of dwarf shrubs and flattened plants. Permafrost, a short growing season, thin soils, and other factors keep vegetation close to the ground on the tundra. Yet tundra and taiga support a surprising amount of wildlife, including all three North American bear species (black, grizzly, and polar) and huge numbers of migrating birds.

Trips to the far north take special planning. You can drive to only a handful of sites up here; many can be reached solely by canoe, kayak, raft, or by air, though one is available by train. Depending on your destination, you must be prepared to handle problems that range from the annoying (biting insects) to the life-threatening (angry polar bears). Average outdoorspeople who know what hypothermia is and have the sense not to air out sardine sandwiches in bear country will do fine on their own at many sites. But other areas are so remote and so hazardous that unless you're a hardened adventurer, you'll be better off visiting them on a guided tour or from a wilderness lodge. Fortunately, many such tours and lodges exist in the far north. One way or another, even a devout urbanite can find a way to enjoy this far-off land. ■

Wrestling polar bears

Churchill Area

■ Northeast Manitoba, 600 miles (965 km) north of Winnipeg ■ Year-round ■ Bird-watching, whale-watching, wildlife viewing, boat tours, northern lights, polar bears ■ Be prepared for biting insects July-Aug. and cool subarctic climate. Reserve ahead for visits June-Aug.; reserve a year in advance for prime polar bear season Oct.–mid-Nov. Access by train or plane only ■ Contact Wapusk National Park, Box 127, Churchill, MB R0B 0E0, phone 204-675-8863, www.parkscanada.gc.ca/wapusk; or Churchill Chamber of Commerce, P.O. Box 176, Churchill, MB R0B 0E0, phone 888-389-2327, www.cancom.net/~cccomm

IF YOU HAVE HEARD OF the small, remote town of Churchill, it is probably in connection with the area's main claim to fame: polar bears. Although the bears that congregate here in the fall are a compelling phenomenon, they are only one of many natural blessings the area enjoys. Depending on the season, visitors also can see an overwhelming concentration of beluga whales, a fine array of migratory birds, and an unsurpassed display of the northern lights. You can also explore a wild slice of Arctic tundra—an ecosystem that typically is hard to reach.

Churchill sits on the western shore of Hudson Bay in a region known as the Hudson Bay Lowlands. Some 9,000 to 8,000 years ago the continental ice sheet retreated, leaving behind the vast basin now known as Hudson Bay. Relieved of the ice sheet's stupendous weight, the land around the bay's margins began to spring back. In fact, the ground around Hudson Bay continues to rise at the rate of about a yard a century, as seems evident at Sloop Cove, across the estuary from Churchill. In the 1760s Hudson's Bay Company employees moored their boats in this cove; today it's a meadow.

Churchill is located in the subarctic, the meeting place of four biomes. In addition to the stunted spruce, tamarack, and other boreal species typical of this latitude, visitors can enjoy the unique marine, tundra, and taiga habitats. This mix of bioregions gives Churchill a great diversity of plants and animals.

Reaching the area is not a matter of loading up the station wagon and driving; no roads go to Churchill. You must travel by train or plane. Thompson, Manitoba, has the nearest railway station that can be reached by paved road, and it's a 23-hour ride from there. Many people come all the way from Winnipeg by train, a two-night journey. On the other hand, if you've got the money but not the time, you can fly from Winnipeg to Churchill in 2.5 hours on regularly scheduled flights (*flights more frequent during prime polar bear season*).

The Churchill area is defined by the activities that are available. It consists of some cultural and natural features right around the town; several dozen square miles of tundra and taiga that can be explored via a small network of paved and gravel roads; the Churchill River estuary and accessible areas of the Hudson Bay coastline, which can be visited by tour boats out of Churchill; and the westernmost parts of Cape Churchill Wildlife Management Area and Wapusk National Park. Huge, balloon-tire tundra vehicles that look like cousins to monster trucks provide tours to a small section of these wildlife protection areas.

What to See and Do

Start at the new **Parks Canada Visitor Centre** in Churchill's historic railway station, just off Kelsey Boulevard. The visitor center has information for the area in general and offers an in-depth look at the cultural and natural history of Wapusk National Park, as well as the area's historic fur trade. Be sure to learn about safe behavior in polar bear country before you venture out (see pp. 84–85).

Within a few blocks of the visitor center you can discover more about the area's rich cultural history at the **Eskimo Museum** (*242 LaVerendrye Ave. 204-675-2030*). Find out about local tour companies at the Chamber of Commerce booth located across from the Parks Canada Visitor Centre. For in-depth, multiday courses, contact the **Churchill Northern Studies Centre** (*P.O. Box 610, Churchill, MB R0B 0E0. 204-675-2307*). Although the center's primary purpose is to support Arctic research, it also mounts programs for laypersons about the Churchill area's main attractions: birds, the tundra, beluga whales, polar bears, and the northern lights.

Birding and Nature Trips

When spring rolls around—usually at the end of April—the birds begin arriving in Churchill. With them come bird-watchers, especially during the prime birding month of May. Some hard-core birders travel thousands of miles with the hope of seeing a Ross's gull. This small Arctic species, rare in North America, began nesting in the Churchill area in 1980.

Several operators run tours that cater to small groups of birders. In addition to the Ross's gull, you might see common eiders preening atop ice floes that float about the estuary and bay in the weeks following the late spring breakup of the pack ice. Near them you may spot ruddy turnstones bustling about the mudflats exposed by low tide, flipping small rocks and debris in search of food. Svelte gray arctic terns, having worked up an appetite by migrating from the tip of South America to get here, hover above the estuary watching for bite-size fish.

Birders also chase their quarry right out onto the water. Local outfits will take people on two- or three-hour boat trips to watch seabirds at sea level. These tours often give equal time to other members of the natural community, such as seals. You may see harbor seals sunning themselves near the river's mouth, bearded

A Chilling Warmth

Polar bears gather near Churchill in October and November, anticipating the formation of pack ice on Hudson Bay. A decade or two from now, however, the bears might not gather until December or later. Eventually pack ice might not form on the bay at all—and the polar bears could vanish into the high Arctic, or wherever suitable habitat remains.

The agent of these potential changes is global warming. According to a paper by Peter Scott, Scientific Coordinator for the Churchill Northern Studies Centre, global warming will hit northern climes earliest and hardest.

The cold, dense air called the Arctic air mass, which largely produces the northern climate, is expected to warm up and shrink, perhaps even disappear. This change will ripple through the Arctic, altering other age-old rhythms such as the migration of caribou and the flowering of tundra plants. Established food chains will be significantly disrupted.

The North could be affected more than most southern areas because for much of the year it is covered by snow and sea ice, which reflect sunlight into space. As that snow and ice cover less area for a shorter time, the surface will absorb more heat and warm more quickly, reducing snow and sea ice even further.

Warming in the North could have drastic consequences for the rest of the world. Scientists estimate that northern peatlands store up to 30 percent of the Earth's surface carbon. If warming affects the ability of peat to store carbon—if, for example, there were more peat fires, which would release carbon in the form of methane into the atmosphere—the planet's energy balance could be disrupted.

Common carrier: a floatplane

seals cruising through the water, or ring seals hauled out on ice floes.

Some tour companies run general nature trips. **Cape Merry National Historic Site,** the point of land on the east side of the mouth of the Churchill River, has beautiful views of the Hudson Bay and the mouth of the river. Take a close look at the abundant lichens that brighten the site. The color of the setting sun, the orange star lichen requires more than a thousand years to grow to the size of a quarter—so avoid stepping on it, or on any of the delicate flowers that grow here.

Tundra

Whether with a tour or on your own in a rental vehicle, you might want to leave the waterside and drive a few miles into the tundra in the warm months. Tundra is characterized by ground-hugging vegetation. Permafrost—permanently frozen ground—underlies most tundra and stops water from percolating through the soil. As a result, ponds, bogs, and lakes dot the land, and the low ground areas are generally soggy.

The best place to see the tundra is along the main road that leads east 16 miles (26 km) from Churchill to the Churchill Northern Studies Centre and the Churchill Research Range. Wildflowers—including the Lapland rosebay, a member of the rhododendron family; white mountain aven; and grass-of-Parnassus—bask in the sun throughout the short, intense summer. You might spot wildlife, though it's well camouflaged. If you see a pudgy little rodent scurry across the road, it's probably a lemming—and, no, they don't really commit mass suicide by running off cliffs.

The tundra also teems with birds. If you scope the ground with binoculars, you may see parasitic jaegers, willow ptarmigan, Canada geese, plover, and whimbrels.

Sea Canaries

While you're at Cape Merry looking for that common eider, you may spot a sea canary. No, it's not another bird. "Sea canary" is a nickname for the beluga whale. Belugas earned this nickname by being among the world's most

Windswept conifers in frozen landscape of Churchill

vocal cetaceans. Even while standing on Cape Merry's shoreline rocks you may hear the belugas breathe through their blow holes and chirp, whistle, and squeal as they communicate with one another. But they are best heard on board a tour boat equipped with hydrophones. Belugas have been known to take the mike into their mouths before calling. Sea canaries indeed!

Belugas migrate to the Churchill River estuary for warmth, breeding and calving, and food. They start gathering in the estuary by mid- to late June, depending on when the ice breaks up. By mid-July some 3,000 of these snow white, 16-foot-long mammals throng the river between its mouth and Mosquito Point, 7 miles (11 km) upriver. Their numbers then dwindle until the end of August.

Great White Bear

At last, late in the year, when an autumnal chill enters the air, it's polar bear season. Actually, the great white bears start coming ashore in the Churchill area in late June or July, when their preferred habitat—the pack ice on Hudson Bay—breaks up. But they're widely scattered during the summer, so polar bear viewing season doesn't really kick in until around the beginning of October, by which time hundreds of the bears have congregated in sections of **Cape**

Churchill Wildlife Management Area and **Wapusk National Park** close to Churchill.

This exceptional concentration of polar bears stems largely from two factors.

First, the pack ice near Churchill usually is among the last to melt each summer, so bears gather there in order to stay offshore and feed longer. When the late-melting ice finally disappears, the bears swim to the area near Churchill, the nearest shore.

Second, polar bears are creatures of habit. They typically return to Churchill because that is where they were born and raised. The western Hudson Bay population, centered around Churchill,

numbers between 1,000 and 1,200.

Seeing polar bears in the wild is thrilling—under the wrong circumstances, *too* thrilling. The world's largest terrestrial carnivore, the polar bear can reach a height of more than 11 feet (18 m) and a weight exceeding 1,500 pounds (680 kg); an average male in the Churchill area tips the scales at about 850 pounds (385 kg). The polar bear is fast, fearless, powerful, and can slip across the tundra as quietly as a snake. It has good hearing, sharp eyes, and an excellent sense of smell. And much more so than the black bear or grizzly bear, the polar bear is very curious—and has been known to stealthily approach people.

You needn't be afraid to visit the Churchill area if you follow the rules. Manitoba Conservation has developed a polar bear safety program and no one has been killed by a bear for almost 20 years. But government efforts alone aren't sufficient; visitors also must do their part by reading and following the safety literature and discussing the matter with Parks Canada staff and locals.

For most of the year, and especially during late autumn, you need to observe standard bear country precautions (see pp. 84-85), such as making noise to avoid surprising bears and never running away from a bear. But polar bears require additional measures. Never go walking alone. Don't even drive down back roads without carrying a cell phone or letting someone know where you're going, because if your vehicle breaks down you shouldn't walk back for help.

The easiest way to see polar bears safely is to take an organized trip. In the fall, tour companies take people into the heart of polar bear habitat aboard tundra vehicles. From these massive vehicles, which carry dozens of passengers high above the ground, you can see as many as 20 bears in a day. During the height of the season, each buggy typically has several bears to itself. There's even a mobile motel holding more than 30 people that parks overnight in polar bear country. ■

Northern Lights

The northern lights, or aurora borealis, begin and end each year's cycle of natural events in Churchill. Nature's scintillating light show can take place in any season; above Churchill, it occurs about 300 nights a year. But winter—say, January or February—is the best time to view it because it's dark for most of each 24-hour day. Some Churchill outfits offer special (i.e., warm) viewing facilities.

Churchill earns its reputation as one of the best places in the world for aurora-watching for several reasons. It is remote and lacking in light pollution, its winter skies are often clear, and it is located under the Northern Hemisphere's auroral oval—a ring of auroral activity around the north geomagnetic pole.

As you gaze skyward on a February night, watching the undulating greenish white lights, you may wonder about their origin. The phenomenon starts 93 million miles away. Explosions on the sun hurl charged particles into the solar system, where they travel along magnetic field lines toward the planets in an outpouring known as the solar wind. In a day or two this star-born breeze reaches Earth, where some of the charged particles rain down along the planet's geomagnetic field lines. As they collide with molecules in the uppermost atmosphere, the particles glow. It is this shimmering light display—in the form of red, yellow, blue, and green sheets, curtains, or ribbons—that we admire as the northern lights in the winter skies over Churchill.

The Thelon

■ Eastern Northwest Territories/western Nunavut, 200-400 miles (320-640 km) northeast of Yellowknife ■ Best months July–mid-Sept. ■ Primitive camping, canoeing, fishing, wildlife viewing ■ Access by boat or plane only ■ Contact NWT Arctic Tourism, Box 610, Yellowknife, NT X1A 2N5; phone 800-661-0788, 867-873-5007, or 867-873-7200. www.nwttravel.nt.ca

THE THELON IS NOT A PRECISELY DEFINED AREA, which is an indication of its isolation and wildness. It is anchored by the **Thelon River,** which runs some 600 miles from Whitefish Lake, in the Northwest Territories, to Baker Lake, in Nunavut. Its centerpiece is the enormous **Thelon Wildlife Sanctuary.** But the Thelon extends beyond the river and the sanctuary to embrace undetermined millions of acres of subarctic tundra.

Yellowknife is the gateway to the Thelon. You will need to arrange transportation, logistical support, and probably guides through a tour company. Trips typically last from one to two weeks and involve either a river journey or a flight in a bush plane to a remote camp, which serves as a base for exploring the area by foot, boat, and plane.

Once there, you will see tundra and boreal forest oases that teem with life, including caribou, musk-oxen, grizzlies, moose, and white-coated tundra wolves, sometimes with pups. All this in an unspoiled landscape of big-sky vistas and utter solitude. ■

Bathurst Inlet

■ Northwest Nunavut, 360 miles (580 km) northeast of Yellowknife ■ Best months late June–late July ■ Hiking, boating, canoeing, fishing, wildlife viewing, flight-seeing ■ Access by plane only ■ Contact Bathurst Inlet Lodge, P.O. Box 820, Yellowknife, NT X1A 2N6; phone 867-873-2595 or 867-920-4330. www.bathurstarctic.com

THIRTY MILES NORTH OF THE ARCTIC CIRCLE, Bathurst Inlet carves a deep notch in the Arctic coast of Nunavut. During its brief but intense summer, the hills erupt with arctic poppies, white mountain avens, and purple arctic lupine—some 120 species of wildflowers in all. Yellow-billed and red-throated loons, eider ducks, and tundra swans join ringed seals in the inlet's clear waters, while peregrine falcons, golden eagles, and rough-legged hawks nest on the cliffs. Caribou and musk-oxen graze the hills, and wolves and grizzlies make an occasional appearance. Ice-cold rivers roar into spectacular waterfalls; 161-foot-high (49 m) **Wilberforce Falls** on the Hood River is the highest falls north of the Arctic Circle.

Any visit to this remote location will likely involve the renowned **Bathurst Inlet Lodge.** Located at the head of the bay, the lodge partners with the local Inuit community to offer various ecotourism experiences. ■

Wood Buffalo National Park

■ 11 million acres ■ Southern Northwest Territories/northern Alberta, 100 miles (161 km) southeast of Hay River ■ Best months June–mid-Sept. (fewer biting insects late Aug.–Sept.) ■ Camping, hiking, boating, canoeing, wildlife viewing ■ Contact the park, Box 750, Fort Smith, NT X0E 0P0; phone 867-872-7900. www.parkscanada.gc.ca/buffalo

THERE'S A LOT MORE TO WOOD BUFFALO PARK than wood buffalo. The park is five times larger than Yellowstone, making it the largest national park in Canada and the second largest in the world (Greenland National Park is bigger). No wonder it can easily contain one of the world's largest free-roaming bison herds (they're not really "buffalo"), some 2,500 strong. Incidentally, these animals aren't the wood bison suggested in the park's name, but a hybrid between wood bison and plains bison.

What are bison of any sort doing up here in the far north? A peninsula of northern boreal plains, the northernmost extension of the Great Plains, juts up into the region's taiga. These boreal plains are a flat jigsaw puzzle of muskeg, shallow lakes and bogs, winding creeks, and typical boreal forest of spruce, jack pine, poplar, aspen, and balsam fir. Three major rivers curve through the park; two, the Peace and Athabasca, form a huge and tremendously productive delta in the southeast part of Wood Buffalo. One of the largest inland freshwater deltas in the world, it attracts migratory birds from all four North American flyways.

Most visitors approach the park from the north, via Hwy. 5 (gravel), which runs across the northeast section of Wood Buffalo to Fort Smith. This small town just east of the park houses park headquarters and the visitor center. Pine Lake Road (gravel) runs into the park from Fort Smith and Parson's Lake Road (sand; inaccessible when wet) connects Pine Lake Road to Highway 5—and that's it for vehicle access. The vast majority of this remote wilderness is available only to experienced backcountry travelers or to visitors led by a guide.

What to See and Do

Much of your visit to Wood Buffalo will center around Hwy. 5. Though encountering the free-roaming bison herd is far from guaranteed, there is a fair chance of seeing these Great Plains icons along this route. In fact, sometimes they'll be right on the road. If so, stop at a safe distance and wait patiently; never nudge them out of the way with your vehicle. Don't honk your car horn. Never approach bison on foot, either. Be especially cautious during the rut, starting around mid-July, when bulls get particularly irascible.

In addition to woolly walls of bison, several interpretive pullouts may entice you to stop along Hwy. 5. Just inside the park's north entrance is the **Angus Fire Tower and Day-use Area.** This pullout

Aurora borealis above Wood Buffalo's Salt Plains

Bison

features a sinkhole with interpretive signs. Such sinkholes—along with underground streams, solution valleys, salt flats, and saline streams—typify karst topography. Because Wood Buffalo is flat and has porous bedrock, most water seeps into the ground instead of flowing away in surface streams. The water slowly dissolves the bedrock, especially where it meets highly soluble gypsum (the pale mineral found in plasterboard). This forms underground caves, which sometimes collapse to create sinkholes. The park has some of the finest gypsum karst landforms in North America—one of the reasons why the United Nations bestowed World Heritage status on the park.

Another factor in gaining World Heritage status is evident at a pullout about midway between the north entrance and Fort Smith. The **Whooping Crane Pullout** celebrates the fact that Wood Buffalo is the last remaining natural nesting area for the endangered whooping crane. Don't expect to spot the elusive whoopers, though, because their nesting grounds lie far removed from the road. You will see many other typical boreal birds in the park.

Turn south on Parson's Lake Road shortly before reaching Fort Smith and you can take in yet another unusual natural phenomenon. Proceed a few miles to the **Salt Plains Viewpoint.** From atop a steep escarpment, you look across a blindingly white salt flat. Deposited by cold, salty mineral springs, the salt has formed mounds where the spring water reaches the surface. A quarter-mile-long (0.4 km) trail leads steeply down to the salt plains.

Back on Hwy. 5, drive to Fort Smith and check out the exhibits at the visitor center. Then head back into the park on Pine Lake Road. Just inside the boundary, stop at the **Salt River Day-use Area,** which serves as the hub for several day hikes. The **Karstland Loop,** a half-mile (0.8 km) interpretive path, visits some excellent examples of karst landforms. In one caved-in spot, red-sided garter snakes have established the northernmost hibernaculum of this beautiful and harmless species.

This Place Is Bugged!

You're cocooned in your sleeping bag when one of the most dreaded sounds in the great outdoors reaches your ears: the whine of an approaching mosquito. You can remind yourself that mosquitoes and other biting insects play an essential role in the web of life, but that's small comfort when a mozzie is sucking your blood at three in the morning. And when the bugs are out in droves—a distinct possibility in Western Canada—they can easily mar or sabotage an entire vacation.

It therefore makes sense to consider the pesky critters while planning your trip. The first step in solving the problem is simply to avoid it whenever possible. Close encounters with biting insects vary greatly depending on location, time of year, elevation, and other factors. Contact the place you plan to visit and find out when black flies, no-see-ums, and other six-legged tormentors usually hatch in the area—and how long they persist in bothersome numbers. Ask about specific sites in the area, too; you'll want to know if the campground you fancy is next to a marsh that doubles as a mosquito hatchery.

If you can't avoid the biting insects—during spring and summer, at least some of these critters occupy most of western Canada—you'll have to get along with them. But before you reach for the repellent, consider that appropriate clothing—loose-fitting long-sleeved shirts, long pants, hats—usually suffice. Where the bugs are swarming, try a head net.

If you're compelled to break out the bug spray, note that repellents without some DEET (N, N-diethyl-metatoluamide) don't work well on many insects. Be careful, though, because improper DEET usage may lead to health concerns. To stay on the safe side, be sure to follow the repellent's directions for use.

For a longer and moderately vigorous hike, take the 4.6-mile **North Loop,** which climbs to the top of an escarpment for fine views of **Salt Pan Lake** and the countryside.

Continue down Pine Lake Road to the **Pine Lake Recreation Area,** about 40 miles (65 km) from Fort Smith. Here in the boreal forest you'll find the park's only road-accessible campground plus opportunities for swimming, boating, and canoeing.

Walk some or all of the easy, 4-mile (6.4 km) round-trip **Lakeside Trail** and you'll get a good look at **Pine Lake,** formed by five clustered sinkholes and fed by underground springs.

At the southern tip of the lake, about halfway along the Lakeside Trail, you can turn off onto the **Lane Lake Trail.** This goes deep into the forest along a chain of small sinkhole lakes, where you may spot beavers, loons, ducks, and shorebirds. Measured from the start of the Lakeside Trail on Kettle Point Road, the Lane Lake Trail is 16 miles (26 km) round-trip. If you like, you can also drive to the end of Pine Lake Road, where **Peace Point** overlooks the Peace River. ▪

Nahanni National Park Reserve

■ 1.1 million acres ■ Southwest Northwest Territories, 150 miles (241 km) west of Fort Simpson ■ Best months mid-June–mid-Sept. ■ Primitive camping, hiking, rafting, kayaking, canoeing, flight-seeing ■ Adm. fee ■ Access by float-plane ■ Contact the park, Box 348, Fort Simpson, NT X0E 0N0; phone 867-695-3151. www.parkscanada.gc.ca/nahanni

In 1978, Nahanni National Park Reserve appeared on the first list of World Heritage sites. That tells you something about the natural virtues of a land with colossal waterfalls, the largest tufa (mineral deposit) mounds in Canada, 3,300-foot-deep (1,000 m) limestone canyons, hot springs, alpine tundra, and abundant wildlife—including grizzly bears, trumpeter swans, wolves, and caribou.

One of Nahanni's virtues—and one of its drawbacks—is its remote-

Backpackers hiking above Ram Canyon

ness. Almost everyone enters the park by chartered floatplane. These charters fly out of several regional communities, including Fort Simpson and Yellowknife; make sure the operators have a national park license. You can go in for the day to **Virginia Falls,** where the **South Nahanni River** drops 300 feet (91 m)—a plunge one and a half times that of Niagara Falls. A 20-minute stroll takes you to a viewpoint on the cliffs.

Most people explore the park by paddling the South Nahanni River in canoes, kayaks, or rafts. These voyages last from 7 to 21 days, depending on your put-in and take-out sites. Unless you're an experienced river runner, go with a licensed outfitter. You must reserve ahead of time, and you'll also need to register and de-register your trip.

As you drift along, you'll pass through gorgeous mountain valleys and beneath towering limestone cliffs. Watch for Dall's sheep on the slopes, moose along the shore, and golden eagles overhead. At several places you can land and hike into the wilderness. ■

Following pages: Virginia Falls

Dempster Highway Scenic Drive

■ Northern Yukon and northwest Northwest Territories, 457 miles (735 km) from Klondike Hwy. to Inuvik ■ Camping, hiking, canoeing, fishing, bird-watching, wildlife viewing, auto tour, northern lights ■ Best months June–mid-Sept. ■ Through traffic impossible during freeze-up and thaw; for travel conditions call 800-661-0750. www.gov.nt.ca/transportation/hwyinfo/index.html ■ Contact Tourism Yukon, Box 2703, Whitehorse, YT Y1A 2C6, phone 867-667-3540 or -5036, www.touryukon.com; or NWT Arctic Tourism, Box 610, Yellowknife, NT X1A 2N5, phone 867-873-5007 or 800-661-0788, www.nwttravel.nt.ca.

DRIVE TO THE ARCTIC? That sounds as likely as swimming to Mount Everest. But since 1979, one public road in Canada—the Dempster Hwy.—has beckoned drivers into the remote beauty of the far north. The Dempster carries motorists more than 200 miles (320 km) beyond the Arctic Circle and ends within 40 miles (64 km) of the Arctic Ocean, allowing travelers to experience an exotic realm usually accessible only to adventurers in bush planes and canoes.

Many people imagine the Arctic as an icy, lifeless plain. But a journey along the Dempster reveals a rich and varied landscape. You'll see lush river valleys, mountains, muskegs (bogs), "drunken" forests of stunted spruce growing at gravity-defying angles, and wide expanses of tundra—the area above tree line where many plants grow but few rise above your knees.

Nearly uninhabited and little developed, the land embracing the Dempster nurtures considerable wildlife; the scarcity of trees often makes the critters easy to spot. Depending on the season, alert visitors almost surely will see moose and arctic ground squirrels; you're likely to see grizzly bears, arctic hare, caribou, hoary marmots, and collared pikas; and you may spot wolves, red foxes, beavers, and Dall's sheep.

Some of the Dempster's more than 150 bird species include golden eagle, northern hawk-owl, tundra and trumpeter swans, peregrine falcon, arctic tern, and red-throated loon; many birds migrate to the tundra and boreal forest to breed and feed in the summer, and a few hardy species live there year-round.

What to See and Do

Getting Ready

Before you leave, you need to prepare for this road; this is not the Trans-Canada. The Dempster's remoteness magnifies mishaps. There are only two little settlements at which you can get a tire fixed, a windshield replaced, or buy gas and food. An incident that would be a minor annoyance at home is a major inconvenience along the Dempster Hwy.

The term "highway" is in fact a bit generous for this gravel road. The surface isn't badly rutted; plenty of people take passenger cars on the Dempster (a rare few even ride bikes), but rugged vehicles can be reassuring. You can drive 40 to 50 mph (65 to 80

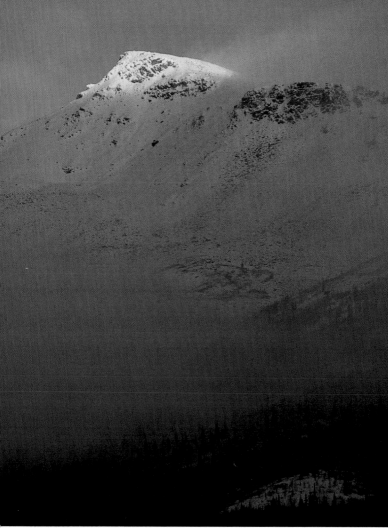

View of Ogilvie Mountains from Dempster Highway

kmph) most of the time, but on some stretches and in bad weather your speed will drop to half that—notably when it rains and the highway gets slick.

Fortunately, it doesn't rain much along the Dempster; most precipitation falls during winter as snow. However, even after that melts off—typically in June—you may encounter snow along mountainous portions of the road. More typically, summer temperatures climb into the 60s and 70s, and the Dempster is dusty. The dust can be

slippery, too; avoid sudden turns or abrupt stops.

Some hardy souls tour the Dempster during the winter. This sounds insane, but winter aficionados note some advantages: You get to see the northern lights at their brightest; you can continue from the end of the Dempster north 108 miles (175 km) to Tuktoyaktuk and the Arctic Ocean on seasonal ice roads; and, according to some people, the driving conditions are better.

There's not a lot of daylight in

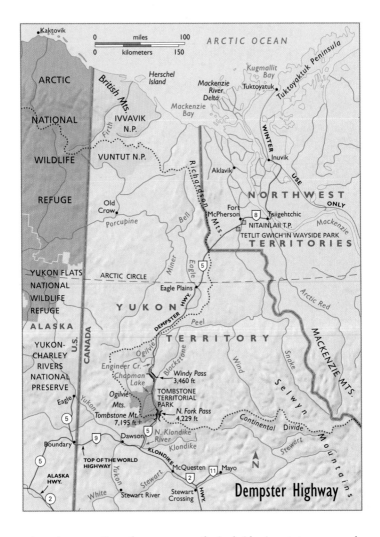

winter, however. Few others are out on the highway to help in an emergency, and the cold and winds can be extreme. For these reasons, don't attempt a winter tour without getting advice from Dempster veterans.

At two times of year no one can drive the length of the Dempster. During thaw and freeze-up, car ferries can't cross the two rivers that interrupt the highway—and the ice bridge is not strong enough to drive on. Breakup ordinarily lasts from late May to early June and freeze-up from early October to early November (check with highway department for road conditions).

Fill up with gas before you start, and fill up again whenever you get the chance—which won't be often. Drive with your headlights on; it's safer and it's the law.

Spruce bog, Tombstone Territorial Park

Pick the best pair of tire tracks on the road, even when it's in the middle (often the case), and follow that path; this keeps you out of the sharp, tire-eating shale that sometimes covers other parts of the highway. If the shale gets you anyway, check your spare tire before leaving—and make sure you bring a second spare. When another car approaches (every 20 minutes, on average), slow down while you're still in that smooth track, then ease over to your side of the road.

Having heeded this litany of warnings, it may surprise you to learn that you can drive the Dempster Hwy. in a single, long day. (This is especially true in mid-summer, with its 24 hours of daylight north of the Arctic Circle.) But don't. Devote at least two days for each way and soak up this rarely visited landscape.

Take advantage of the numerous pullouts and overlooks and the nearly infinite number of wide spots in the road. Stop the car and stand outside in the stillness. Perhaps you may opt to take a short stroll out onto the tundra or along a creek. If you know how to navi-

gate through trackless wilderness, you can use the highway as a jumping-off point for backcountry hikes and canoe trips.

Lodging is available in Eagle Pass or Fort McPherson, or you can pitch a tent at one of several campgrounds. There's plenty of lodging at the end of the road in Inuvik, where you can rest up before your drive home. Or you can leave the planning to someone else entirely: Take the biweekly bus to Inuvik, or take a guided tour of the Dempster.

Along the North Klondike River

The drive begins at the southern terminus of the Dempster Hwy., where it meets the Klondike Hwy. 25 miles (40 km) east of Dawson. Unofficially called Dempster Corner, this intersection is occupied by a gas station/garage, a motel, and a restaurant. You won't find another gas station for 230 miles (370 km) as you head north on the Dempster. (The following description of the drive gives distances in both miles and kilometers, but uses the Dempster Hwy. kilometer markers as points of reference.)

Boreal forest ablaze with autumnal color, Campbell Lake, South of Inuvik

The highway starts along the North Klondike River, passing through the poplar, spruce, and birch that blanket this river valley. Watch for moose feeding in the backwaters and bald eagles perched above, scanning for fish. You'll cross creek after creek running down from the **Ogilvie Mountains,** which shoulder their way into the horizon 15 miles (24 km) or so ahead.

Soon you'll rise into the Ogilvies where, around kilometer marker 67, the road climbs close to tree line and patches of tundra begin to appear. Grizzlies occasionally show up on the slopes above the highway, though rarely are these footloose predators are rarely predictable *(in general, keep your distance from them and from all wildlife).*

A couple of miles later you'll reach the craggy **Tombstone Range,** the most dramatic mountains along the Dempster. Unlike other mountains along the Dempster, the Tombstones are composed of igneous rock. About 92 million years ago, molten rock gushed up through the sedimentary materials that predominate in this region and hardened into granite. Erosion then carved away the softer sedimentary rock over time, leaving behind the dark granitic peaks you see today.

Tombstone Territorial Park

To start an exploration of the Tombstones, turn off just before kilometer 72 at the Dempster Interpretive Centre *(June–early Sept.)* and campground for 535,000-acre Tombstone Territorial Park. Interpreters staff the modest visitor center during the summer and conduct campground talks and guided hikes. The campground rests in a wooded area by the banks of the North Klondike and offers an easy, half-mile (0.8 km) trail from the back of the campground near the river. Watch for moose, beavers, and bears.

The interpretive staff can recommend many longer outings that lead from the forested valley bottoms up to the open alpine tundra on the hills and mountains. Though these are cross-country routes, the openness of the terrain makes navigation relatively easy; visitors with a modicum of outdoor skills can manage the shorter hikes. Bear in mind that cross-country travel, even on the open slopes where most vegetation hugs the ground, generally is much slower than walking on a trail. In fact, it is frequently easier to hike when the ground is still partially frozen *(as in late May)* than during peak summer days.

As you continue north on the Dempster, you'll be in Tombstone Territorial Park for about the next 30 miles (48 km), until just past Chapman Lake. After ascending 1 mile (1.6 km) from the visitor center, you can stop at an overlook and gaze at **Tombstone Mountain** itself, the park's highest at 7,195 feet (2,193 m). Tombstone Mountain reigns over the upper **North Klondike River Valley,** which spreads out beautifully below this pullout.

From the overlook, the highway keeps climbing for the next 5 miles (8 km) until it reaches **North Fork Pass Summit.** Here, at the highest point of the Dempster Hwy., you're astride the Continental Divide; water on the south side flows into the Yukon River system and ends up in the Pacific Ocean, whereas water on the north side flows into the Mackenzie River system and ends up in the Arctic Ocean.

At 4,229 feet (1,289 m), North Fork Pass lies above timberline, in the tundra. Normally found a couple of hundred miles farther north, this high-Arctic-like tundra exists here due not only to the elevation but also to the shape of the land, which funnels frigid polar air through the area. Most of the plants stay within 6 inches of the ground, where it's warmer. Beneath that ground lies permafrost—a layer of soil that never thaws.

Permafrost makes life tough for plants. For example, roots can't penetrate the frozen ground, so tundra plants must make do with shallow root systems. But the moist, nutrient-rich soil produces miniature shrubs—lowbush cranberry, Labrador tea, and bearberry—and wildflowers such as moss campion and sweet coltsfoot (*flowers peak late June–early July*). Without trees and tall bushes, the tundra offers long views and a liberating sense of openness. Golden eagles, finding this openness conducive to hunting, are often sighted gliding above the pass.

From North Fork Pass the Dempster stays high for about the next 28 miles (45 km). At kilometer 71.5 the highway crosses the **East Fork Blackstone River** and then follows this waterway through the wide-open spaces of the **Blackstone Uplands.** Slow down and keep your eyes open, for these uplands teem with wildlife. Woodland caribou, members of the Hart River herd, can often be seen in the summer as they graze on grasses and sedges. Grizzlies also roam the rolling tundra in the summer and fall, munching berries and digging for roots and arctic ground squirrels.

Many people come to the Blackstone Uplands just to see the birds. Positioned near the dividing line between the Arctic tundra to the north and the boreal forest to the south, the uplands feature species from both zones. You may see a plump willow ptarmigan strolling beside the road, a red-throated loon paddling about in one of the small lakes, or a male snow bunting, resplendent in black-and-white breeding plumage, warbling away.

You'll see even more birds if you pull over and carefully scan the tundra, where nesting birds may be sitting quietly, trying to be inconspicuous. With a single

Tundra Moose

The largest subspecies of moose on the continent, the tundra moose (also called the Alaska or Yukon moose) measures up to 7 feet (2 m) at the shoulder and weighs as much as 1,800 pounds. In summer, you'll typically spot these impressive mammals in the shallow water of ponds and lakes, dunking for aquatic plants. You can identify the bull moose by their size and broad, palmlike antlers, which they shed every winter—only to grow a larger pair each spring.

sweep of the binoculars you may spot long-tailed jaegers, American golden plover, and whimbrels.

At kilometer 102 pull off and spend some time on the wooden deck overlooking **Two Moose Lake.** As the name implies, you may indeed see moose here: to be precise, the big "tundra" moose subspecies, munching on pond weed, their favorite repast.

Many other creatures thrive here and in other, similar lakes in the uplands. At the base of the

whirligigs, sharply dressed in their russet-tan-black-and-white summer plumage, swirl atop the lake near the platform. They swim about crazily, changing course every second, frantically stabbing the water with their bills as they gobble up insects.

As you continue through the Blackstone Uplands, you'll pass more lakes. They lack observation platforms, yet each harbors its fair hare of moose and birds. **Chapman Lake,** at kilometer 116, is the

Porcupine, denizen of the Yukon

bountiful food chain is a rich algal bloom that occurs each spring and summer. Another vital link in the chain is the multitude of bugs that swarms over the lake—a boon to avians but a blight to humans.

Some 30 species of waterbirds use the lake and surrounding area, including bright white tundra swans, trumpeter swans, Canada geese, many duck species, and a host of shorebirds, such as the hyperactive red-necked phalarope. Knots of these blackbird-size

largest lake on the Dempster. Loons often nest on its little island. A famous migrant, the barren-ground caribou (see sidebar p. 269), also passes this way—and along other parts of the Dempster—from October to April.

Windy Pass & Ogilvie River

Around kilometer 130 the highway starts gradually rising from the uplands toward 3,460-foot (1,055 m) **Windy Pass,** which awaits at kilometer 154. At first glance the pass looks barren, but botanists and lepidopterists could happily spend months here because the area brims with rare Beringian endemics. During the last great ice age, when the rest of Canada and much of the Northern Hemisphere lay beneath vast sheets of ice, Beringia—composed of eastern Siberia, the land bridge that today lies under the Bering Strait, Alaska, and much of the Yukon from here west—escaped the era's frozen touch. It is estimated that more than 50 species of butterflies can be spotted within a 2-mile circle. Species such as Eversmann's Parnassian butterfly have survived from the last ice age until now, inhabiting Windy Pass and other sites along the Dempster.

North of Windy Pass the highway leaves the Blackstone River drainage and moves into the Ogilvie-Peel watershed, starting with several miles along **Engineer Creek.** Especially from kilometer 170 to 180, note the strong red color of the soil—the result of iron oxide—in and around the creek.

Erosion pillars decorate many hills along the road. As one of the unglaciated areas of Canada, the landscape before you was shaped by wind and water, not ice. If this area strikes your fancy, pull over at **Engineer Creek Campground** at kilometer 194. Train your binoculars on nearby **Sapper Hill** and look for peregrine falcons and golden eagles, but please do not hike here: Most arctic birds are ground nesters.

Just past the campground, Engineer Creek and the Dempster join the **Ogilvie River** and head north amid hills marked by rock towers and stony fins. At kilometer 244 the road climbs up and away from the river and runs along the spine of a high ridge to the **Ogilvie Ridge Viewpoint,** at kilometer 259. You can see far to the north and east, across the braided waterways of the Ogilvie and Peel Rivers to the Richardson Mountains and lands north of the Arctic Circle.

Closer at hand—right at your feet, to be exact—lies more tundra. Note that it's not really treeless. Contorted miniature spruces dot the landscape, their upper branches—which protrude above the snow in winter—scarred by wind-driven ice crystals.

Eagle Plains

Five miles (8 km) past the viewpoint the highway descends slightly and starts across the high, wavy hills of the Eagle Plains. Once again above tree line, travelers get a top-of-the-world sensation as they curve along to the Eagle Plains Hotel *(867-993-2453),* at kilometer 369 the midpoint of the drive. You can get a room, park a trailer, pitch a tent, eat in the restaurant, repair your tires, or launder your clothes—that's all optional. But everyone should fill up with gas at this oasis.

Leaving the hotel just north of Eagle River, you'll encounter one of the oddities of this remote highway as you suddenly find yourself driving down the middle of an airstrip. Don't worry. Though the Dempster occasionally widens to accommodate airplanes, planes rarely land here—and when they do, they go out of their way to avoid landing on travelers.

Over the next 20 miles (32 km)

Tombstone Mountain

the highway slowly rises from muskeg (bog) through drier, sparse forest until you return to the tundra. Soon thereafter, at kilometer 405.5, you arrive at latitude 66°, 33': the **Arctic Circle.**

From here north the sun never sets at the summer solstice and never rises at the winter solstice. One of several interpretive signs explains that, contrary to what many people think, the Arctic Circle does not divide Arctic tundra from boreal forest. Many factors influence the transition from forest to tundra. The dividing line cuts raggedly across Canada, dipping as far south as Manitoba and rising north almost to the Arctic Ocean. But here, at the crossing of the Arctic Circle, the elevation has defeated the trees and the long views are beautifully unobstructed.

From the Arctic Circle the road proceeds across the tundra on a raised berm. Within a few miles the highway narrows and sprouts more ruts and rocks, so you'll want

to slow down. You'd probably have slowed down anyway to watch a camouflaged flock of whimbrels eating their way across the tundra or a long-tailed jaeger raiding another bird's nest.

In fact, you may just want to stop, cut the engine, and let the spaciousness, the remoteness, the grand quiet wash over you. You can venture onto the tundra and feel its hummocky unevenness tugging at your ankles, its sponginess trampolining you slightly with each step. Or you can watch for intriguing things that you'd never notice from a moving car.

While driving, you may spot an arctic ground squirrel racing across the highway, but you won't see one feeding on foxtail barley unless you stop. What a show! Rushing to limit exposure to predators, a ground squirrel zooms into a stand of this foot-high grass and starts frantically gathering seeds. Grabbing the base of a barley stem with both paws, the squir-

Fox, Tombstone Territorial Park

rel puts its mouth over the bottom of the stem and quickly pulls the plant through its teeth, stripping the seed heads and jamming them into its cheeks. Then it bolts to the next foxtail barley and repeats the routine. After about five minutes, the squirrel's cheeks are hairy balloons that stretch from its face to the top of its front shoulders. Stuffed to the max, the arctic squirrel then hightails it—literally, with its black-tipped tail thrust stiffly into the air—back to its burrow.

Richardson Mountains

If you get addicted to the idea of stopping, the Rock River Campground, at kilometer 446, will accommodate you. From there the Dempster Hwy. continues across the tundra and climbs into the stark, weather-worn Richardson Mountains. At kilometer 465 the highway crosses into the Northwest Territories. Pull off at the interpretive displays and savor the mountain views. This, once again, is the Continental Divide.

For the next 15 miles (25 km) the Dempster winds through the burly Richardsons, flanked by the blue-black, rocky mountains, their bases a shower of fallen shale. Lower on the slopes the green summer tundra provides a fresh contrast to the dour mountaintops. Narrow creeks cut frothy white slices in the fabric of hillside and tundra. Arctic ground squirrels scurry about and the sky is alive with ravens, jaegers, and arctic terns—those indefatigable travelers that are at the northern end of their 11,000-mile migration from Antarctica.

Peel and Mackenzie Rivers

Around kilometer 490 the Dempster begins a 30-mile (48 km) descent to the **Peel River,** losing 2,300 feet (700 m) in elevation and changing dramatically in character: The mountains and tundra fade and, in the bottomlands, the boreal forest returns. Just 1.5 miles (2.4 km) from the Peel, at kilometer 536, tarry at **Tetlit Gwich'in Wayside Park** to enjoy the views of the Peel River Valley and the Mackenzie Delta (see pp. 270-72).

A mile and a half later, drive aboard the free government ferry

The Porcupine Herd

During the winter the region that includes the Dempster Hwy. hosts one of the world's great wildlife spectacles. Migrating from the edge of the Arctic Ocean, the Porcupine caribou, 123,000 strong, seek shelter in the boreal forest. As early as late September and as late as May, Dempster travelers see the animals along the highway between Chapman Lake (around kilometer 116) and the Northwest Territories border (around kilometer 465).

The Porcupine caribou are named for the Porcupine River of Yukon and Alaska. They use Alaska's Arctic National Wildlife Refuge (ANWR) as part of their calving ground—a central factor in the controversy around plans to drill for oil in ANWR.

Called the "deer of the north," these barren-ground caribou survive the harsh Arctic winters not only by migrating to the forest but by a variety of adaptations. A caribou's huge hooves, for example, seem to belong to an animal twice its size, but these clown feet serve as snowshoes. The hooves also have sharp edges that enable their owners to paw through hard-packed snow to reach the lichen that gets them through the winter. Heat-retaining hairs cover every part of a caribou, even its big hooves.

If you watch caribou quietly, you'll hear strange clicking noises coming from the herd. With each step a caribou takes, tendons rub across the bones of its foot, producing a loud, knuckle-cracking sound. Some scientists speculate that this allows the herd to stay together in snowstorms or fog. Indeed, no other member of the deer family hangs together like barren-ground caribou. Though the Porcupine caribou occupy a vast area, they tend to gather in enormous aggregations—as many as 80,000 in a single mass.

and chug across the Peel, bordered by a broad floodplain of muskeg. A mile (1.6 km) from the ferry lies **Nitainlaii Territorial Park,** which features a campground and a small visitor center. Four miles (6.4 km) from the park, the highway reaches the little town of Fort McPherson; here you can find food, gas, and tire repair—but you'll have to turn off the highway and drive into town for these services.

At kilometer 608 you come to the mighty **Mackenzie River** and at kilometer 613 the second ferry crossing. As you cross, you can choose to make a side trip to the tiny hamlet of Tsiigehtchic for a glimpse of Gwich'in life. Continue to the end of the Dempster, skirting the eastern edge of the vast Mackenzie Delta, where the river fractures into a maze of channels and islands before emptying into the Arctic Ocean. Here the terrain is a sprawl of drunken forest, though some uplands, creeks, and lakes offer relief.

Finally, at kilometer 736, you'll roll into **Inuvik** (the last few miles on paved road, no less). This 50-year-old hub of the far north marks the end of the Dempster Hwy., but Inuvik and environs are an adventure all their own (see pp. 270-72). ■

Mackenzie River Delta & Inuvik

■ 614 million acres ■ Northwest corner of Northwest Territories, on Arctic Ocean ■ Best months mid-May–mid-Sept. ■ Camping, hiking, canoeing, fishing, wildlife viewing, boat tour, flight-seeing ■ Contact NWT Arctic Tourism, Box 610, Yellowknife, NT X1A 2N5, phone 800-661-0788, 867-873-5007 or -5036, www.nwttravel.nt.ca; or Town of Inuvik Tourism, Box 1160, Inuvik, NT X0E 0T0, phone 867-777-4321 or -2607, www.town.inuvik.nt.ca

THE MACKENZIE RIVER FLOWS GRANDLY northwest across the Northwest Territories, pulling river after river into its embrace. The Mackenzie drains a fifth of Canada, making it the third largest watershed in the Western Hemisphere, exceeded only by the Amazon and Mississippi Rivers. As it approaches the Beaufort Sea and the Arctic Ocean, this immense mass of water fans out to create a delta 150 miles long and 60 miles across. Half of the delta is water—a labyrinth of broad channels, sinuous backwaters, lakes, and ponds. The other half consists of islands, green with spruce, willow, poplar, and horsetail. Because of the Mackenzie's relatively warm water, the delta is an oasis in these latitudes of Arctic tundra.

Exploring the delta is not easy. Only a few locals live here, fishing in summer and trapping in winter. But out-of-towners can fly to Inuvik, on the delta's eastern edge, from several Canadian or Alaskan cities. Or they can drive the Dempster Highway, then venture out on guided boat and airplane trips. Visitors can also explore the boreal forest around Inuvik.

Aerial view of Mackenzie River Delta

What to See and Do

Inuvik is the hub of the western Arctic. With a population of 3,500, it is the largest town for hundreds of miles around. You can start your exploration right in town. Check out the **Western Arctic Visitor Centre** *(867-777-4727. June-Sept.)*, which has displays on the natural and human history of the region. You might also ask at the Parks Canada office *(867-777-8800)* or the **Aurora Research Institute** *(867-777-3298)* to see if they're offering any programs or outings while you're in town.

Several hiking trails begin in town. Starting near the hospital on the east end of town, the **Jimmy Adams Peace Trail** follows the perimeter of **Boot Lake** for a couple of miles—it doesn't quite complete the circle, so hikers have to backtrack a bit. From the chamber of commerce in the middle of Inuvik, the **Midnight Sun Tundra Nature Hike** leads almost 4 miles (6.4 km) uphill to **Three Mile Lake,** passing through boreal forest and up into the tundra. Locals recommend that during the summer hikers take this trail late at night so they can witness the lowest arc of the never-setting midnight sun. A couple of miles southeast of town on the airport road lies **Chuk Park,** which features a campground, a canoe launch, and a quarter-mile (0.4 km) interpretive trail that introduces visitors to the northern boreal forest.

Chuk Park also has a viewing tower from which you can gaze upon hundreds of square miles of the Mackenzie Delta. You can see 80 miles (129 km) to the **Richardson Mountains,** which form the western boundary of the delta. To the north, however, no mountains limit the horizon; all you see is the green maze of the delta sliding over the Earth's curve toward the Arctic Ocean.

From Inuvik you can take a guided delta tour on a small boat. A typical trip lasts about four hours, starting from the town dock and heading south into the channels of the Mackenzie. In the course of the trip you may spot at least a dozen bald eagles, tundra swans, and other birds.

Local scientists figure that at least 100 species—more than 90 percent of them migratory—use the delta, but the area is so wild and little studied that no authoritative species list exists yet. If you're lucky you'll also spot muskrat, moose, red fox, and black bear. In July and August you'll meet so many mosquitoes whenever the boat stops that you'll always be thankful to get under way again.

If you want to visit the heart of the delta, during the summer you can take one of the daily flights out of Inuvik to the little settlement of **Aklavik.** The low-level flight lasts about 20 minutes (one-way) and provides a quick look at the delta. For a more in-depth experience, take a 2- to 3-hour boat ride to Aklavik, then fly back to Inuvik.

The most popular airplane outing from Inuvik takes visitors 80 miles north to Tuk, properly known as **Tuktoyaktuk,** a tiny Inuvialuit (western Arctic Inuit) community on the Arctic Ocean. The plane passes low over the eastern side of the delta and out onto the **Tuktoyaktuk Peninsula.** Though largely a cultural tour, natural attractions include the world's highest concentration of pingos (ice-core hills); a view of wildlife, including beluga whales, caribou, and swans; and a rare opportunity to swim in the Arctic Ocean—or, more commonly, to dip a toe into that frigid water. ■

Bearded seal, East Channel, Mackenzie River Delta

Aulavik National Park

■ 3 million acres ■ Northern Banks Island, Northwest Territories, about 500 miles (805 km) northeast of Inuvik ■ Best months mid-June–mid-Aug. ■ Primitive camping, hiking, kayaking, canoeing, fishing, wildlife viewing, wildflower viewing ■ Adm. fee ■ Remote wilderness travel; contact Parks Canada about extensive preparation and precautions ■ Contact Parks Canada Western Arctic Field Unit, P.O. Box 1840, Inuvik, NT X0E 0T0; phone 867-777-8800. www.parkscanada.gc.ca/aulavik

TIRED OF CROWDED NATIONAL PARKS? Try Aulavik. Teetering on the edge of North America, Aulavik National Park is larger than Yellowstone, yet it gets fewer visitors per year than a Yellowstone restaurant gets at lunchtime.

The gateway for Aulavik is Inuvik, the NWT town at the end of the Dempster Hwy. From there tour companies and air charter services can fly you to Aulavik, about 500 miles (805 km) northeast on the northern end of Banks Island, the westernmost island of the Arctic Archipelago. This is, to state the obvious, an exceedingly remote park. This means that visitors who are not veteran Arctic wilderness adventurers should go with a guided tour—and even then you should be fit and fairly experienced.

The eastern area of Aulavik is made up of badlands and canyons; the western portion has upland plateaus and rolling hills. The park lies at a higher latitude than the middle of Greenland, so the landscape is treeless, windswept, cold, and harsh. Arctic willow is the redwood of Aulavik, sometimes soaring to heights of more than 10 inches. Spring comes around mid-June and fall hits in early August, though the fact that the sun doesn't set between mid-May and late July makes highs in the 60s possible in midsummer. At any time of day or year, snow can fall and the temperature can plunge below freezing.

Once the tundra has dried out (around late June), the flat terrain and low vegetation make Aulavik moderately easy to hike, if you're accustomed to navigating trackless wilderness. Aulavik adds the danger—and it's a considerable one—of polar bears. These fearsome predators patrol the park's north coast and sometimes venture inland, so travelers must be alert and take precautions (see pp. 84–85).

Most visitors to Aulavik use the **Thomsen River** as their trail, putting in a canoe at either the park's southern boundary or at Green Cabin; it's about 112 miles (180 km) to **Castel Bay** on the coast from the former and about 75 miles (121 km) from the latter. Thought to be the world's northernmost navigable river, the Thomsen is an easygoing waterway that runs north up the middle of the park, which also is the lushest part of Aulavik. More than 150 species of flowering plants light up the tundra in summer. You may spot ptarmigan, geese on nests, and perhaps a dainty arctic fox. Occasionally the howls of arctic wolves reverberate across the landscape. Most notable of all are the musk-oxen. The population on Banks Island exceeds 65,000 (about 25 percent inside the park), making this the planet's largest concentration of the shaggy beasts. ■

Ivvavik National Park

■ 2.5 million acres   ■ Northwest Yukon, 120 miles (193 km) west of Inuvik
■ Best months mid-June–mid-Aug.   ■ Primitive camping, hiking, white-water
rafting and kayaking, fishing, wildlife viewing, wildflower viewing   ■ Adm. fee
■ Remote wilderness travel; contact Parks Canada about extensive preparation
and precautions   ■ Contact Parks Canada Western Arctic Field Unit, P.O. Box
1840, Inuvik, NT X0E 0T0; phone 867-777-8800. www.parkscanada.gc.ca/ivvavik

IVVAVIK MEANS "A PLACE FOR GIVING BIRTH, A NURSERY," in the language of
the Inuvialuit. Living up to that name, Ivvavik National Park serves as a
calving ground for many of the 123,000 barren-ground caribou that constitute the Porcupine herd (see sidebar p. 269). Located on the Yukon
North Slope about 120 miles (193 km) west of Inuvik, Ivvavik exhibits
a great variety of ecosystems, including mountains, river valleys, and a
coastal plain on the Arctic Ocean.

What to See and Do

To reach this remote park, take a tour or charter plane from Inuvik. Like Aulavik and Tuktut Nogait National Parks, Ivvavik is isolated and without amenities; unless you're an experienced Arctic out-doorsperson, go with a guided tour. Your party should register with the Parks Canada office in Inuvik before you leave and de-register upon your return.

Typically, visitors explore the park by rafting or kayaking down the 80 navigable miles of the **Firth River,** which flows from the park's southern end to the sea. Trips take anywhere from 4 to 14 days, putting in at Margaret Lake and taking out at Nanaluk Spit. River travelers must have considerable skill in order to negotiate the many Class III and Class IV rapids.

When they are not bashing through white water, kayakers and rafters can enjoy a visual feast of convoluted canyon walls, taiga (the scraggly transitional forest be-tween tundra and boreal forest), and tundra. Notably from late June to early July, brilliant wildflowers grace the surrounding tundra.

At certain times of the year *(notably first two weeks of July),* the Porcupine caribou cross the firth. You may also spot grizzlies, moose, gyrfalcons, wolves, and snowy owls. Near the end of the trip, as the firth winds through the coastal plain, you're likely to see musk-oxen and perhaps even polar bears (preferably at a safe distance), though the latter generally don't come ashore until winter. Smaller tundra mammals include lem-mings and the remarkable singing vole, whose high-pitched trill can be heard across the tundra.

Smaller still, but far more an-noying, are mosquitoes. Especially during July, bring insect repellent and bug-resistant clothing (see sidebar p. 253). ■

Rafting Firth River's Sheep Creek Canyon

Springtime melt of aufeis (overflow ice)

Tuktut Nogait National Park

■ 4 million acres ■ Northern Northwest Territories, 275 miles (443 km) east of Inuvik ■ Best months mid-June–mid-Aug. ■ Primitive camping, hiking, kayaking, canoeing, bird-watching, wildlife viewing ■ Adm. fee ■ Remote wilderness travel; contact Parks Canada about extensive preparation and precautions ■ Contact Parks Canada Western Arctic Field Unit, P.O. Box 1840, Inuvik, NT X0E 0T0; phone 867-777-8800. www.parkscanada.gc.ca/tuktutnogait

LIKE IVVAVIK, TUKTUT NOGAIT NATIONAL PARK was established in large part to protect the calving grounds of caribou, in this case the 80,000-head Bluenose West herd. Also like Ivvavik (see pp. 274-75), Tuktut Nogait offers much more to visitors than that wild herd.

Tuktut Nogait lies about 275 miles (443 km) east of Inuvik. Travelers can fly from Inuvik directly to the park or to the hamlet of Paulatuuq (Paulatuk on most maps), about 25 miles (40 km) west of the park, then make arrangements to hike or boat to the park. The boat will drop you at the mouth of the Brock River; from there you can hike 12.5 miles (20 km) through the river's scenic canyons. As you would in other far north parks, check with the Parks Canada office in Inuvik before you leave to learn the proper precautions for exploring this remote area. Unless you are an experienced wilderness traveler, go with a licensed guide.

What to See and Do

This park brims with broad waterfalls, deep stony canyons, vast expanses of tundra, dazzling wildflower displays, and comely rivers. The main river, the **Hornaday,** tempts kayakers and canoeists with a navigable—and gentle—100-mile (161 km) stretch that runs through the heart of the park and ends near **Cache Lake,** not far upstream from

Musk-oxen

Polar bears, tundra wolves, arctic foxes—they're all familiar emblems of the far north. Less familiar, but equally totemic of the northern wilderness, is that outlandish creature, the musk-ox.

As so often happens, the common name makes no sense: Musk-oxen are not oxen, nor do they possess musk glands. Goats and sheep are their closest relatives. You can see the resemblance if you squint at a musk-ox and imagine a dark, 800-pound (363 kg) horned sheep that hasn't been sheared in 20 years.

If you think musk-oxen have a prehistoric look about them, you're right. Dating back about 600,000 years, the species came to North America over the Bering land bridge in the company of saber-toothed cats and woolly mammoths. At the height of the Ice Age, musk-oxen ranged as far south as present-day Ohio. Today, by contrast, they are confined to the far north—notably Greenland, northern Alaska, and northern Canada. Driven to extinction in Alaska (but since reintroduced) and once imperiled in Canada, musk-oxen have slowly been recovering thanks to conservation efforts; tens of thousands of them now roam Canada.

Despite their slow, docile appearance, musk-oxen can be swift and fierce if the need arises. When attacked by wolves, they form a defensive circle to shield their hindquarters and their calves; few wolves are willing to take on that bulwark of horns. As the breeding season approaches, pairs of bulls settle the pecking order by butting heads. Following ritualistic displays of bullhood—pawing the ground, walking stiff-legged—the two combatants back up until they are a couple of hundred feet apart. Then they thunder toward each other at 35 miles an hour and clonk heads. A dozen such collisions may be required to settle the matter.

the spot where dramatic **La Roncière Falls** drops over a sedimentary rock shelf. The river is not navigable beyond this point. Many people will put in at the confluence of the Little Hornaday and the Upper Hornaday. Trips usually take 8 to 12 days, with the best paddling in July.

Tuktut Nogait also offers reasonably easy hiking, though it doesn't have established trails. The routes mostly cross hard-packed terrain and sometimes follow well-worn caribou paths. Any difficulties you encounter will stem from the trails' remoteness and the navigation skills required, not from the strenuousness of the hiking itself. Even in summer, be prepared for heavy fog, rain, icy winds, frost, and snow.

Wildlife abounds. If you drift down the leisurely Hornaday, you'll have plenty of time to survey the cliffs for nesting peregrine falcons, golden eagles, gyrfalcons, and rough-legged hawks. In the hills and valleys look for wolves, grizzly bears, arctic ground squirrels, wolverines, musk-oxen, and, of course, the caribou. ∎

Other Sites

The following is a select list of additional Western Canada sites.

Pacific Coast

Desolation Sound Marine Provincial Park

A renowned haven for boaters and kayakers, who poke around in the sheltered bays and snug coves of this coastal wilderness. Above the relatively warm waters loom the big-shouldered Coast Mountains. Access is by water only, but those without their own watercraft can rent boats or kayaks and arrange drop-offs in the sound area. This largest of B.C.'s coastal marine parks is located on the north end of the Sunshine Coast, in the southwestern part of the province. Contact BC Parks, Garibaldi/Sunshine Coast District, P.O. Box 220, Brackendale, BC, V0N 1H0; phone 604-898-3678. wlapwww.gov.bc.ca/bcparks/explore/parkpgs/desolation.htm

Carmanah Walbran Provincial Park

This 40,000-acre park is famed for its colossal and ancient trees; in this relatively small space it protects two percent of all the old-growth forest remaining in B.C. You'll find 800-year-old Sitka spruce that top out above 300 feet and shorter, gnarly cedars that have been growing for well over 1,000 years. This grand forest houses wolves, black bears, pileated woodpeckers, salmon, and a host of other wildlife. Although it is almost untouched wilderness, the park does feature some hiking trails. Driving to the park is tricky, so contact BC Parks at the following address for important access and safety information: South Vancouver Island District, 2930 Trans-Canada Hwy., Victoria, BC V9B 6H6; phone 250-391-2300. wlapwww.gov.bc.ca/bcparks/explore/parkpgs/carmanah.htm

Interior Mountains and Plateaus

The Pocket Desert

Sagebrush, prickly pear cactuses, rattlesnakes, western skinks, kangaroo rats; these are not the plants and animals you expect to find in Canada. But here in the 30,000-odd acres of the nation's only true desert, you'll find such flora and fauna because the Pocket Desert is the extreme northern tip of the Great Basin Desert (it hugs the Washington border near the southern British Columbia town of Osoyoos). The area gets less than 10 inches of rain a year, and summer temperatures climb into the 90s, even the 100s. Contact Osoyoos Desert Society, P.O. Box 123, Osoyoos, BC V0H 1V0; phone 250-495-2470 or 877-889-0897 www.desert.org

Kokanee Glacier Park

This 80,000-acre park features classic sharp peaks, glaciers that feed more than 30 lakes, and vast meadows brimful of wildflowers. Old mining trails make this otherwise little developed park easy to hike. Tucked into the Selkirk Mountains, Kokanee lies at the heart of the Kootenays, 15 miles north of Nelson in southeast British Columbia. Contact BC Parks, Kootenay District, Wasa, BC V0B 2K0; phone 250-422-4200. wlapwww.gov.bc.ca/bcparks/explore/parkpgs/kokangla.htm

Creston Valley Wildlife Management Area

The marshes of the Creston Valley Wildlife Management Area are known for their birds. More than 250 species have been sighted here. An unusually dense concentration of ospreys nests in the area. A wildlife center offers interpretive hikes and canoe trips through this 17,000-acre refuge in southeast British Columbia, located six miles west of Creston between Kootenay Lake and the U.S. border. Contact the management area, P.O. Box 640, Creston, BC V0B 1G0; phone 250-428-3260. www.crestonwildlife.ca

Canadian Rockies

Mount Robson Provincial Park

"On every side the snowy heads of mighty hills crowded round, whilst, immediately behind us, a giant among giants, and immeasurably supreme, rose Robson's Peak." (Milton and Cheadle, 1865) Today this peak is named Mount Robson, but it's still the tallest mountain (12,969 feet) in the Canadian Rockies. Mount Robson anchors this 555,419-acre park known for its alpine scenery, its abundant wildlife, and its wide-ranging accessibility, with activities for everyone from car campers to backcountry explorers. Mount Robson presses against the Alberta border and adjoins Jasper National Park; you can hike from one park to the other. Contact BC Parks, Mount Robson Area Office, P.O. Box 579, Valemount, BC V0E 1Z0; phone 250-566-4325. wlapwww.gov.bc.ca/bcparks/explore/parkpgs/mtrobson.htm

Prairie

Kimiwan Lake

Situated at the confluence of three major flyways—the Mississippi, the Central, and the Pacific migration corridors—Kimiwan Lake serves up a smorgasbord for birdwatchers; the species list exceeds 200. Annually some 250,000 waterfowl and 27,000 shorebirds pass through or nest around Kimiwan Lake. The Kimiwan Birdwalk and Interpretive Centre make observing birds easy and informative. Located in west-central Alberta, Kimiwan Lake abuts the town of McLennan ("Bird Capital of Canada"). Contact Kimiwan Birdwalk and Intertpretive Centre, P.O. Box 606, McLennan, AB T0H 2L0; phone 708-324-2004 or 708-324-3010. www.inetnorth.net/org/mclennan/mclennan.htm

T-rex Discovery Centre

Out here in the badlands rises a gleaming new edifice dedicated to dinosaurs. The resident star is "Scotty," a Tyrannosaurus rex unearthed in the vicinity, but the exhibits cover many dinosaurs and provide plenty of information. You can take a guided tour of the center, go on a three-hour tour of a nearby active dig site, or sign up for the "Day Dig Program," which can be a half-day, full-day, or week-long opportunity to work alongside paleontologists as they hunt for fossils. Scotty and the gang can be found in southwest Saskatchewan, just outside Eastend. Contact the center, P.O. Box 520, Eastend, SK S0N 0T0; phone 306-295-4009. www.dinocountry.com

Turtle Mountain Provincial Park

This 46,000-acre park gets its name from the abundance of western painted turtles that call it home, but the 200-plus lakes and lush hardwood forests in these rolling hills attract many other animals as well. The lakes and marshes feature moose, salamanders, muskrats, mink, and, it seems, at least one beaver lodge on every body of water. In the uplands watch for elk, badgers, white-tailed deer, red foxes, and loads of birds. Hike the Turtle's Back Trail up to the summit of Turtle Mountain; from the viewing tower you can look over southwest Manitoba and south into North Dakota. Contact Manitoba Conservation, P.O. Box 22, 200 Saulteaux Crescent, Winnipeg, MB R3J 3W3; phone 800-214-6497. www.gov.mb.ca/natres/parks/regions/western/turtle.html

Boreal Forest

Meadow Lake Provincial Park

Long and narrow, Meadow Lake Provincial Park stretches along the course of the Waterhen River for about 60 miles. At 410,000 acres, this park is one of Saskatchewan's largest. Noted for its dozens of clear-water lakes, the park offers canoeing, rafting, boating, fishing, and a number of white-sand beaches. Visitors can choose from a wide range of recreational activities—everything from golf to backcountry camping in the verdant boreal forest. Meadow Lake Provincial Park lies in west-central Saskatchewan. Contact the park, P.O. Box 70, Dorintosh, SK S0M 0T0; phone 306-236-7680. www.serm.gov.sk.ca/parks/meadowlake

Grand Beach Provincial Park

Blessed with white-sand beaches on the eastern shore of Lake Winnipeg and located only 50 miles north of Winnipeg, this park gets summer crowds intent on recreation. But if you head back to the lagoon and marshes behind the beaches and dunes you'll find a pretty, natural setting. The lake, the lagoon, the marsh, and the boreal forest provide diverse habitats that in turn harbor a range of animals, especially birds. Try the Wild Wings Trail, a short but worthwhile loop where you may spot bald eagles, common loons, white pelicans, osprey, great blue herons, and many other birds, particularly during the spring migration, in May. Contact Manitoba Conservation, P.O. Box 22, 200 Saulteaux Crescent, Winnipeg, MB R3J 3W3; phone 800-214-6497. www.gov.mb.ca/natres/parks/regions/central/grandbeach.htm

Atikaki Provincial Wilderness Park

The name provides the defining information: "wilderness" park. This undeveloped expanse of prime boreal forest is a haven for wolves, woodland caribou, moose, and otters—and for the traveler who wants to see them in a totally natural setting. No roads reach Atikaki. You must go by air or water. A number of outfitters run guided canoe trips into the park; you can make your way by canoe or plane to several lodges within Atikaki. The park sits in southeast Manitoba on the Ontario border, just north of Nopiming Provincial Park. Contact Manitoba Conservation, P.O. Box 22, 200 Saulteaux Crescent, Winnipeg, MB R3J 3W3; phone 800-214-6497. www.gov.mb.ca/natres/parks/regions/eastern/atikaki.htm

The Far North

The Ingraham Trail

Its name notwithstanding, this is a road, not a hiking trail. There aren't many roads in the unsettled vastness of the Far North, so a scenic drive like the Ingraham Trail is notable. The first half is pavement, the second half gravel. It runs 45 miles (one way) through a pleasant landscape that is half woods and half water. The rivers and lakes along the way offer more than a dozen campgrounds, boat launches, hiking trails, picnic areas, and viewpoints. The Ingraham Trail starts in Yellowknife, in southern Northwest Territories, and runs east. Contact Northern Frontier Country, #4 4807 49th St., Yellowknife, NT X1A 3T5; phone 877-881-4262 www.northernfrontier.com/ingraham.htm

Herschel Island Territorial Park

Starkly beautiful Herschel Island lies just a couple of miles off the northwest coast of the Yukon, in the Beaufort Sea, which is part of the Arctic Ocean. Flights from Inuvik take visitors to the island for day trips. In the cold waters you may spot bowhead whales, beluga whales, and ringed seals. Dozens of bird species nest on the flowering tundra, where you may also occasionally spot a musk-ox, caribou, or arctic fox. Contact Parks and Outdoor Recreation Branch, Dept. of Renewable Resources, Yukon Government, Box 2703, Whitehorse, YT Y1A 2C6; phone 867-667-5648. www.renres.gov.yk.ca/protected/herschel.html

Resources

The following is a select list of resources. Contact provincial and local associations for additional outfitter and lodging options.

Nationwide resources

National Parks and National Historic Sites
888-773-8888
www.parkscanada.gc.ca/
Planning information on Canada's national parks and historic sites.

Alpine Club of Canada
Indian Flats Road
P.O. Box 8040
Canmore, AB T1W 2T8
403-678-3200
www.alpineclubofcanada.ca/
Provides information, trips, and lodging at various premier destinations throughout Western Canada.

VIA Rail Canada
P.O. Box 8116
Station Centre-Ville
Montreal, QC H3C 3N3
888-842-7245
www.viarail.ca
For a scenic ride through Western Canada.

PACIFIC COAST

Federal, Provincial, and Local Agencies

Tourism British Columbia
Box 9830, Stn. Prov. Govt.
Victoria, BC V8Z 2G3
800-435-5622
www.helloBC.com
Travel information on sites, outfitters, and lodging.

Department of Fisheries and Oceans, Pacific Region
555 W. Hastings St.
Vancouver, BC V6B 5G3
604-666-0561
www.pac.dfo-mpo.gc.ca
For saltwater fishing licenses. Fishing licences are also available through many sporting goods stores.

Pacific Rim Tourism Association
3100 Kingsway
Port Alberni, BC V9Y 3B1
250-723-7529 or
866-725-7529
www.pacificrimtourism.ca
Assists with explorations of the area of Vancouver Island and Pacific Rim National Park.

Victoria and Vancouver Island Tourism
812 Wharf Street
Victoria, BC V8W 1T3
250-754-3500
www.tourismvictoria.com
www.islands.bc.ca
In-depth information on both the city and the island.

Tourism Vancouver
Plaza Level
200 Burrard St.
Vancouver, BC V6C 3L6
604-683-2000
www.tourismvancouver.com
Recommendations on local hotels and travel.

Ferries and Rail

BC Ferries
1112 Fort St.
Victoria, BC V8V 4V2
250-386-3431
www.bcferries.ba.ca
Provides service on the Inside Passage, to the Queen Charlotte Islands, and between Tsawwassen and the Gulf Islands.

Washington State Ferries
2911 Second Ave.
Seattle, WA 98121
205-464-6400 or
888-808-7977
www.wsdot.wa.gov/
For ferry information from British Columbia south to Seattle.

BC Rail
1311 West First St.
North Vancouver, BC
V7P 1A6
604-984-5505 or
800-663-8238
www.bcrail.com
Explore BC by rail. Helps plan vacation that involve rail explorations of B.C.

Outfitters

Lady Rose Marine Services
P.O. Box 188
Port Alberni, BC V9Y 7M7
250-723-8313 or
800-663-7192
Provides transportation to Pacific Rim National Park and its vicinity.

Majestic West Coast Wilderness Adventures, Ltd.
Box 287
Ucluelet, BC V0R 3A0
250-726-2868 or
800-889-7644
www.island.net/majestic
Explore the Broken Islands, Johnstone Strait, and Ucluelet Harbour by sea kayak.

Strathcona Park Lodge
P.O. Box 2160
Campbell River, BC
V9W 5C5
250-283-3122
Specializes in wilderness courses and outdoor adventures on Vancouver Island.

Tourism Whistler
4010 Whistler Way
Whistler, BC V0N 1B4
800-944-7853
www.whistler-resort.com
Check with this area tourism authority before exploring the area with skis or hiking boots.

For tours of Gwaii Haanas National Park Reserve and Haida Heritage Site, contact the park for a listing of currently approved outfitters.

South Moresby Air Charters
Box 969
Queen Charlotte City, BC
V0T 1S0
250-559-4222 or
888-551-4222
www.smair.com
Offers tours into the heart of the ancient village sites.

Rose Harbour Guest House
Box 437
Queen Charlotte City, BC
V0T 1S0
250-559-2326
www.roseharbour.com
Operates in southern Gwaii Haanas. Nature observations and bird-watching opportunities.

Queen Charlotte Adventures
P.O. Box 196
Queen Charlotte, BC
V0T 1S0
250-559-8990 or
800-668-4288
www.qcislands.net

/qciadven/
Ecotours by boat, sea kayak, and land in Gwaii Haanas and other areas of the Charlottes.

Haida Gwaii Charters
P.O. Box 191
Skidegate, BC V0T 1S1
250-559-8808
www.haidagwaiicharters
.com
Experience the magic of Haida Gwaii with those who have inhabited it for thousands of years.

INTERIOR MOUNTAINS & PLATEAUS

Federal, Provincial, and Local Agencies

Northern British Columbia
P.O. Box 2373
Prince George, BC
V2N 2S6
800-663-8843
www.northernbctravel
.com
Recommendations and ideas for traveling Trans-Canada 16 and the area to the north.

Tourism Northern Rockies
Bag 399K
Fort Nelson, BC
V0C 1R0
250-774-2541
www.northernrockies.org
Provides area-specific information on outfitters serving the northern parks of Stone Mountain, Liard River, and Muncho Lake.

Outfitters

Cathedral Lake Resort
250-226-7560
Operates a lodge and cabins within the core area on Quiniscoe Lake. Provides transportation from parking area to Lake Quiniscoe.

Main Current Expeditions
Box 784
Rossland, BC V0G 1Y0
250-362-2172
www.maincurrent.com
Small-group white-water rafting expeditions along the Liard and Tatshenshini Rivers into some of the most remote areas of

northern British Columbia.

Manning Park Resort
Manning Park, BC
V0X 1R0
250-840-8822
Rents canoes and rowboats for trips on Lightning Lake.

Manning Park Corral
Manning Park, BC V0X 1R0
250-840-8844
Provides guided trail rides to some of Manning's stellar sights.

Northern Rockies Lodge
Mile 462 Alaska Highway
Box 8
Muncho Lake, BC
V0C 1Z0
250-776-3481 or 800-663-5269
www.northern-rockies-lodge.com
Introduces the scenery, wildlife, and culture of this remote area on Liard Air's daily fly-outs and tours from a lodge on Muncho Lake.

Redfern Lake Adventures
RR 1 Mile 108, P.O. Box 30
Fort Nelson, BC V0C 1R0
250-774-6457
www.pris.bc.ca/walkabout
Backcountry cabin accessible only by air, horse, foot, or ATV. Guided hiking and other backcountry recreation experiences.

Scoop Lake Lodge (fly-in only)
5615 Deadpine Dr.
Kelowna, BC V1P 1A3
250-491-1885
Wilderness escapes on a lovely lake near the Liard River.

CANADIAN ROCKIES

Federal, Provincial, and Local Agencies

Travel Alberta
319 Innovation Business Centre
9797 Jasper Ave.
Edmonton, AB T5J 1N9
800-661-8888
www.travelalberta.com
Information on vacation

opportunies of all kinds in the Rockies and prairies.

Banff/Lake Louise Tourism Bureau
P.O. Box 1298
Banff, AB T0L 0C0
403-726-8421
www.banfflakelouise.com
Helps with lodging and trip planning.

British Columbia Forest Service
Nelson Forest Region
518 Lake St.
Nelson, BC V1L 4C6
250-354-6200
Provides information on the forests surrounding some of Western Canada's national parks.

Calgary and the Canadian Rockies Tourism
200, 237 Eighth Ave. SE
Calgary, AB T2G 0K8
800-661-1678
www.tourismcalgary.com
Provides information on lodging and outfitters.

Edmonton Tourism
9797 Jasper Ave., NW
Edmonton, AB T5J 1N9
800-463-4667
www.tourism.ede.org
Assists in planning visits to the provincial capital and neighboring attractions.

Outfitters and Lodging

Prince of Wales Hotel
Glacier Park, Inc.
P.O. Box 2025
Columbia Falls, MT 59912
406-892-2525 (reservations)
403-859-2231 (lodge)
www.glacierparkinc.com
Stunning 1927 hotel overlooking Upper Waterton Lake.

Rocky Mountaineer Railtours
1150 Station St.
1st Floor
Vancouver, BC V6A 2X7
800-665-7245
www.rockymountaineer
.com
Provides an opportunity to see the area by rail.

Chateau Lake Louise
111 Lake Louise Dr.
Lake Louise, AB T0L 1E0

403-522-3511 or
800 866-5577
The frequently photo-
graphed hotel sits right
on the lake.

Maligne Tours
626 Connaught Dr.
Jasper, AB T0E 1E0
780-852-3370
www.malignelake.com
Guided hikes and white-
water rafting trips within
Jasper National Park.

Pyramid Riding Stables
P.O. Box 1200
Jasper AB T0E 1E0
780-852-3562
Opportunities to explore
Jasper National Park on
horseback.

Warner Guiding and
Outfitters
Box 2280
Banff, AB T1L 1C1
403-762-4551 or
800-661-8352
www.horseback.com
Travel on horseback to
areas inaccessible by road.
Journeys of one to six
days, some with natural-
ists or other experts.

THE PRAIRIE

Federal, Provincial, and Local Agencies

Travel Manitoba
7-155 Carlton St.
Winnipeg, MB R3C 3H8
800-665-0040
www.travelmanitoba.com
Information on planning
trips in the province.

Tourism Winnipeg
279 Portage Avenue
Winnipeg, MB R3B 2B4
800-665-0204
www.tourism.winnipeg
.mb.ca
Helps visitors make reservations and locate travel
information.

Manitoba Conservation
200 Saulteaux Crescent
Winnipeg, MB R3J 3W3
800-214 6497
www.gov.mb.ca/natres
/parks
Up-to-date information
on camping and trails in
the provincial parks.

Outfitters

Canoeski Discovery
1618 9th Ave. N
Saskatoon, SK S7K 3A1
306-653-5693
Rents canoes and leads
ski trips to Prince Albert
park.

Eagle Point Resort
P.O. Box 1349
La Ronge, SK S0J 1L0
306-425-2273 or
888-332-4536
www.eaglepoint.ca
Houseboat and cottage
rentals; kayak, canoe, and
paddleboat rentals; and
golf course in Lac La
Ronge Provincial Park
area.

Rabbit Creek Outfitters
RR 1
Shellbrook, SK S0J 0E0
306-747-3182
Horseback trips into
Prince Albert park.

Spirit Sands Covered
Wagon Tours
Box 512
St. Claude, MB R0G 1Z0
204-827-2800 or
204-379-2007
Day and overnight trips by
covered wagon through
Spruce Woods Provincial
Park.

Upland Crosscountry Skiing
611 Albert Avenue
Saskatoon, SK S7N 1G6
306-982-2213
Assistance with planning
ski trips in Prince Albert
park.

Waskesiu Lake Marina
Waskesiu Lake, SK
S0J 2Y0
306-663-1999
Canoe, kayak, and boat
rentals in Prince Albert
National Park. Guides/
outfitters for the park.

BOREAL FOREST

Federal, Provincial, and Local Agencies

See listings under "The
Prairie" chapter

Outfitters

Horizons Unlimited/

Churchill River Canoe
Outfitters
P.O. Box 1110
La Ronge, SK S0J 1L0
877-511-2726
www.churchillrivercanoe
.com
Canoe rentals and guided
trips on the Churchill
River.

Thompson's Camps, Inc.
P.O. Box 419
La Ronge, SK S0J 1L0
306-635-2144 or
800-667-5554
Boat excursions in Lac
La Ronge area.

Air Service

Jackson Air Service
Channing Airport
Flin Flon, MB
204-687-8247
or Skyward Aviation
Thompson Airport
Thompson, MB
204-677-1737
For trips to and around-
Grass River Provincial Park.

Transwest Air
800-667-9356 or
800-665-7275
Service to Lac La Ronge
Provincial Park.

Osprey Wings
Thompson's Camps, Inc.
Box 419
La Ronge, SK S0J 1L0
306-635-2144
Operates out of
Thompson's Camps.

THE NORTH

Federal, Provincial, and Local Agencies

Tourism Yukon
100 Hanson St.
P.O. Box 2703
Whitehorse, YK Y1A 2C6
867-667-5340
www.touryukon.com

Department of Renewable
Resources
Parks and Outdoor
Recreation Branch
P.O. Box 2703
Whitehorse, YK Y1A 2C6
867-667-5648
www.renres.gov.yk.ca
Provides information on
parks and campgrounds
in the Yukon.

Northwest Territories
Tourism
  P.O. Box 610
  Yellowknife, NT X1A 2N5
  800-661-0788
  www.nwttravel.nt.ca
  Assists travelers with trip
  arrangements.

Nunavut Tourism
  Box 1450
  Iqaluit, NU X0A 0H0
  867-979-6551 or
  866-686-2888
  www.nunatour.nt.ca
  Helpful information in
  preparing for a trip to the
  Far North.

Yellowknife Tourism
  #4 4807 49th St.
  Yellowknife, NT X1A 3T5
  877-881-4262
  www.northernfrontier.com
  Information on outfitters
  and lodging available in
  the northern parks.

Outfitters

Bathurst Inlet Lodge and
Bathurst Arctic Services
  P.O.Box 820
  Yellowknife, NT X1A 2N6
  867-873-2595 or
  867-920-4330
  Accommodations, eco-
  tourism experiences,
  and air charter services
  to Bathurst Inlet area.

Horizons Unlimited /
Churchill River Canoe
Outfitters
  P.O. Box 1110
  La Ronge, SK S0J 1L0
  877-511-2726
  www.churchillrivercanoe
  .com

Cabin and boat rentals,
guides, and shuttle service
along the Churchill River.

Nahanni & Whitewolf River
Adventures
  Box 4869
  Whitehorse, YT Y1A 4N6
  867-668-3180
  www.nahanni.com
  Licensed park operator
  offering guided canoe and
  rafting trips through Nahanni NPR and Ivvavik NP.

Nahanni Wilderness Adven-
tures
  Box 4, Site 6, RR1
  Didsbury, AB T0M 0W0
  888-897-5223
  www.nahanniwild.com
  Guided canoe and rafting
  trips through Nahanni
  NPR.

Wilderness Adventure
Company
  RR3
  Parry Sound, ON P2A
  2W9
  www.blackfeather.com
  Guided canoe trips
  through Nahanni NPR.

Air Service

Alkan Air
  Box 4008
  Whitehorse, YK Y1A 3S9
  867-668-2107
  or P.O. Box 1190
  Inuvik, NT X0E 0T0
  867-777-3777
  www.yukonweb.com
  /tourism/alkanair
  Serves the Yukon and
  Northwest Territories and
  provides air charters from
  Inuvik to Aulavik, Ivvavik,

and Tuktut Nogait
National Parks.

South Nahanni Airways
  P.O. Box 407
  Fort Simpson, NT
  X0E 0N0
  867-695-2007
  Air charter services to
  Nahanni National Park
  Reserve.

Arctic Wings and Rotors
  P.O. Box 1916
  Inuvik, NT X0E 0T0
  867-777-2220
  Air charter services from
  Inuvik to Aulavik, Ivvavik,
  and Tuktut Nogait
  National Parks.

Canadian Helicopters
  Box 2689
  Inuvik, NT X0E 0T0
  867-777-2424
  Air charter services from
  Inuvik to Aulavik, Ivvavik,
  and Tuktut Nogait
  National Parks.

Outdoor Education

Churchill Northern Studies
Centre
  P.O. Box 610
  Churchill, MB R0B 0E0
  204-675-2307
  www.cancom.net/~cnsc/
  Offers summer learning
  vacations that focus on
  the flora and fauna of the
  Hudson Bay region. Also
  offers Elderhostel
  courses.

About the Author and Photographer

From his home in Oregon, **Bob Devine** writes about conservation, natural history, and outdoor travel. He is also the author of *Pacific Northwest,* in this series, and of *Alien Invasion: America's Battle with Non-native Animals and Plants.*

Freelance photographer **Raymond Gehman** specializes in outdoor and natural history subjects. A frequent contributor to *National Geographic* and *Traveler* magazines as well as National Geographic Books, he now lives in central Pennsylvania with his wife and two sons.

Illustrations Credits

All photographs by Raymond Gehman, except:

p. 49, Andrew Gehman; pp. 90-91, Sam Abell, National Geographic Photographer; p. 95, Sam Abell, National Geographic Photographer; p. 96, Sam Abell, National Geographic Photographer; pp. 104-105, Michael Yamashita; p. 108, Michael Yamashita; p. 242, Norbert Rosing/NGS Image Collection; pp. 246-247, Maria Stenzel.

Index

Abbreviation
National Park = NP

National Geographic Guide to America's Outdoors: Western Canada
by Bob Devine
Photographed by Raymond Gehman

Published by the National Geographic Society
John M. Fahey, Jr., *President and Chief Executive Officer*
Gilbert M. Grosvenor, *Chairman of the Board*
Nina D. Hoffman, *Executive Vice President,*
   President, Books and School Publishing

Prepared by the Book Division
Elizabeth L. Newhouse, *Director of Travel Publishing*
Allan Fallow, *Senior Editor and Series Director*
Cinda Rose, *Art Director*
Barbara Noe, *Senior Editor*
Caroline Hickey, *Senior Researcher*
Carl Mehler, *Director of Maps*

Staff for this Book
Allan Fallow, Caroline Hickey, *Book Managers*
Charles Kogod, *Illustrations Editor*
Kay A. Hankins, *Designer*
Janet Cave, Robin Currie, Patricia Daniels, Jarelle Stein, Jane Sunderland, *Text Editors*
Michelle Harris, Victoria Garrett Jones, Amy Mack, Jane Sunderland, *Researchers*
Lise Sajewski, *Copy Editor*
Nicholas P. Rosenbach, *Map Manager*
Matt Chwastyk, Sven M. Dolling, National Geographic Maps,
   Mapping Specialists, *Map Edit, Research, and Production*
Tibor G. Tóth, *Map Relief*
R. Gary Colbert, *Production Director*
Meredith Wilcox, *Illustrations Assistant*
Connie D. Binder, *Indexer*
Larry Porges, *Editorial Coordinator*
Deb Antonini, *Contributor*

Manufacturing and Quality Control
Christopher A. Liedel, *CFO*
Phillip L. Schlosser, *Managing Director*
John T. Dunn, *Technical Director*
Vincent P. Ryan, *Manager*
Clifton M. Brown, *Manager*

One of the world's largest nonprofit scientific and educational organizations, the National Geographic Society was founded in 1888 "for the increase and diffusion of geographic knowledge." Fulfilling this mission, the Society educates and inspires millions every day through its magazines, books, television programs, videos, maps and atlases, research grants, the National Geographic Bee, teacher workshops, and innovative classroom materials. The Society is supported through membership dues, charitable gifts, and income from the sale of its educational products. This support is vital to National Geographic's mission to increase global understanding and promote conservation of our planet through exploration, research, and education.

For more information, please call 1-800-NGS LINE (647-5463) or write to the following address: National Geographic Society, 1145 17th Street, N.W. Washington, D.C., 20036-4688 U.S.A.

ISSN 1539-0896

Visit the society's Web site at http://www.nationalgeographic.com

The information in this book has been carefully checked and is accurate as of press date. However, details are subject to change, and the National Geographic Society cannot be responsible for such changes, or for errors or omissions. Assessments of sites are based on the author's subjective opinions, which do not necessarily reflect the publisher's opinion. The publisher cannot be responsible for any consequences arising from the use of this book.